D0261773

BERNARD-HENRI LÉVY

WHO KILLED DANIEL PEARL?

BERNARD-HENRI LÉVY
WHO KILLED DANIEL PEARL?

TRANSLATED BY JAMES X. MITCHELL

DUCKWORTH

First published in the UK in 2003 by
Gerald Duckworth and Co. Ltd
First Floor, East Wing
90-93 Cowcross Street
London EC1M 6BF
Tel. 020 7490 7300
Fax 020 7490 0080
email: inquiries@duckworth-publishers.co.uk
www.ducknet.co.uk

A CIP catalogue record for this book is available
from the British Library

ISBN 0 7156 3261 2

Printed in Great Britain by
TJ International Ltd, Padstow, Cornwall

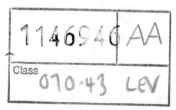

FOR ADAM PEARL

TABLE OF CONTENTS

PART THREE CRIME OF STATE

PART FOUR AL-QAIDA

PART FIVE "OVER INTRUSIVE"

FOREWORD

This book begins 31 January 2002, the day of the death of Daniel Pearl, the American journalist kidnapped, then decapitated, in Karachi, by a gang of religious madmen.

I will say, when the time comes, where, and in what circumstances, I was when I saw for the first time the image of his decapitation.

I will tell how and why I decided that day, though I didn't know the man, to take the time necessary to grasp the mystery of his death.

The investigation lasted one year.

It took me from Karachi to Kandahar, New Delhi, Washington, London, and back to Karachi.

This is the story.

It is the account of his investigation, of his search for the truth, that is the material of this work: as raw as possible; as close as I can to what I saw and experienced; the role of doubt and that of conviction; the dead-ends and small steps forward; the true and false witnesses; those who talk because they know you know; the hidden actors who confide their part of the secret or, on the contrary, mislead you; the moments when the hunter, the investigator, has the impression of being the hunted; fear like an ominous feeling or fair warning—the fear without which the report fails to convey the atmosphere of the gray areas, of shadows in stark light, typical of dubious places; the facts, only the facts, and, when the real was not available, some involuntary part of the imaginary looms.

The first subject of this investigation was, of course, Pearl himself.

The enigma of those "gentle men" of whom Dostoyevski speaks.

The life of this fine journalist, an American and a Jew, but who was many other things as well: a citizen of the planet, a man curious about other men, at home in the world, friend to the forgotten, living life to the fullest, standing in solidarity with the downtrodden, detached and engaged, generous and irresistibly optimistic; a luminous character who made it his duty, if need-ed, to think counter to himself; he was a man who had chosen to answer evil with good and, above all, to understand.

His death, then.

A chronicle of this death.

Who he saw.

What he did.

If there was enough in the investigation he was conducting to explain that they should want him silenced and killed.

So, an investigation of the investigation.

Begin again, from the evidence he left, and in a sense in his place, the investigation that cost him his life.

Retrace his steps. Find, from Islamabad to Karachi, the trail of this man who unwittingly entered a world of darkness. Walk like him. Observe like him. Try to think like him, to feel what he felt, and so to the very end, the instant of death and what he lived in that instant—one year to try to reconstruct the instant of the death of a man I have never met.

Then, there are the others, those who assassinated him, and one in particular, the brains behind the crime, Omar Sheikh.

The dread this individual inspires.

The horror of his hatred of everything humane.

But also, as with his victim, my stubborn will to understand—the will to enter, not into his reasons, but into his passion, his glacial delirium, the way he lives and reacts, the way he wanted and prepared his crime.

Physics of bloody passions.

Chemistry of a murderous vocation.

Not the devil in the mind, but in the mind of the devil, to try to fathom something of this assassin's torment of which others before Pearl were victims—and which others after him, alas, will be.

How does it work, in this day and age, the demonic?

What happens in the soul of a man who, without reason, *in cold blood*, chooses to espouse evil, to aim for the absolute crime?

What is it that, in the start of this century, makes the abject become desire and destiny?

Who are these new possessed who think anything is permitted, not because God doesn't exist, but precisely because He exists and this existence drives them to madness?

Distance and proximity.

Extreme disgust and the will to understand.

Omar, the laboratory.

And then, finally, their world.

This world which is also ours and in which the atrocious death of Daniel Pearl was possible.

This unknown world, without points of reference, whose gestation I have never, for the past ten years, tired of observing, between forgotten wars, the Bosnia engagement and the *Rapport Afghan;* a world whose new compartments the Pearl affair, with all it implies and everything it puts into play, with its unexpected ramifications, has allowed me to discover.

This world of radical Islam with its codes and passwords, its secret territories, its nightmare mullahs breathing madness into souls, its minions, its field marshals.

The universe of the new terrorism and, in particular, bin Laden, who we shall see had his place in this story and whose shadow, dark mystery, weapons of subtle or mass destruction, comings and goings, necessarily haunt these pages.

And then these questions: the clash or not of cultures; one Islam or two; how can the Islam of light triumph over this cadaver-hungry God, grinding bodies and souls in the crucible of a distorted law; are the cold monsters of today still States? What response to hatred when it is the cement of a country adrift? What defense against theological politics fired white-hot? Is the spirit of crusade and the combat against the "Axis of Evil" the appropriate response? Must we resign ourselves to the fact that the failure of the Universal, the global will for vengeance, the regression, are the only echo to the affliction of the soul?

A final word.

If this book began at the beginning of the year 2002, the fact is that it ended in April 2003, in the middle of the Anglo-American war in Iraq.

Completing it, I understand better why this war, from its initial premises, inspired in me such a feeling of malaise.

It is certainly not that I am a pacifist.

It is not that I am less sensitive than others to the idea of seeing the Iraqi people, who were dying a slow death forgotten by the world, delivered from their tyrant.

But there I was, returning from that other world. During the entire time of the debate over the question of the priority of overthrowing Saddam and whether the planet's fate was at stake in Baghdad, I was in the black hole of Karachi. And I couldn't, and still can't, help imagine that this war in Iraq—beyond its human and political costs, beyond the civilian deaths and the new spin it will give to the wicked wheel of the war between civilizations—attests to a singular error of historical calculation.

A regime already largely disarmed while in the depths of Pakistan's cities, nuclear secrets were traded.

A tyrant in his autumn, a phantom of 20th century history, while, back there in Karachi, tomorrow's barbarous configurations were being concocted.

One of the last political dictators being consigned to ancient bestiaries—and, on the other side, beasts of unknown species rising up, with limitless ambitions, for whom politics is at best a useful fiction.

And against this dictator, supporting this circus of a war served up to feed world opinion, a makeshift coalition where—supreme joke—we pretended to enlist this same Pakistan that I saw turning into the Devil's own home.

That also is the Pearl case.

An invitation not to mistake this century for another.

An opportunity to explore this silent hell, full of the living damned, where our next tragedies are hatching.

WHO KILLED DANIEL PEARL?

PART ONE
DANNY

CHAPTER 1 A NIGHT IN KARACHI

Arrival in Karachi.

The first thing that hits you, even inside the airport, is the complete absence of Westerners.

There was an Englishman on the plane, doubtless a diplomat, who embarked with me in Islamabad. But a bullet-proof car was waiting for him at the end of the tarmac and whisked him away, across the runways, before the other passengers had even begun to leave the plane.

And then, the closed faces and the calls to prayer mixed with announcements of arrivals and departures. From the customs officer to the porter, from the beggars to the taxi drivers swooping down on me amid the helmeted soldiers patrolling the perimeter, a harsh, hostile expression lights up their eyes as I pass, an air of surprise also, or of incredulous curiosity, which says much about the incongruous nature of the presence here, in this spring of 2002, of a Western traveller. No women. This is striking, this impression of a world entirely devoid of women. And, lost in the crowd, eyes lined with kohl, hair the color of dark honey, a dark blue, stained and rumpled double-breasted suit, the pockets crammed with improbable papers—but with a carnationlike blossom at the lapel, as a sign of welcome, I suppose—

the driver sent by the Marriott, who leads me to his car on the other side of the airport. Traffic is snarled. The police just found a bomb and took it outside near the parking lot to detonate it, forcing a massive gridlock of vehicles to one side.

"American?" he asks after a long moment, observing me in the rear-view mirror.

"No, French."

He seems relieved. France's stance on Iraq, perhaps. France's policy in the Arab world.

"First time in Karachi?"

"First time."

I am lying, of course. But I am not about to tell him that yes, I know Pakistan. I am not about to tell him he wasn't even born the first time I was here, in 1971, when Zulfikar Ali Bhutto, in all his majesty and glory, was on the very threshold of power. His style, his allure, the cultured air of a colonial Pakistani, product of the finest British public schools, who in his indomitable optimism never imagined he could end up at the end of a rope eight years later… Giscard fascinated him… and Servan Schrieber, whom he wondered if people my age in France were reading. This culture, the unveiled women in the party meetings… Ayub Khan, Yayha Khan, the ruling military…. Those brutes, you'll see, it won't last. The war over Bangladesh, and then, supporting the oppressed Bengalis seceding from increasingly Westernised Pakistan. Entering Dacca with the Indian army… President Mujibur Rahman, and his big glasses gleaming with irony… my first job, as a policy consultant, my first book, in other words, my first involvement with what was, for me, a war of national liberation but remains, for the Pakistanis, the ultimate trauma—the carving up of their country, an irrevocable Alsace-Lorraine. I know that one of the most significant entries on Pearl's résumé was his posting in India before coming to Karachi. Worse still, in the minds of the Islamists, and perhaps of the Pakistani intelligence services, was the fact that he "kept an apartment in Bombay." In the crazy logic where the smallest sign is transformed into proof or confession, this confirmed him as an enemy of the country, the agent of a foreign power and, therefore, a man to eliminate. So, I say nothing. I am not about to reveal that in another life, thirty years ago, I was an active, militant adversary of the Pakistani regime. He seems once again relieved.

"And your religion? What is your religion?"

This I was not expecting. Or, in any case, not like that, not so fast, nor with such assurance.

Again, I think about Pearl and his last words, fixed on the video taken by his captors: "My father's Jewish. My mother's Jewish. I'm Jewish."

I think about the incredible story I read on the "Reporters Without Borders" website just before leaving. Aftab Ahmed, editor of a Peshawar newspaper, had published a letter to the editor mildly critical of the anti-Semitic wave engulfing the country, a suggestion to let up on the constant publication of article after article dragging Jews through the mud. Scandal! Trial for blasphemy! Huge demonstrations by religious leaders and Islamists before the courthouse. Newspaper shut down. Printing press burned down. Kill him! Hang him! Get rid of this infidel, we can hate whomever we want and for whatever reasons we deem appropriate. The editor, narrowly escaped the death penalty and, after fifty-four days, was released from jail, but only after writing a "letter of apology to the Muslim people." Publication was suspended for five months, and his colleague, editorial page editor Munawar Hasan, is still in jail a year later.

In fact, I think about all I have been told about the virulent anti-Semitism of the Pakistanis and about this second piece of advice: "Don't speak about it. Ever. There are anti-Semites who, as is often the case, have never seen a Jew in their lives and will not put two and two together when they hear your name. So silence, OK? Never respond to questions or provocations. With India in your past and, on top of that, being Jewish—it's a lot for one man, so don't mention either, no matter what."

The taboo subjects in Pakistan: India; Kashmir, which must be "liberated" from Indian domination and which they perceive as a modern-day Bangladesh, bleeding but still dormant; and of course, Judaism.

"Atheist," I finally say. "My religion is atheism."

The answer surprises him. I see his incredulous glance as he scrutinizes me in the rear-view. Atheist, really? Is that possible, to be of the atheist religion? Indeed it seems possible, since I don't appear to be joking, and so I suppose he concludes his passenger is a Western eccentric. That's better than a Jew, a Catholic, or a Hindu. He extracts an old cigarette, gone limp with sweat, from his pocket and offers it to me as a sign of friendship.

"No thanks," I say, "I don't smoke."

And now it's my turn to question him about his religion, his life, his children, about the beggars at the airport exit, the post card vendors selling photos of Bin Laden, the man perched on the scaffolding painting "Bush=Butcher" in black letters on a wall, and another man, his beard neatly tucked into a hair net, who offers to sell me some heroin as we stop at a red light. Are there as many drug addicts as they say in Pakistan? And bin Laden? Is bin Laden alive? I hear he's a hero for most people here in Karachi, is it true? I read that in the city there are two million Afghans, Bengalis, Arabs, Sudanese, Somalis, Egyptians, Chechens, in short, foreigners without papers forming an army of natural candidates for al-Qaida recruiting agents—what does he think? And those old men there, half naked, sooty with the years and dust, shaggy, hoisting bundles of sticks, appearing from a side street like a column of ants? And this other man, crouched by the side of the road, an apron around his waist, a straw hat crushed on his head, patiently rummaging in the ruins of a house? And this one with the scabby face and a crutch raised like a weapon menacing the cars? And that one, rigid, his arms outstretched like a scarecrow that the wind will blow away? I thought Karachi was a rich city, I didn't imagine there was so much misery, rubble, vagabonds.... I couldn't imagine these faces of the half-dead, their backs bent like teetering specters in the dying light of the coming night—do you know, my friend, they look like a pack of wolves? And that one, scratching his leprosy, do you know what he reminds me of? And this squatting skeleton? In short, I ask him everything, all the questions possible and imaginable rather than allow him his, the one I know is coming, the one that asks what an atheist Frenchman on his "first trip to Pakistan" is doing here, in this city, at a time he knows to be on the edge of apocalypse: whether I'm here as a "tourist" or on "business," and, if that's the case, why?

Isn't the idea, for this first trip, to say nothing? To begin the investigation by remaining incognito as long as possible? Luckily I had kept the "multiple entry" visa given me in February, during my "Afghan mission." So I didn't have to say anything to anyone. Nothing asked. I didn't have to go by the Pakistani embassy to explain myself. And now that I'm here, I'm determined not to say more than I have to. That will last as long as it lasts. It will cause problems, of course, with various contacts and, especially, with officials. But too bad for the officials. I'll have other occasions for them to tell me what I already know: that Pearl had been here since Christmas. That he was on the trail of the man with the shoe bomb on the Paris-Miami airbus, Richard Colvin Reid. That he had been "overly intrusive," too "prying," sticking his nose into delicate matters that don't concern foreigners. That he was wrong to trust Omar Sheikh, who had hoodwinked him by promising to lead him to Reid's guru, Mubarak Ali Shah Gilani, leader of Jamaat al-Fuqrah, the terrorist sect on the FBI's list of terrorist organizations, and who on said day, instead of leading him to Gilani, took him to a house in the suburbs of Karachi where, after eight days, on 31 January, he was executed. That Omar Sheikh was arrested. That he is at this very moment on trial. That it is through his trial that the regime decided to focus on Islamism in Pakistan—we are following the case, Mr. Lévy! Let justice run its course! Don't be too nosy yourself....

For now, there are the places. The atmospheres. The air Pearl breathed, every day, after his arrival on a winter morning at the Karachi airport. There's the Marriott, where I also have taken a room. The Hotel Akbar, in Rawalpindi, where he met for the first time his future executioner, Omar Sheikh, and where I must go myself. The Village Garden, in the lower city, their rendezvous the evening of his abduction. There is the place of his ordeal. The place where his body was found, cut in ten pieces, then put back together for burial: the torso, the head placed at the base of the neck, the arms severed at the shoulders, the thighs, the legs, the feet. All the places he had been, tragic or ordinary, where I want to try to find, to sense, his presence. And for all of that—all the mystery surrounding Pearl, to retrace his steps, to imagine what he felt, lived, and suffered—I don't need a visa or meetings in high places, or, especially, too much visibility.

The role of an ordinary tourist suits me fine. At least it allows me to ward off the real risk of being taken for a "journalist": a category not only defamatory, but unintelligible in a country which I know (and which I will soon have the occasion to verify) is drugged on fanaticism, doped on violence, and has lost even the very idea of what a free press could be. Daniel Pearl.... The group of English journalists stoned in December in the Pashtun hills of Chaman.... The BBC team attacked around the same time somewhere on the Afghan border.... The journalist from *The Independent* , Robert Fisk, beaten and injured by a crowd of fanaticized Afghan refugees.... Shaheen Sehbai, the courageous editor of the Karachi *News* threatened with death by the secret service for going too far on, precisely, the Pearl affair.... In fact, he was forced to flee to the United States.... So, low profile. I'm content with a low profile.

"Sorry, it's the police," the driver says suddenly as he pulls over to the side.

I had asked him to leave the main road, using the traffic as a pretext, but in fact what I wanted was to find a guest-house down a side street where I had stayed thirty years ago, just before leaving for India and Bangladesh. I was absorbed in my recollections—the bizarre feeling of having already seen these streets, these low houses, but as if in another life, as if in a dream—engrossed, also, in grim reflections on the freedom of the press in Pakistan and on the disappearance of this city's languid past, a city I once liked but which now seemed horribly metamorphosed. So I hadn't noticed the policeman stepping out of the half-light—long hair, wrinkled peacoat, bloodshot eyes lined with kohl, young but not juvenile, hard features, a machine-gun held nervously at arm's length and, in the other hand, an absurd flashlight, whose beam isn't larger than a pencil, which he aims at us.

"You'll have to get out. He's going to ask you something. I was going too fast."

The cop—a real cop?—pulls me out of my seat a little roughly, looks me up and down, surveys with some distaste my old leather jacket and three-day beard, and then takes from my pocket the handful of rupees I had changed at the airport, and my passport.

The passport visibly surprises him.

"Lévy?" he says incredulous. "Are you Lévy? Is your name really Lévy?"

Instantly I tell myself: "Catastrophe! Immediate invalidation of the theory according to which the Pakistanis never having seen a Jew in their life, my name, etc...." And then, the memories of Bangladesh come back to me and I remember that "Lévy" is the name of a prestigious paramilitary battalion, created by the

English to police the borders. (To be more precise: the "Levy Malakand," named for the Malakand, the semi-tribal zone near Afghanistan, where the regular army won't go, leaving it to the "Levys" to maintain order.) I remember the homonym, almost cheered by it, and sense it will help me out again, like thirty years ago in Jessore when, having gotten somewhat lost, I found myself face to face with an elite unit of the Pakistani army.

"Two thousand rupees," he says, softening, in the tone of a merchant giving you a real good deal. "Speeding, your situation is not in order: but, for you, only two thousand rupees."

I think about protesting. I could get on my high horse, invoke the respect due the Levy Malakand, call on the driver who has remained in the car with his head on the steering wheel pretending to sleep during the whole incident. But no. Above all, no. I leave the two thousand rupees. And as if nothing had happened, without a word of reproach or the slightest comment to the driver, I get back in the taxi, only too happy to step into the role of a swindled tourist. All is well. Good beginning. Balthasar Gracian: "The things of this world must be looked at in reverse, to be seen the right way round."

CHAPTER 2 HOUSE OF TORMENT

I am in the house where Pearl was held captive.

Well, I say "the" house as if there had been only one and as if I were certain that he was detained, tortured, dismembered and buried in the same place.

In reality no one knows for sure. There are people in Karachi who believe that, both for purposes of blurring the trail, thwarting the searches of the FBI and Pakistani Rangers, and reducing the risks of being reported by the neighbors, the kidnappers might have moved him from hideout to hideout during those seven days in this sprawling agglomeration of fourteen million people that is Karachi.

But there is one place, at least, that everyone thinks of, because it is there, on May 17, after months of searching every cemetery in the city, that buttons from Daniel Pearl's shirt were found, and the car seat where he was seated in the photos sent to the press by his captors—and then, in the garden, three feet under the ground, his body in ten pieces. It is there, in the heart of the neighborhood of Gulzar e-Hijri that in all probability the execution took place, and that is where, one conjecture leading to the next, I suppose he was held from the first night.

It takes almost an hour to get there by car.

Ask nothing of anyone, just send the Pakistani "fixer" ahead to make sure there's no police patrol around the site still deemed highly sensitive, and to be on the safe side, announce oneself to the informal authorities in the vicinity and to the Aghan refugee camps one passes through.

From the Village Garden in the middle of the city—where Omar Sheikh, the leader of the abductors, had fixed their rendezvous— take Sharah e-Faisal, the avenue of King Faisal, which goes up toward the airport and follow it about twenty minutes. It's a good road, reassuring, going through the business quarters, a marine base, retired veterans' residential neighborhoods, the Air Force museum, the Jinnah museum as well as the Finance and Trade Center where the main offices of several large Pakistani banks are grouped.

Then make a left on Rashid Minhas Road, which is again a large avenue with a strong army presence: on the right, the "ordnance depot," on the opposite sidewalk, another group of residences for retired officers, a cinema, the "Aladin" theme park, with its aquatic playgrounds, its video and shopping arcades, the crowded Iqbal gardens, the National Institute of Public Information, a university for adults where upper-level bureaucrats are retrained. Here, too, the traffic is light, a perfectly calm road. An impression of normal life, at least on the day of my passage— and why would it have been otherwise the day Pearl made the trip?

After about ten minutes, maybe fifteen, we turn east and get on the Super Highway, a four-lane highway, the "lifeline" of Pakistan, which heads toward Hyderabad. We pass through the Sorhab Goth quarter with its terminal for buses and trucks, a vegetable market, an interminable kind of compound without trees or vegetation, built on the ruins of the Pashtun areas destroyed in the 1980s, a village of Afghan refugees, numerous little restaurants where *pulao* and tea is served with, as in Kabul, dishes of sugar-coated almonds, a restaurant under construction; modest buildings, poorer than on Rashid Minhas, but no more or less than certain quarters in central Karachi. Nothing there, either, that might alert Pearl. Nothing that would lead him to think he was entering some far-off and terrifying no-man's-land.

Left again just after the restaurant under construction. Another large artery, in worse condition, but quite acceptable; Mehran Avenue. A sign indicates the Karachi Institute of Information Technology, another, Dreamworld Family Resort, a sort of playground where young Pakistanis organize the equivalent of our rave parties. Others announce Maymar Apartments, or Ghulshan e-Maymar Complex, or Karachi Development Authority, a quasi-governmental institution for urban development, or, visible on the left, the Dawat Academy International University, whose construction is at a standstill, with only the adjacent mosque completed. Here, suddenly, the landscape turns bleak. There is something sinister in these vacant lots and half-finished houses whose lower floors are squatted, the eucalyptus trees that never quite finish dying of thirst. But it's still not the end-of-the-world atmosphere, the hell, the impenetrable and sordid lower depths that was described to us when it became necessary to explain the failure of the Pakistani police to find the American journalist.

And then, left again on a narrower street, Sharah e-Mullah Jewan Road, where for the first time—by now we've been on the road almost an hour—the landscape really changes. More vacant land and rocky terrain with scattered garbage dumps, few houses, the street deserted, no cars, no pedestrians. A few minutes more, then we park and walk the last 200 meters. Off to the right about 500 meters away is a large abandoned house topped with a television antenna. Eight hundred yards further is the *madrasa* Jamia Rashidia with its soccer field, and behind it, hovels, apparently abandoned. Finally, between the big house with the antenna and the *madrasa*, are two farmhouses facing each other and surrounded by the same wall of cement brick about five feet high. It's in the first farmhouse that Daniel Pearl was held prisoner.

This is the route (another exists, but longer, from the other side, and with lots of police) he must have taken.

And such is the time (one hour, maybe less) of his last journey. A police report based on the deposition of one of the conspirators, Fazal Karim, and repeated by the Pakistani press, speaks of several hours and a change of vehicles—but why? What's the point, since the victim was trusting?

These are the principle stages of his transfer into a zone about which too much has been said, but I repeat—it must be remembered when the question is posed as to what the Pakistani police did or did not do to find him alive—that it was said that the zone was out of reach, a jungle. Well, it's doubtless a lowly place, a disreputable and dangerous area, propitious for all sorts of trafficking and full of the same sort of houses as this one, and where the industry of kidnapping, which flourishes in Karachi, has always had its hideouts. But everyone knows that most of the so-called farms are the refuges of criminals or Islamists. I made the journey and can testify that, apart from this last little stretch, we never leave the city.

What did Pearl do during this time?

What could he have been thinking? What went through his mind all along this journey?

Did he understand that he had fallen into a trap and was not being taken to the interview he had sought with Gilani?

Did he ask questions? Was he anxious, impatient, angry? Did it become necessary to threaten him? Block the door? Subdue or hit him ?

A neighbor, whose son is enrolled at the *madrasa*, says Pearl was seen arriving blindfolded at the gates of the house.

Of course anything is possible.

And, assuming this was the case, assuming that after the Super Highway, as they entered the less frequented Sharah e-Mullah Jewan Road, where the flow of traffic ebbs, they took the precaution to tie a scarf over his eyes—it wouldn't necessarily be cause for alarm. It wouldn't be the first time a journalist had undergone such measures on his way to meet some personality whose hideout must remain secret. It happened to me in Colombia, when I was being driven deep into Cordoba to see Carlos Castaño the notorious leader of the paramilitary fascists... and thirty years ago in Bangladesh, when I was being taken into the western outskirts of Calcutta to the Maoist leader Abdul Motin, wanted by the police of both Bengals. . . .

But deep down I don't believe it.

I can't see his captors taking the risk of driving around with a blindfolded foreigner.

Nor do I believe that Pearl, on this route, which I have seen as though through his eyes, found any reason to be afraid.

My feeling is that he remained more or less confident throughout a journey that a reporter with some experience of Karachi would find normal.

Possibly some apprehension, a few dark thoughts crossing his mind, but dismissed. I imagine him finding the way a little long, chaotic, but also questioning his companions, scribbling in the pages of his notebook, crooked lines as always when riding in a car, even joking, noting what he sees; PNS Karsaz, Kentucky Fried Chicken, Gulberg, Knightsbridge Restaurant, Bundoo Khan, North Karachi Sind Industrial Estate, Karachi Development Authority. And then, in the last stretch, if he was really blindfolded, a little nervous, on his guard, but continuing to take mentally the notes he can no longer take by hand: noises, odors, the probable distance traveled. And at the very end, after getting out of the car, the last snare—the uneven path he feels under his feet that takes him to the house where at last he will have his interview, happy to be there, taking a deep breath and shaking off the ride in this enclosed space where, according to the kidnapper's testimony, his first question was, "Where is Gilani? Where is the man I'm supposed to meet?" At this point Bukhari, who led this little convoy on his motorcycle and would soon direct the execution, put a fraternal arm around Pearl's shoulders and with the other hand stuck a gun in his ribs. But even then, he didn't believe it. Even with a gun in his side, even hearing Bukhari tell him with a big smile, "Now, you are kidnapped," he still believed it was a kind of joke and waited until he was taken in to the house, searched and undressed, before beginning to comprehend what was happening to him.

Behind him—and today behind me—the house of Saud Memon, the owner of the property.

Next to it, the two-story house of Fazal Karim, Memon's driver who witnessed the scene and most likely held Pearl's head during the execution, and eventually cut the body into ten pieces.

A few hundred yards away, the *madrasa* Jamia Rashidia, whose students testify they neither saw nor heard anything until the sixth day—two days before the murder—when the American took advantage of a trip to the toilet to try to escape through an air vent. From the roof of the school they saw Fazal Karim and another retaliating with blows and a bullet fired into his leg: "You're going to pay now, you're going to crawl like a worm in the dirt...."

On the other side of the street, curtained by acacias with white plastic bags hanging from their branches, are two buildings under construction that wouldn't have been there at the time. Desire of the police to see the area inhabited? To encourage development?

There, under his feet and today under mine, so perfectly quiet that the echo of my steps on the twigs and palm leaves that cover the ground is deafening, the small courtyard, planted as well with acacias, palms, bamboo, and mango trees, is where the remains of his tortured body were found. Like the bodies of saints, it was accompanied by meager relics: three pieces of faded green rope, anti-diarrhea pills, two car seats, a piece of the top of his track suit, three bloodstained plastic sacks used to wrap his dismembered body. What learned art of torture! How, with a knife, and before rigor mortis, does one cut a body into so many pieces?

And here, sheltered by a wall with large black letters indicating the direction to the National Public School and further hidden from sight by another dense row of green acacias, is the concrete block building, a narrow rectangle with its two rooms and no electricity (although the rest of the neighborhood is electrified), low ceilinged (I have to lower my head, I imagine he did too), damp and smelling of rotten apples and wet plaster (water from rudimentary cistern overflows into the room). Here is where he spent six days and six nights, where he was interrogated, brought back after trying to escape, and where he was finally killed, then dismembered, on the night of the 31st, although his killers still had the effrontery to demand a ransom from the *Wall Street Journal* and his family. The Golgotha of Daniel Pearl. The scene of his Calvary. Daniel Pearl naked, pitiful and bleeding, like the Chinese youth who by order of Prince Ao-Han-Ouan was sliced up alive, and whose agony, eyes rolled up, face ecstatic, his smile stiffened by suffering, had so impressed Georges Bataille—the famous "torture of a hundred pieces" from *Coupable* and *The Interior Experience*.

Has the place been changed? Reoccupied?

I don't think so; everything seems, on the contrary, as it was.

The same metal gate, padlocked and sealed by the police, with its cascade of white and red bougainvilleas that now cover half of it.

The same surrounding wall that I scale at the very place where I imagine Pearl tried to escape, among the trees near the trench dug along the wall to serve as a septic ditch, and the mound of well-tamped dirt he must have noticed upon his arrival.

The same abandoned garden, full of insects, and the odors of jasmine mixed with those of the pestilent trench. A kind of outdoor bathtub that must have served as a water reservoir and is probably now used by the police when they pass.

And as for the room itself, it's the same cement floor blotched with wax and soot showing where candles and lanterns were placed. The same thick, cement-brick walls, a badly washed brown blood stain on one of them; a handful of hair; a transom facing the road and closed by a metal shutter that was then boarded over; a wooden door without keyhole or handle, barred with a beam slid through padlocked iron rings; construction material in a corner; fishing nets; clumps of straw mixed with mud; mattress stuffing with spider webs; old clay pots thrown in a corner under the transom; colonies of red ants; cockroaches; two discarded spoons and a plate; a candy-pink alarm clock with just one hand; crumpled cigarette packs; a cold brazier; a bed made of cords.

This is Daniel Pearl's prison.

This is the scene of his martyrdom, his tomb.

I remain there for an hour, letting the silence of the place slowly penetrate me, forever, in this terrible setting of the ordeal of the ten times sundered. And inside me, a feeling of friendship moves me to tears—for a man who was ordinary and exemplary, normal and admirable, who found here his last point of contact with life.

CHAPTER 3 A MYSTERIOUS SMILE

In the photos of Pearl taken by his captors in the place where he was held hostage, which have been kept at the British consulate in Karachi, there is a very strange detail.

I'm not referring to the photos everyone knows about, which went around the world when the kidnappers sent them by e-mail to the editors of various outlets of the international press.

I'm not talking about the one, for instance, in which he's sitting on an old car-seat, his head on his lap, his hair tousled, with a gun just inches from his temple.

I'm not talking about the photo that is almost the same, where the gun has come even closer and the man holding it has grabbed Pearl's hair with his other hand to push his head down even farther. In the foreground, his chained wrists, another chain on his ankles. His body is curled up into a ball. You can sense weariness, despair, fear.

I'm not talking about the third one either, probably part of the same series, in which he has straightened up and, still against the same blue background, which is probably a sheet hung up to preclude identification of the wall and the house, he's looking at the camera. His hair has been combed. He has pulled himself together, but his eyes are out of focus, the lower part of his face is swollen. He is pale with the pallor your skin gets in prison. He looks as if he's been drugged, or beaten. (In my opinion these three pictures were taken the day he tried to escape; or maybe the next day when he tried again, during his walk; or maybe the day when a student from the *madrasa* next door came and knocked on the farm door, and Pearl started calling for help, screaming like a lunatic—not the kind of stuff, of course, his kidnappers appreciate....)

No, I'm thinking about two other photos that as far as I know weren't published in the international press, which were taken the next day—the day before his execution.

In one, he is holding a copy of *Dawn*, the big Karachi daily, in order to date the photo and prove that the captive is still alive. He looks calm. His hair is tidy, freshly cut like a child's. On his parted lips a faint smile lingers. His clear gaze faces the camera. His chains have been removed and he is holding the paper in both hands, steadily, just in the right spot so that neither photo nor headline is concealed. On that face, on that body—with control seemingly regained over his expression, the look in his eyes, and his posture—I can detect no trace of fear or anxiety.

The other is even more surprising. The same newspaper is behind him. Except this time they must have taped it to the dark blue fabric and so his hands are free. I can't see the fingers on the right hand, hidden beyond the top of the frame. But I do see his arm, upheld in a strange gesture that could be triumphant, or saying goodbye, or obscene. As for the fingers of his other hand, they're hidden by his thigh and invisible to the jailers standing on his left—but if you look closely, particularly at the position of the ring finger, which seems to me to be slightly stiffened and pulled back from the other fingers, I have the distinct impression that he is discreetly miming a "Fuck you!" visible only to us, who will receive this image. Is Pearl joking? "V" for victory on one hand... "Fuck you" on the other.... Is he sending us a message, and what is it? One thing is unmistakable. It's his mischievous, almost joyous face. It's that perfectly relaxed smile. It's that hair standing up, as if in flames. It's that relaxed, almost nonchalant stance. At that point, he's been a prisoner for six days. He's somewhere deep inside Karachi in a squalid room of only a few square feet. He's in the hands of men he obviously realizes are not only Islamists but killers. His glasses have been taken away from him. They may have been broken. He's badly fed. According to the testimony of one of his guards, after hearing his kidnappers use the word "injection," and fearing they were going to inject poison into his food, he even went on a hunger strike for two days, and started eating again only on the condition that one of his guards taste his sandwiches first. His hands have been tied, his legs chained. Now he's going to die in a few hours. And yet he has the relaxed look of a guy who decides, finally, that the situation he's in is interesting—he has the look you put on when you want to reassure your loved ones, or when you have good reason not to worry.

There are other mysteries, many other mysteries, which I won't elucidate, in the Pearl affair.

There's the police report, for instance, that I read in Karachi, in which Fazal, who doesn't speak English but understands it, testified that on the very last day he saw one of the Yemenis who had come to kill Pearl go up to him, and talk to him in a language which Fazal could not understand—and Pearl's face lit up, then clouded over again, and then he gave a long answer, shouting, in the same language. What language, then? French? Hebrew? Those were the two other languages Pearl spoke. But a Yemeni speaking French… or Hebrew…. And saying what? How very strange.

There are all those images that present other kinds of problems to the investigators, to the forensic labs in Lahore and other places, and now, to the writer—starting, of course, with the famous video sent by the kidnappers, after the execution, to the American consulate in Karachi and which I watched, and watched again. Why doesn't Pearl struggle more when the hand with the long knife enters the frame? Why don't you see the blood flow? Why does his face, in the last phase of the throat slitting, already have that corpse-like rigidity? When the other hand comes from behind, grabs hold of his head, does it again to get a better grip, and when the fingers leave a sallow imprint on the forehead, visible in the picture, isn't that proof that the blood has stopped flowing and Pearl is already dead when he is being decapitated? Another hypothesis: Was Pearl drugged? Has he, like Bataille's ecstatic Chinese youth, been injected with a dose of opium before being decapitated? Or should we believe the testimony of the man who led investigators to Pearl's grave, Fazal Karim, when he says: "We had a problem with the camera. We noticed at the last minute that the cassette had jammed. We had to start all over again. We were halfway done and the head was almost completely severed. We had to put the knife back into the cut and redo the whole scene."

But here's the first mystery.

Here is the thing I've been thinking about since I found those two photos.

Pearl, when they were taken, is confident.

There must have been a particularly difficult moment the day before, when the first series of photos were taken. Surely he must have smelled, at least on arrival, the odor of catastrophe. But my feeling is that, on that day when these last two photos were taken, everything had more or less fallen into place: He doesn't believe he's going to be killed. It's as if the idea hasn't even occurred to him. He's looking at his executioners—but he's looking at them as if he were fascinated rather than troubled by what is happening to him.

Is he naïve?

Does he live—as do most of the journalists I know and as I do whenever I take on this occupation—with a magical belief that he is intrinsically invulnerable?

Did the killers reassure him, and have they themselves at that point decided to let him live?

Is it the same kind of moment of "disquiet, uncertainty and indecision" noted by Leonardo Sciascia in his description of the long ordeal of Aldo Moro, kidnapped and murdered by those 1970s fundamentalists, the Italian Red Brigades?

In all situations of this kind, does there invariably come a moment—and is it the reason for what we see in the pictures—of vagueness and perhaps compassion, which in Moro's case occurred on 15 April 1978, when the Brigade sent their famous "Communiqué Number 6," declaring, "The time has come to make a choice"?

Had the kidnappers reassured Pearl? Did they tell him, "Don't worry, you are our guest, the negotiations are going on"? Did they give him books, a Koran, a chessboard, cards?

Contrary to what the Western press has written, I believe that the execution and its videotaping were not necessarily planned, and may have become imperative at a particular point during his captivity, for reasons we do not know.

My theory is that for the time being, between Pearl and his killers, between the great journalist—liberal, tolerant, open to the cultures of the world and a friend to Islam—and the jihadists, a relationship has formed of trust, of near complicity, and understanding.

I am convinced that what happened was the same kind of phenomenon that Sciascia noted (I see, in fact, that Pearl in these photos has something of the same look that Moro had in the famous photo sent to the newspaper *La Repubblica* on 20 April, in which he too held up the previous day's paper)—"the daily familiarity which inevitably sets in" within the depths of the "people's prison," the "exchange of words," the "common partaking of food," this symbolic sharing. The game involving "the prisoner's sleep" and "the guard's watch," the care they must take of the "health" of the man they have "condemned to death." These "trivial gestures," these "words" that they "inadvertently" say to each other, but that "emanate from the most profound movements of the soul." The "eyes that meet at the most vulnerable moments," the "unexpected exchange of spontaneous smiles"—all of these opportunities, day after day, "for jailer and prisoner, victim and executioner, to fraternize."

Knowing him to be a relentless journalist, I'm ready to wager that he takes advantage of these few days to talk, make jokes, and, one thing leading to another, to finally ask the questions that have been on the tip of his tongue for weeks.

To be precise, let's say that there was the shock of the first day, his mind reeling, an instant of panic. But I'm sure the situation developed as it always does when journalists confront trouble: a moment of dread, yes, and then you get used to it, your reflexes return, you completely forget the danger. I am sure that he quickly came to his senses and that even in the shack where he had to sleep on a pallet, eat out of a mess tin, and put up with the cold, he never lost that devouring curiosity that now he had the opportunity to satisfy: Aren't these the very jihadists he's been trying to find since he arrived from Bombay? Isn't he observing them living their lives, going about their business, arguing, reacting to the news, praying? Doesn't he have entire days and nights to not only observe them but to question them, get them to confide in him, and understand them? Even better: What if he succeeded in solving the mystery of the notorious Gilani, the man he wanted to interview, and as we shall see, was obsessed by? What if that was the meaning of the raised arm in the last photo?

Something happened at that moment.

Something happened that made the kidnappers change their minds and send for three Yemenis, professionals in this kind of crime, with orders to execute him.

The question is, what? What exactly happened? At what exact moment during his captivity?

Did Omar Sheikh's men have a change of mood?

Was it—as Omar himself kept repeating with peculiar insistence from the very first day of his trial—that they could not, after thinking it over, forgive him his attempt to escape the day before?

Was there deliberation? A trial?

Was there an external event that turned things awry?

An accident?

An order from above, and why?

An interference, but what?

A collision of convictions, of which he became the victim?

That is the subject of this book.

It is the mystery that must be solved—its framework, the threads of its plot.

CHAPTER 4 MISE À MORT

What time is it?

Night?

Day?

The video doesn't say.

It doesn't appear on the Pakistani police report.

So, let's say it is at the end of the night.

Or, to be precise, daybreak, five A.M., just before the cock crows.

Karim, the caretaker of the farm who has been keeping a close watch over him for the past week, comes to wake him up.

He gets along well with Karim. He has gotten used to their long conversations in the evening, after the lamps have been put out and the others have gone to bed. In his poor English, the Pakistani tells him about his five children, his little house in Rahim Yar Khan, his problems. And he, in turn, asks over and over the same questions: What do you have against us? Why do you hate us so? What crime has America committed that deserves such terrible reprobation, and what can we do, or be, to earn back the trust of your people, of all poor people?

But this time, something is wrong.

Even groggy with sleep, he senses this is not the same Karim. He is stony, closed. He can tell from the way Karim tears off the covers and orders him to get dressed that he is no longer the companion of yesterday who gave him his daily lesson of Urdu. And then, when he fumbles at his shoe laces with stiff, clumsy fingers, the Pakistani speaks with a tone he's never used before and it sends a chill through his body.

"Don't bother with that. Where you're going, you won't need laces," he says, tight-lipped, without looking at him.

And with that, with these words, and especially with the way he says them, he understands that something has transpired during the night, that they have made a decision, and the decision is not to set him free.

Suddenly, he feels fear.

He feels a glacial rush flow through his body—and for the first time since he has been here, he feels fear.

And yet, at the same time, he cannot believe it.

No, again, he does not believe it—he cannot believe that, in the space of one night, the situation could have deteriorated to this extent.

To begin with, he is their ally. Their a-l-l-y. A hundred times over the past eight days he has told them that if there were but one American and one Jew left in the world to extend a hand to Muslims in general and those of Pakistan in particular, to reject the absurd theme of the clash of civilizations, and to believe in peace with Islam, he would be that man. Daniel Pearl, Jew, liberal, hostile—as his entire career has demonstrated—to everything stupid and arrogant about America, friend of the neglected, of the downtrodden, of the disinherited.

And he is lucky. He has always been one of those people protected by an uncanny kind of luck. His father is telling the press the same thing at this very moment, and it's what he himself has always said, throughout his fifteen years as a journalist. Danny has a lucky star. Danny has an angel on his shoulder. It would be a fine thing if his luck deserted him now, in Pakistan, on the eve of the day he is due to leave for America! What an ironic turn of events that would be, if his luck turned just as he and Mariane learned they were going to have a son!

To think you could find a Muslim gynecologist in Karachi willing to do a sonogram and tell them the sex of their unborn child, and then not be able to convince these Islamists that they've got the wrong man, that he is not the Zionist Jewish spy denounced in the press. No, it is too absurd! And since all that is absurd is, to the inveterate rationalist, stupid, impossible, unreal, he decides this will never happen and that, ultimately, he'll make his jailers listen to reason.

The door leading to the second room, where the others are, is open. Karim, still obstinate, still evasive, motions to him to move forward. Forget about the shoes. He follows without too much apprehension, breathing in the sweet scent of the nearby bougainvillea and mango trees.

When he reaches the room, he understands.

He still cannot believe it, but he understands.

First of all, their faces.

Their careful air this morning.

This communion of terror he senses in their body language and in the way they watch him enter.

He knew, from talking with them, that Bukhari, the commando, had the blood of at least a dozen Shiites on his hands. He knew that Amjad Hussain Farooqi, or Lahori, the head of

Lashkar i-Janghvi, had ties with al-Qaida. But he knew it without knowing it. They may have told him, Bukhari may have retorted, the other night, with a childlike laugh; "You, you may have an angel, but I've got a devil!" —they looked too nice to be killers.

But suddenly, that's it.

Silent, hands crossed behind their backs, their sinister expressions revealed by the unsteady light of the oil lamps, they show their other faces, the ones they wore when they plunged the children of Shiite families who lived near to the Binori Town mosque, in Karachi, into quick lime. He had read an article about it one day. And all at once, he knows.

And, there are three men in the corner of the room, near the door, who weren't here yesterday. Sitting on their heels, with empty soda cans at their feet, they seem distracted, as though their thoughts are elsewhere or they are praying. They wear the red and white scarf of Palestinian fighters, but from the long white tunics pulled up on their calves, their bare feet, and, at their waist, the curved dagger with the handle of horn, the *jambiya* as they call it in Sanaa, he can tell they are Yemenis.

"Lie down!" Bukhari orders in a dull, hollow voice, as though he were talking to himself.

The ground is bare. It's cold. He doesn't see where he is supposed to lie down.

"Lie down!" Bukhari repeats impatiently, a little louder.

And, to his great surprise, Bukhari walks over and gives him a kick in the shins that makes him fall to his knees as the others jump on him, two of them tying his hands with a piece of green rope, a third whipping an enormous syringe out of the folds of his robe and swiftly pulling up his shirt to give him a shot in the stomach.

He struggles. "Are you crazy? What are you doing? I'm your friend."

But now they're hitting him, and Bukhari is yelling "Shut up!" as they kick him in the stomach, in the head. He goes silent, panting. He tries to protect his face. He is stunned with astonishment and terror. And then, when he is in too much pain to get up by himself, they lift him by the arms and pull him to his feet.

He feels strange now. His mind is fuzzy, his ears are buzzing. He feels like he's being sucked into a vortex of sand. But at the same time, mixed with the fear, the pain, the tears and the torpor, he is flooded with euphoria—as though his mind were a bright flame that has escaped his body and is floating next to him.

"They've drugged me," he says to himself. "The syringe. Those bastards, they've drugged me."

He doesn't really know if the idea is reassuring or makes him even more fearful.

"You're going to repeat after me," Bukhari tells him, taking a piece of paper out of his pocket and motioning to one of the Yemenis who has a camcorder that, blinded by tears and the sweat dripping into his eyes, he initially takes for a gun about to kill him point blank: "My name is Daniel Pearl. I am a Jewish-American from Encino, California, USA."

Pearl repeats it. It's hard, he's out of breath, but he repeats it.

"You are going to say, 'I come from, on my father's side of the family is Zionists. My father is Jewish. My mother is Jewish. I am Jewish.'"

Pearl would like to tell the Yemeni that he is too close, that's not the way to film, that the result will be an amateur cameraman's image of a face with "fish eyes." But, despite the strange state they have inflicted upon him, this bizarre mixture of euphoria and pain racking his body and mind, he is lucid enough to realize this is no time to give advice. And so he repeats the phrase again.

"Articulate," says Bukhari. "Speak more slowly and distinctly: 'My family follows Judaism. We have made numerous family visits to Israel. In the town of B'nei Brak, in Israel, there is a street called Chaim Pearl Street which is named after my great-grandfather who was one of the founders of the town.'"

How do they know that, Pearl wonders? Where did they go to dig up that information? B'nei Brak is a small town. And the fame of poor Chaim Pearl, his forebear, has never gone beyond the close circle of his parents and his two sisters. So he's not going to repeat that, he says to himself. He can't let these barbarians put their dirty hands on this little family secret. But Farooqi is already walking over to him, and he sees the huge shoe that hurt him just a moment ago, and so, with a tentative half-smile he hopes will be perceptible on film, he thinks better of it and repeats, "My family follows Judaism. We have made numerous family visits to Israel...."

Bukhari seems content. He clears his throat. He spits on the ground. He congratulates the Yemeni, seeming not to realize that this incompetent is too close—but no matter. And he gestures to Pearl, a sign of encouragement, as if to say "You see! You can do it!" and it gives him a moment's hope.

"Repeat again," he says, after peering at length at his paper. "Repeat this: 'Not knowing anything about my situation, not being able to communicate with anybody, only now realizing that some of the people in Guantanamo Bay must be in a similar situation.'"

That's all right. That's what he really feels. He can agree with condemning the conditions of detention of the prisoners at Guantanamo. The only problem is he's out of breath, and his delivery is too jerky. The Yemeni makes a face. They'll have to re-shoot it.

"Again," Bukhari continues: "I've come to realize that this is the sort of problems that Americans are going to have anywhere in the world now. We can't be secure, we can't walk around free, as long as our government policies are continuing and we allow them to continue."

It's not because he is unwilling. No, he can say this too, if necessary. But the drug must be taking effect, and his head hurts. His legs are like a rag doll's and he's having increasing difficulty concentrating. Can Bukhari understand that? Can he give him some shorter sentences to say now?

Bukhari, suddenly understanding, almost human, chin in hand as though the whole scene deserved contemplation, dictates this sentence: "We Americans cannot continue to bear the consequences of our government's actions...."

And then the rest, one after another, patiently, as though dealing with a child:

"Such as the unconditional support given to the state of Israel... Twenty-four abuses of the veto power to justify the massacre of children... And the support for the dictatorial regimes in the Arab and Muslim world... And also the continued American military presence in Afghanistan."

There. It's done. The Yemeni turns off the camera. Are they going to let him sit down now, give him a little water? He feels so terrible.

And then, an extraordinary thing happens.

Bukhari goes and turns up the oil lamps to provide a much brighter light.

He barks an order to Fazal, who has been sitting curled up, as if he were cold, in the corner with the Yemenis ever since they came into the room. He hurriedly jumps up and crosses the room, eyes wide and staring, and steps just behind Pearl.

At a sign from Bukhari, without a word, the other Pakistanis get up and leave. Before they shut the door quickly behind them, he glimpses the dirty light of dawn, the clouds moving in the sky, a flock of birds scattering. Just for an instant, he can feel the beneficent coolness of the early morning breeze on his swollen face.

The only ones left in the room besides Fazal Karim and the out-of-breath cameraman, fussing with his camcorder, are the other two Yemenis, who get up and unsheathe their daggers. One of them comes and stands behind him, next to Fazal Karim, the other stands close at his left, practically pressed against him, the dagger in his right hand.

And then, all of a sudden he sees him.

He couldn't see him until now, because he was in the shadows, and anyway, without his glasses, he can't see more than six feet in front of him.

He sees his eyes, bright, feverish, too deeply set, and strangely pleading—for half a second, he wonders if he too has been drugged.

He sees the weak chin, the barely perceptible trembling of the lips, the outsized ears and bony nose, and the straight, tar-black hair.

He sees his hand, large, hairy, with its gnarled joints and its dirty fingernails, and a long, grainy scar that runs from thumb to wrist and seems to cut it in two.

Then finally, he sees the knife. He has never seen a knife so close up, he says to himself. The handle of cow horn, the leather. A chip near the handle, a bit of rust. And then, there's another thing. The Yemeni sniffles. He blinks and sniffles simultaneously, as if he were keeping time. He can't seem to stop sniffling. Does he have a cold? No. It's a tic. He thinks: That's funny, this is the first time I've ever seen a Muslim with a tic. And then he says to himself: The executioners, in the past... it was a good idea to put a hood over their heads, to hide their faces.... It's hot. His head hurts. He wants desperately to sleep.

The green light on the camera flashes on.

Fazal faces him and ties his wrists together and then, stepping behind him, grabs him by the hair.

The nape of the neck, he thinks, shaking his head and trying to free himself—the center of voluptuousness, the weight of the world, the hidden eye of the Talmud, the executioner's axe.

And the gaze of this man, he thinks, looking at the Yemeni with the knife. For a fraction of a second their eyes meet, and he realizes, at that instant, that this man is going to slit his throat.

He would like to say something.

He feels he must tell them, one last time, that he is a journalist, a real one, and not a spy. He wants to shout—"Would a spy have trusted Omar Sheikh? Would a spy have come here so confidently, without any cover?"

But it must be the drug, having its final effect.

Or else it's the rope cutting into his wrists and hurting him. The words won't come.

Talking becomes difficult, like breathing under water.

He tries to turn his head, to beseech Karim with his eyes one last time. The cigarette, remember the cigarette you offered me last night? Don't you remember everything I told you about the way we American journalists helped the Afghan mujahideen during the jihad against the Russians? Don't you remember, you were so moved by it, you put your hands on my shoulders, your brusque and brotherly embrace? But Karim holds him with an iron hand so that he can't move an inch.

And then, like static jamming his mind, thoughts seem to slither in lazily from obscure corners: His bar mitzvah, in Jerusalem. His first ice cream, in a café on Dizengoff, in Tel Aviv with his father. George, the Bulgarian shoe salesman he met in the tube in London. His friend, the Belgian bass player. The Irish fiddler he had played with last year in a Soho bar. The soft, whiney sounds of the shelling by the liberation army of the Tiger, that last night at Asmara. His wedding to Mariane, in a chateau near Paris. And Hemingway's matador, leading with his left shoulder, the sword that strikes the bone and refuses to go further. Yet it takes only a third of the blade, if it comes from high enough, and if the matador's aim is true, to reach the aorta of the bull, if he is not too massive. His father, again, carrying him on his shoulders coming home from a walk. His mother's laugh. A round loaf of French bread, the deep, tasty crevices of its crust.

As the Yemeni killer grabs the collar of his shirt and rips it open, he thinks for a moment of other hands. Caresses. Games of his childhood. Nadour, the Egyptian friend at Stanford he used to spar with, between classes, for fun—whatever became of

him? He thinks of Mariane, that last night, so beautiful, so desir-
able—women want what, in the end? Passion? Eternity? She was
so proud, Mariane, when he got his Gilani scoop! And he misses
her so! Had he really been reckless, should he have been more
wary of this Omar? But how could you know? How could you
suspect? He thinks of the dying Kosovar refugee who clutched
his hand. He thinks of the sheep he saw suffocate, last year, in
Teheran. He thinks he prefers Bombay and the *Secret Book of the
Brahmin* to Karachi and the Koran. His memories are like horses
on a carousel whirling round in his head.

He feels the hot, slightly rank breath of the panting Yemeni.

From the courtyard, he smells a sweetish odor that, until
now, he hadn't noticed and that, absurdly, bothers him: Funny,
he thinks, when you haven't bathed for eight days... you can
easily get used to your own stench... but that of others....

He hears strange noises that come from far away and sound
like the echo you hear when you put a conch shell to your ear.
He even thinks, for an instant, are those footsteps? Voices?
Someone coming to save me?

It's funny, up until this morning he would have thought the
courtyard was silent, you couldn't hear anything. But now, he
hears everything. You can hear a rustling, a furious murmur of
sounds, all blending together. An avalanche of unsuspected
sounds. Never before had he listened so closely to the background sounds of silence, the sounds he wishes would block out
the breathing of the Yemeni.

A moment of dizziness.

His sweat turning cold.

His Adam's apple that struggles in his frail neck.

He is seized by a huge hiccup, and he vomits.

"Straighten him up!" says the Yemeni killer. The other Yemeni, behind him, grabs him under the arms like a sack of potatoes and sets him up straight.

"Better than that!" he says, stepping back, like an artist getting a better view of his painting. And now it is Karim's turn to pull his head up, face towards the ceiling, the bared neck straining with the shout that is about to come, though leaning a bit to the side.

"Get out of the way!" the killer says to the Yemeni with the camera, who is too close and will hamper his movements. The man with the çamera steps aside, very slowly, as though filled with a sacred terror at the thought of what is about to happen.

His eyes closed, Pearl feels the motion of the knife as it approaches his throat. He hears a rustle in the air next to him and realizes the Yemeni is practicing. He still cannot believe it. But he's cold, he's shivering, his entire body recoils. He would like to stop breathing, make himself small, disappear. At least, he would like to lower his head and cry. Has he done this before, he wonders. Is the man a pro? And what if he's not? What if he bungles it and has to start over again? His sight is going foggy. His last vision of the world, he tells himself. He is sweating and shivering at the same time. He hears a dog barking, far away. A fly buzzing, close to him. And then, the squawk of a chicken that gets mixed up with his own cry, astonishment mixed with pain, inhuman.

And that was it. The knife entered the flesh gently. Gently, ever so gently, he began under the ear, far back on the neck. People have told me it is something of a ritual. Others, that it's simply the classic method for cutting the vocal chords and preventing the victim from screaming. But Pearl reared up. He gasped furiously for air through his butchered larynx. And his reaction was so violent, the strength he finally summoned so great, that he bucked out of Karim's grip, roaring like a beast, and collapsed with a groan in his own blood, that gushed like water. The Yemeni with the camera is shouting too. Half way through, his hands and arms covered with blood, the Yemeni killer looks at him and stops. The camera was jammed. Because of the camera, they have to stop, and begin all over again.

Twenty seconds, perhaps thirty, go by, time for the Yemeni to start over again and reframe the image. Pearl is lying down on his stomach now. The half-severed head is separated from the torso and lies far back on the shoulders. The fingers of his hands dig into the ground like claws. He is no longer moving. He moans. He splutters. He is still breathing, but in fits and starts, a groan cut with gurgles and whines like a puppy's. Karim puts his fingers in the wound to clear the way for the knife. The second Yemeni inclines one of the lamps in order to get a better look and then, feverishly, as though drunk on the sight, the odor, the taste of hot blood that spouts from the carotid as though from a broken pipe, splashing in his face, he cuts Pearl's shirt and then rips it off. The killer, too, finishes his task. The knife slides back into the first wound, the cervical vertebrae crack and blood spurts in his eyes again, blinding him. The head, rolling back and forth as though it had a life of its own, finally comes off and Karim brandishes it, like a trophy, for the camera.

Pearl's face, crumpled like a rag. His lips, at the moment the head is detached, seem animated with a last movement. And the black liquid, of course, flows from his mouth. I've often seen people who had been killed. None, for me, can be worse than this one face I did not see and continue to imagine.

CHAPTER 5 WITH THE PEARLS

"No, that's not it. . . ."

I'm in Los Angeles, Mulholland Drive. Sky that color you see only here. Light that hurts your eyes. A small house by the side of the road, with a garage, potted flowers hanging from balconies, a profusion of small cacti. Cautiously, discreetly, with all possible tact, I am in the process of sharing my preliminary conclusions with Daniel Pearl's parents, including my version of their son's death.

"No, no, that's not it," interrupts the father, Judea, who looks to me like the genial French humorist Francis Blanche, with kind intelligent eyes that occasionally flash with infinite sadness. "It's true there was a video tape. But it was in two parts. I'm sure it was taped at two different times of the day. You can't go ahead as if the two parts say the same thing, or as if they're said in the same tone."

What are these two parts? And what does that change?

"Everything," he replies. "It changes everything. You have the part when he talks about the United States, the prisoners in Guantanamo. There he actually talks like a robot. The words are obviously dictated. Maybe he's even being shown cue cards, off camera. He trips over certain words. He puts in these long 'uhhhs' between words. He deliberately mispronounces things. He says 'Amrica,' for instance, which is what they must have written on the card. What I mean is that he's doing everything to let us know, we who are going to get the message, that he doesn't believe a word of what he's saying. And then you have the second part, where he says, 'My name is Daniel Pearl.... I am a Jewish-American.... I live in Encino, California.... On my father's side I come from a family of Zionists.... My father is Jewish.... My mother is Jewish.... I am Jewish."

Judea knows these words by heart. I sense that he could recite them to the end, like a poem. At certain points he takes on intonations and a voice that are not entirely his but Danny's, his son's.... As for the other part of the message, which concerns Guantanamo and American policy, I find it strange that he seems so certain that it was dictated and that Danny is reciting it against his will. I would have thought otherwise. I had thought and written otherwise, but I let him speak.

"Just listen to this second part. Listen...."

His face has brightened. He's smiling. He's looking at his wife who is smiling too. She's fragile, heartrending, a sharp pretty face half hidden by a fringe of jet-black hair and a pair of glasses, a tiny figure who floats in her shift, halfway between the living and the dead. He takes her hand, strokes it imperceptibly. They have the same look that they have in the magnificent photo in the staircase to the office, dating from the time, forty-three years ago, when they arrived from Israel. The house is full of photos of Danny, of course. But there are also photos of his sisters, Michele and Tamara. Of Mariane, his wife, and little Adam. And there are two magnificent, glorious, resplendent portraits of them—the little Iraqi Jewish girl and the little Polish Jewish boy landing in America like the Ellis Island immigrants, because they know that this is the land of liberty. And suddenly that's what they look like.

"That part about being Jewish, he said that. Those are his words. Those are his sentences. Nobody is forcing him to do anything at that point. There are no cue cards. How many times do I have to tell you that two plus two makes four, that I'm a Jew, that I'm proud of it—that's what he's telling them. I imagine at that point he still trusts them. He doesn't know what's going to happen. So he's talking to them, telling them where he comes from, his background. We all have roots, don't we? And these are mine. You're Moslems. I'm a Jew. But ultimately we're human before anything else."

Another glance towards his wife, who has the same fond look she had when she showed me her son's room earlier, with his stuffed animals, his football trophies, and the diary he kept when he was little and was making New Year's resolutions: to not pick his nose and to do better in math. The next day he wrote, "I am doing better in math but I am still picking my nose."

"And then... in that first part of the message, there's something that's absolutely incredible. It's the sentence where he says, 'In B'nei Brak, in Israel, there is a street called Chaim Pearl Street, named after my great-grandfather....'"

"Yes," I say. "It was a sentence that I found very odd, too. First of all, is it true? Is there really a street with that name in B'nei Brak? And if so, how the hell did they know about it?"

"Exactly!" exclaims Judea. "Exactly!"

Now he seems euphoric. His expression is that of a great scientist making a major discovery—this must be what Professor Pearl, member of the National Academy of Engineering, world authority on artificial intelligence, looks like in his great moments of heuristic victory.

"They couldn't have known—exactly! No one in the world could have known that! Of course it's true. My grandfather was a local hero in B′nei Brak, a town ten miles outside of Tel-Aviv where he settled in the 1920s, with twenty-five other Hassidic families who, like him, were from Ostrowitz in Poland. But nobody knows that except us. Nobody. Which means...."

His face darkens. Often, with both of them, I see euphoria alternating with profound sadness. I assume those are the moments when the most unbearable images return, when everything is erased, everything—the tales and the testimony, the analysis, the courtesy towards the French stranger who is investigating the Pearl affair, the exchange of ideas, effort to understand—and suddenly nothing exists except the face of their child, tortured, calling out.

"Which means that sentence is a message. To his kidnappers, he's saying, 'This is who I am, I'm proud of it, I'm from a family who built cities, for whom building cities, digging wells and planting trees was the most beautiful thing you could do on earth—take that, you who love death and destruction!' But primarily it's to us, his mother and me, the only ones in the world who remember that in B′nei Brak there is a street named after my grandfather. So what is he saying to us? As you can imagine, I've asked myself that question thousands and thousands of times, for months. And my theory is that it's a coded message that means 'I'm Danny. Everything is OK. I'm being treated well. I'm speaking freely, since I'm saying something that nobody else could know except you and me. I am your beloved son. I love you.'"

Ruth has tears in her eyes. Judea's looking up at the ceiling and holding back tears of his own. He gets up and goes to get me a plate of cookies. A hair-dryer for her because her hair is damp and he's afraid she'll catch cold. I'm thinking about those Isaac Babel characters in *Red Cavalry* who, until the very last minute when the cossack is about to slash their faces or cut them to pieces keep repeating, "I am a Jew." I'm thinking about that old rabbi in I-don't-remember which Isaac Bashevis Singer novel, confronted during a pogrom by a brute about to strike him, cut his beard off, humiliate him, who surreptitiously repeats his prayer and with a thousand little gestures too subtle for the thug to perceive and visible only to He Who Sees All, persists in affirming, without arrogance, calmly, with that inner steadfastness that forges great heroes and martyrs, his unswerving loyalty to his hated community. Why didn't I think of this sooner? How could I have kept saying, like everybody else, and even here in this book, "Forced to proclaim his Jewishness, humiliated"? It was the opposite! A gesture of pride! A moment of dignity! Completely in keeping, in fact, with many of the stories I had heard about him: the party in Islamabad at the home of Khalid Khawaja, bin Laden's former pilot and friend, where everybody started to condemn Israel and the Jews, and he froze the assembly simply by saying "I'm a Jew"; the conversation in Syria with seven militants from Hezbollah discussing the "two religions," Islam and Christianity, and he chimes in, speaking softly and without emphasis, to add a third, his own, Judaism. But Judea is coming back. And I sense that it's my turn to speak.

"What you're saying sheds so much light, suddenly. It's perfectly obvious. Because I saw the video. I watched it dozens of times, frame by frame, image by image. And there were things I couldn't decipher. Disruptions of tone and rhythm... different expressions... the beard that wasn't the same, the state of his clothing.... Times when Danny is talking to the camera and others when he's oblivious to it.... Shots facing the camera, others in profile. When he lowers his eyes.... He's sarcastic when he's saying 'nowhere where Americans will be safe, nowhere where they will be able to go freely'... convincing when he's talking about his great-grandfather... bizarrely brutal, adamant, the words cracking like a whip, in that crucial part where he says 'my father is Jewish, my mother Jewish, I am Jewish....' Sarcastic again, or no, delighted, smiling like a child, when he utters the words that in theory condemn him: 'On my father's side I come from a family of Zionists....' If you're right, my dear Judea, everything becomes clear. It's a long interview, isn't it, almost a conversation, shot over a period of time, maybe hours or even the whole day, or even several days—and then afterwards the cuts, the editing."

Judea nods his head. He looks worn out, ten years older in ten minutes, but he's nodding his head silently.

"There's something else I was thinking that goes with what you're saying. I too was struck by how self-assured he looks in certain shots. I'm not talking about the video any more, no. Although when you think about it even in the video he doesn't have the look of a man who knows he's going to die. In the last sequence, for instance, about the relationship between the U.S. and Israel, he really seems to be making fun of them. No. I'm talking about the photos. You know those photos where he's wearing the top of his track suit and he has chains on his legs, the ones they sent to the media when he was being held. There are two photos that were not published in which—"

Judea's face changes once more. He leaps up again.

"What do you mean, not published? There were photos of Danny that weren't published, are you sure?"

"I think so, yes. That's my impression. At least I didn't see them anywhere. I read and saw just about everything that was published on your son's death and those two photos, in which he seems so confident, almost happy, I don't think I saw published anywhere...."

The truth is that I don't know any more. His emotion, his excitement, and the importance he is giving to this detail are starting to perturb me and make me uncertain.

"Is it so important?" I ask him.

"Yes, of course. Think about it—there are four photos. Four. Imagine there's a fifth. Where did it come from? Who gave it to whom? You see—what a difference it makes! Come with us, we'll check."

He gets up. Ruth gets up. They take me into the next room, which functions as the modest headquarters of the Daniel Pearl Foundation they have created in memory of their child, and where they keep, on the floor, in cardboard boxes, all the folders, everything that was written, the tributes, the articles. And there we are, all three of us crawling around, moving boxes, searching, looking for every single photo published, even in the most obscure paper. "Maybe in this box. No, the one underneath. Further down. Wait, let me do it, it's too heavy. Take that folder instead, the one with the Israeli clippings...."

I'm suddenly ashamed to have unleashed this frenzy.

I can feel that they are in the same state of agitation at the idea of an unpublished photo as they must have been last year, when Danny's death was not yet a certainty and one clutched at every clue, a detail, any fragment of information to rekindle hope.

There is something so utterly poignant, given that the tragedy has already taken place, about searching in the past, in a brief episode from a time now sadly irretrievable, for one last retrospective reason to believe and hope, that I am over-whelmed by emotion.

All the more so when, after ten minutes of showing me photos, always the same ones, among which I could never find my supposedly new picture, they finally hand me an issue of the *Jerusalem Post*. And there, I am forced to admit, was indeed the photo; it was rare, but not unpublished. I'm sorry....

"Let's go back to the video," says Ruth, exhausted by our absurd quest. I had noticed immediately that she had respiratory problems. She is very small. Very slight. But she gets out of breath in a way that is usually associated only with diabetics and the overweight. And then it's awful—she struggles to get her breath back. She pants. She looks like a survivor, I tell myself—still so youthful, so graceful, but with the look of a survivor. How do you live after such a disaster? Where do you find the strength to go through the motions of living? "Let's go back," she says. And I can see that she needs to go back to sitting on the couch.

"We haven't seen the video. We were told about it. We were given the transcript. But actually seeing it, no, we haven't seen it—how could a mother watch such a thing? We would have preferred that it not be aired at all. When CBS showed it, and from CBS it got on to the Internet, we were very angry, my husband and I. You have to show what these people are capable of, the CBS 'expert' on Islamic issues said—and showing it will discourage people from turning to Islam. What a joke! It's the opposite. Instead, for a lot of people, it was an incentive. Used for recruiting and propaganda in the mosques. But what do you think?"

I say you can make a case either way. But in cases like this, when in doubt, censorship is the worst solution. She shrugs—as if to say that in any case the battle is lost.

She goes on: "Since you've seen it, I have a question. How is he dressed? Does he wear his top the whole time?"

She sees that I don't quite grasp the meaning of her question.

"What I mean is whether there's any part of the video where he doesn't have his sweat suit top on. Did you see my Danny bare-chested?"

I know that there is indeed such a moment on the tape. I know that when the hand has finished its butchery, when you see it moving around in the wound, he is in fact bare-chested, but then there's a bizarre final shot, where he's wearing his pink and blue top again. But I don't dare tell her. I sense so much pain in her question, such secret entreaty, that I would like to tell her what she wants to hear, what she is hoping for—but what? I am silent.

"And another thing. Can you explain why they killed him the way they did? The way they cut him in pieces then put him back together to bury him."

I hear Judea, the scientist, the man of rigor, grumbling in his corner: "Too many questions at the same time!"

And she's like a little girl who's been scolded, close to shame: "It's true. But I would really like to know."

His voice is dull, constrained:

"They didn't cut him up just so he'd fit more easily into the plastic bags."

I don't know how to respond to that, either. I'd like to tell them what they so much want to hear, what would make them feel better, or at least not as bad. But again, how can I know? So I chanced to say:

"You have to look at the Algerians, who are the great experts at this kind of set-up. It seems to me that it's a message. A proclamation to the West. This is how we will treat you from now on. This is what we will do to you. What's more—"

I am thinking that 31 January, the probable date of Pearl's death, is close to the Islamic holiday on which sheep are sacrificed.

"What's more, it must have been not too long before the Aïd. So perhaps they wanted to tell us that from now on we won't just be slitting the throats of sheep, but also yours, you American, Jewish, European dogs."

I sense that Judea is trying to figure out with his rigorous, scientific mind whether we were in fact close to the Aïd in early February. That's what he used to do when his beloved Danny would call him urgently when a story deadline was looming: Dad, can you figure out for me the dates of Ramadan twelve years ago? What time is high tide in Karachi next week? What kind of weather they had during the battle of Waterloo? The next solar eclipse? What time the sun rose on the day Louis XVI was guillotined?

"As for your second question, Mrs. Pearl, as to why they felt the need to put him back together to bury his—"

She cuts me off. And in one breath, very fast, her little voice choked by oncoming sobs, she says:

"Maybe at the end somebody wanted to take care of him."

CHAPTER 6 DANNY'S FACE

I met again with the courageous parents, Ruth and Judea, and I corresponded with them.

I met Daniel Gill, Pearl's childhood friend, who started a boy's club with Danny at age six or seven, and who was best man at his wedding twenty years later.

I met colleagues, Americans and others, who had crossed Pearl's path in Karachi and in the rest of his professional life.

I read Steve LeVine, his *Wall Street Journal* colleague who was following developments in an investigation for the paper, and who in fact should have been in Karachi instead of Pearl, but, as it happened, he was getting married, and Danny was assigned instead. The assignment also led to a last-minute cancellation of a Pearl family reunion planned for 18 January in San Francisco.

And of course Mariane, almost immediately—I was in New York to show my movie *Bosna!*, and she was there with Tom Jennings, another friend of Danny's. Beautiful, dignified, like a modern Antigone, Mariane was considering making a film with Jennings in Karachi about her husband—a film of duty and truth. Go back to Karachi? To follow Daniel Pearl's path, when your name is Pearl? Yes! Without hesitation! To prevent pain and memory from solidifying, to prevent oneself from becoming rigid with grief, and dissolving in mourning. And then there was

Adam. She had to think about little Adam Pearl, born after his father's death, who had become her reason for living. She sent me a sweet photo of him for New Year's 2003.

So, Mariane Pearl: The virginal demeanor with ash-gray eyes. Curly black hair pulled back into a chignon, as in the photos. The lovely nape of her neck. Such an odd mixture of French, and now American, and a little bit Cuban, and Buddhist, and Jewish because of Daniel. Mariane, in an uncomfortable and empty apartment downtown in the Stuyvesant Towers: I sense it will be a long time before she can accomplish more than the merest gestures necessary to ensure her baby's well-being. Mariane at the restaurant, that night and the following—her olive skin, no makeup, only the mask of misfortune; an old loose T-shirt thrown on, in contrast to how chic she looks in the photos in the Pearl living room showing happy times. Her answers are brief. She resists pathos. She creates a slight distance whenever the questioning gets too precise—"I pass… I can't answer that… no, really, that's not possible… I can't answer that question…." Mariane Pearl, who every time she hears that I'm going back to Karachi sends me a friendly, sisterly little message: *Prenez garde à vous*—"Take care." I remember seeing Mariane in an old BBC interview, when things were at their greatest uncertainty, when everybody was still hoping that the kidnappers had not committed the irreparable: She was six months pregnant, shattered and full of hope, intense. I remember her pleading, "If somebody has to give their life to save him, I'll do it. Please get in touch with me. I'm ready."

With her and the others, I asked the same questions.

Each time I gleaned photos, documents, scraps of memories, shreds of a life.

Searching through a man's past as if I were rummaging in a bag.

Poking, with the end of my pen, through the little heap of secrets and clichés.

I had to look behind the martyred face to find the other, real face—not *Pearl's* face, *Danny's*.

I wanted so desperately to understand who the real Danny was that they had targeted, then killed.

To think of Daniel Pearl as alive.

God, according to the prophets who had given both of us some nourishment, is not the God of the dead but, first and foremost, the God of the living.

There's the splendid child, unexpectedly blond, whose room I had found so touching when I visited it in Los Angeles.

There's the football-playing child, kneeling next to the ball with his big orange socks, hair still blond and long, the face of a little prince, fresh as a daisy, posing for the photo and maybe stifling laughter—only his eyes are smiling, but what a smile!

There's the best friend, the stories of kids on Mulholland Drive, children's clubs, school outings, long intervals under the trees, endless summers, coconut cream pie after violin lessons, a happy life.

And very soon there's the music fanatic—photos of him playing violin, guitar, mandolin piano, drums. Group photos in Bombay. Another group in the Berkshires, a typical '80s rock band. Another splendid black and white photo: age eighteen or twenty, in tux and bow tie, hair cut short à la Tom Cruise, looking out at the audience, a restrained grin—he has just drawn the bow over the strings to play his last note. I can hear the applause, he is about to take a bow, he's happy. Favorite hobbies? asks the

Stanford college application. "Sports and music, windsurfing and violin...." What was your relationship? I asked Gill. "Music, girls, but mainly music. There were a bunch of us and music was the link. Rock, pop, but also at fifteen an Isaac Stern concert, or Stephane Grappelli, or Miles Davis." The delight of Judea, a musician himself, when he discovered that his little boy had perfect pitch! Praise the Lord for this miracle! Thank you for this gift!

Here's the good friend, again—his generosity with colleagues. The headline he makes up for one. The catchy phrase he gives another. His kindness to the youngest reporters. The controlled insolence with his elders. His loyalty to the newspaper, there's only one, it's *the* newspaper, his, and too bad that it also belongs to the Dow Jones Company, which isn't exactly his cup of tea. When the *New York Times*, right before his departure for London in 1998, tried to lure him away with the kind of offer that makes you think twice, particularly in America, he turned it down, saying "I am not a mercenary. I like the *Journal* and I like my friends. I'm staying."

Too good to be true? A pious cliché? Fortunately he's there to correct that impression. He's present in his answers to the questions on the Stanford application—modest, teasing, above all not taking himself too seriously. He calls himself "lazy" in his deliberate, very readable cursive, the letters distinct and sometimes almost separated—the still somewhat childish writing of a man who must have been told a hundred times "Be more careful! I can't read your writing!" My problem is that I am "lazy," he writes, and sometimes, "fortunately not often," I feel "contempt for humanity." Sometimes, too, "petty frustrations" drive me to "generalized pessimism."

There's the charmer. There, too, we have to watch out for the too-good-to-be-true. But the charm and magnetism were real. There are stories, in Paris and London, of women who were captivated. He was funny. He had an irresistible imagination. He could make up a song for a girl he liked in ten minutes. He was capable, also, like Solal, of giving himself an hour to seduce her, and succeeding. Danny, his mother would insist—suddenly very much the "Jewish mother," oh-so-proud of her little boy who had become a ladies' man—had two reasons to be a success with young women. And not just women, in fact. He was charm personified—everybody, male or female, came under his spell. First of all, said Ruth, he was interested in them. He looked at them as if at that moment nothing more important existed in the world. Secondly, he had been loved as a child—he was beloved and he knew it. Nothing better than love to create an adult who feels comfortable in his skin… a charmer.

There are, again, the photos. They're the photos that I have spread out in front of me on the floor of my Los Angeles hotel room. They emanate a vibration and power that suddenly almost frightens me. Here's Danny all by himself, a close-up, with those sparkling, trusting eyes behind his glasses—"the jewel of the eye, truthful and laughing," says the poet. Here's Danny standing with his parents, the good son, the good boy, with a look of infinite tenderness. Danny with a beard, in profile, in front of a window looking out towards the sea; it has rained, the sky is a powdery blue. Danny from the back, in a shaft of light that isolates him. Danny wearing a T-shirt, his eyes bright, a gentle smile, casually elegant, a handsome chiseled face—he looks like a young Arthur Miller. Danny with Mariane, orange T-shirt over beige pants: they're walking in the streets of a big city, maybe Milan, Turin or simply Paris, the arcades of the Palais-Royal. They're young, they look happy, I can hear them breathing, I can make out their animated voices and their laughter, I see the looks they exchange, I feel their light breath. Danny as a baby. Danny as a child, by the sea. Danny as a teen, holding a baseball bat, good as gold, an ironic stillness. Or with his sisters, at the prow of a white boat, a pontoon, glowing warm twilight, a seagull above their heads. With his sister again, in the garden at home, the end of a California afternoon, a light wind, sunshine, teasing her as two friends look on in amusement. Or in another garden, bathed in heat, light breeze, with his violin, reading a Bach score that his friend Gill is holding up for him. Danny with his 92-year-old grandmother Tova, who lives in Tel Aviv, looking at him in ecstasy while he smiles; he adored her. Danny on assignment, in what seems to be an Arab street—his hair has grown and he's wearing a ponytail and all is right with his world.

There's a wedding photo. He's standing in front of a fence, a photographer in the background, friends. Mariane's shoulders are bare. Orange taffeta skirt. Chiffon scarf. A bouquet of flowers in her hand. A perfect silhouette. Her delicate, exposed neck. I can imagine a Chopin prelude or a mazurka as background music. She's radiant. He's dressed up. Slightly artificial. Beige suit, a little stiff. Freshly cut short hair. He's holding her hand. In his eyes, a confident questioning, a tender glow, the youthful pride of happiness achieved. Not the slightest hint that could prompt someone to say later, "There, it was written, the tragedy was lurking beneath the enchanted image." Not even, in their eyes, that slight hesitation, the distance between me and myself that usually testifies to the possibility of misfortune, or, simply, worry. No. They were absolutly present. Joy and beatitude. I have seen few faces, in my lifetime, so fulfilled. It seems to me that few people know they are happy when they're happy, and Pearl was one of the few. (And yet, it's coming back to me, what Ruth confided yesterday as we parted—the day right before or right after his wedding, when he told her that it was too much happiness. Exactly—too much good luck, and he hoped that one day he wouldn't have to pay for so much luck.... Did he really say that? Did she really tell me he said that? Or am I dreaming? Or did I misunderstand? I don't know any more. Too many photos, yes. There are so many I get dizzy and maybe I'm talking nonsense....)

There's the journalist. I have in front of me the commemorative anthology published by his newspaper, *At Home in the World*. His whole life, that title. The inner password, the motto of this tireless globetrotter, as interested in the fate of a Stradivarius as he is in the mystery of Iranian Coca-Cola bottles, in the problems inherent in calculating dates for Ramadan and in the quarrel between Yemenites and Ethiopians on the origins of the Queen of Sheba. Unusual columns. Intrepid reporting. The guy who demolishes NATO's pronouncements on the Kosovo situation in the Eastern establishment's favorite newspaper. The one who, when the White House orders the bombing of a chemical factory in Sudan because it believes that it isn't a chemical factory, but rather a clandestine laboratory making weapons for biological warfare, is the first to go look and shout, "No, it really was a chemical factory. America has committed a tragic error." An assignment in Qom. The rock music trend in Teheran. The battle for generic drugs, particularly for AIDS patients. Al-Qaida's involvement in diamond trafficking in Tanzania.... Daniel Pearl, contrary to what has often been said, was not a war correspondent. "You have to be in practice to cover a war," he'd say. "I'm not in practice. That's why I didn't want to go to Afghanistan and preferred to go to Pakistan." But you can sense the very good, the very great, journalist. You sense the passionate explorer, tirelessly striding through far-away lands, the love of human beings and the world—you sense the news addict who lives his assignments, body and soul.

Was Danny careless? It's been said. During my year of investigation, I kept meeting people in Karachi, Madrid, Washington, who told me: "rash risks... was warned... didn't want to listen... what a pity...." One step away, particularly in Pakistan, from lapsing into the hateful: "got what he deserved... sad but true... too bad for him... that's the way it is." It was the opposite, of course. A good assessment of risks. A healthy fear of the country and the lunatics who disfigure it—proved by his e-mails to his parents. He didn't have protection, granted, but who did, at the time? What journalist prior to "The Daniel Pearl Affair" walked around with one of those armed escorts in orange or blue caps who protect Pakistani bigwigs? Even now there aren't many. I was offered one, during one of my trips. But what I immediately realized is that first, it's the kind of precaution that mostly serves to attract the attention of those who wish you harm; and second, that a retired cop getting ten dollars an hour isn't very motivated, in case of trouble, to take a bullet for you. I repeat, Pearl was not a war correspondent. He had not a trace of fascination for this garbage, the violence of men against men. Caution, he would say, is a dimension of courage.

And another thing. Did you know that it was he, Daniel Pearl, who in 1998, three years before "The Pearl Affair," volunteered to compile for the *Wall Street Journal* a sort of journalistic handbook on security issues? He had thought of everything. The *Journal* used it to brief its reporters. Except for one subject, only one, which he left out: kidnapping! What to do if you were kidnapped! The specialists are categorical. They all say there's one absolute rule, which is don't try to escape. Never. But there you have it. It was the only rule he didn't know. It was the only situation he hadn't considered. He had anticipated everything, except what you're supposed to do if you get kidnapped. What irony! What a coincidence! As is the dream that Ruth had on 23 January, at the same time as the kidnapping. Danny, haggard, disheveled, appearing to her at the bottom of a dead-end street. "What's wrong, darling? What's going on?" "Nothing. They just made me drink water. Lots of water. It's nothing." But he looks so awful. So pale and so awful. Ruth wakes up in a sweat, and goes directly to her e-mail: "Danny, are you all right? Please answer immediately!"

More about carelessness. The theory that he was being manipulated by American intelligence. Who told me that? It doesn't matter. The reasoning is as follows: A *Wall Street Journal* colleague buys a used computer at the Kabul market, right after the American war and the flight of the Taliban. He boots it up. He discovers to his amazement that the hard drive contains a quantity of strange information that smells of al-Qaida. He gives it to the *Journal*. Who pass it on to the American intelligence services. And they, once they've processed the information, come back to the newspaper in the hope—it's classic—that one or several journalists can help them confirm or disprove their preliminary conclusions. It's possible, of course. Everything, absolutely everything, is possible in such a strange story. As for the theory that Danny was in touch with the intelligence agencies, why not? What would be wrong with that? Shouldn't a good journalist, in the search for the truth, look for information anywhere he might find it? Shouldn't he follow up on every lead, make use of anything he can? Turn over every stone? Will I be accused of being a secret agent when I go to New Delhi to ask Indian intelligence what they know about his death? A CIA agent when I go to Washington, check on the investigation, glean there, too, a few clues, scraps of truth, maybe some evidence? The one thing I know is that Danny was a seasoned journalist. Street-smart. He never let himself be taken in by authorities, small-time crooks or spies. The one thing I could never imagine is that he would cross that yellow line between those who love truth and the agents or even militants of any given cause.

There is the Jew who had always thought if he had a son he would have him circumcised and who in 1998 wrote to his mother: "I will pass on to my children all the Jewish tradition I know, and with your help, maybe a little bit more." How Jewish? I asked Ruth and Judea. Jewish. Faithful to that part of his memory. Because to him being Jewish was a way of having a memory. Yom Kippur. The High Holidays. Friday night dinner when he was home in Los Angeles. This other conversation with his mother, or maybe it was the same one, I don't remember, when he asked, "If I married outside of my faith, what would you say?"

He was thinking about Mariane, remembers Ruth. He loved her so much! She made him so happy! And he was so sure that they had the real faith, the two of them, which was the faith of the heart! And that bar mitzvah photo at the Wailing Wall, *kippa*, prayer shawl, holding the Torah, bigger than he is, that pure light flashing from his eyes.

And those questions that he asked us, recalls Judea, his mother and me, especially his mother, about our families and our roots. How are you Jewish, how am I? Obviously it fascinated him. And there was the way he would call from wherever he was in the world every time there was a bombing in Israel to ask about his grandmother Tova and his cousins in Tel-Aviv.

And Israeli? I asked then. I read in France that he was American but also Israeli, dual citizenship—the French sometimes call it *double allégeance*—is there any truth to that? Judea hesitated. Well… I'm the one who has an Israeli passport, and naturally so does Ruth. So it depends how you look at it. From the Israeli point of view, because his mother and father are Israeli, he was too, automatically, in a certain way. But he never thought about it. Neither did we. The only trace of it was when he was three, and he was listed on Ruth's Israeli passport. But does that make you an Israeli?

And politically? I continued. What were his politics? Was he very critical of his country? Anti-American?

Judea laughed at that. Maybe I hadn't expressed myself correctly. Maybe I was wrong to say "anti-American." Because for the first time in the three hours we have been talking, Judea bursts out laughing, yes, hearty laughter—and just as well, in fact, it makes me happy.

Anti-American, you said? Are you joking? Who told you such nonsense? You're not going to tell me that's why he's popular in France and Europe! On the contrary, he loved his country. He was proud to be an American citizen. He knew all the names and biographies of the presidents from when he was a little kid. Do you know why he wanted to call his son Adam? He found out right before he got kidnapped that it was going to be a boy, and he and Mariane decided to call him Adam. And it was because of John Quincy Adams, sixth president of the United States, a fervent abolitionist, who fought against slavery. It's true there was the ecumenical angle, OK. There was the idea that it was a name that could be said in all languages and all religions. But it was also a tribute to a great president who was also a great American. Danny, I assure you, was passionately American. Much more than I am, for instance. I'm still a damn Israeli immigrant.

And apart from that? Besides being proud to be American? About Israel? The Palestinians? What were his fundamental thoughts about Israel and the Palestinians?

Judea hesitates again. I realize—he realizes—that he doesn't really know much about it.

He loved the Jewish people, for sure. Deeply loved Israel. Was inwardly appalled when he witnessed the country being caricatured and stigmatized: He knew Israelis hate war, that they drag their feet when they have to do their stints in the reserves. He had cousins there and he knew they cried in their tanks when they went out on operations. But he also loved justice. He refused to have to choose between Israel and justice. And so, a partisan of two states—does that satisfy you?

The root of the problem, Judea continues to insist, is that Danny didn't have ideas, no positions or opinions, because he was a journalist before anything else. You couldn't expect him to get involved or be a militant for any cause. You couldn't hope that he would take sides for the Jews, or for the Palestinians—the Jews are right because. . . the Palestinians have a point because. . . . The role of the journalist, he would say, isn't to give out prizes for virtue. The journalist's role is to ascertain the facts, period.

I try to get more out of Danny Gill, his childhood friend, who is ill at ease to be talking about his old friend, intimidated to be there at the parents' house, in the role of final witness. I can imagine him as a little boy, already overweight, dominated by his friend. I imagine them getting together in the evenings when they took their dogs for a walk. Who told me that the last e-mail from Pearl, the evening of the 23rd was to ask about his dog? Maybe Gill. His dog was sick, but now he's better. It's Pearl who's gone. His eyes get blurry; he wipes away a tear, an emotional boy's tear. I keep pushing, anyway. Maybe because I don't want to give up my idea of Danny as a true American democrat, I ask him, "The war in Iraq, for instance. I know it's always hard to make the dead talk, but you who knew him so well. . . what would he say if he were here?" And Gill, in front of Ruth and Judea who are listening, like me, without saying a word, confirms, "He'd be critical, of course. Completely critical. Judea is right when he says this idea that he was anti-American is bullshit. But this stupid war, he'd be against it, I guarantee it."

There's the Jewish-American Danny, but he's open to the cultures of the world and to the culture, particularly, of the *other*. This Jew learns some Arabic, in London, at age 30—because of his Sephardic mother, born in Iraq? Certainly, but not only that. Also because of this desire for the other, this openness to the enigmatic otherness of his fellow human, near and far. This American rejects the fashionable theories about the collision of civilizations, the inevitable clash of cultures. He and Omar, his murderer, read Huntington, we will see, at the same time. But the killer subscribes to the idea, loves the death that he is promised—Danny resists, refuses the disaster that is foretold. If there's only one left, it will be me. If there is only one American and Jew left to believe that confrontation with Islam is not fatal, I will be that American and that Jew, and I will do everything in my power to avert the inevitable.

Conversation between Danny and Gill, after September 11, on the Koran: Doesn't the Koran preach hatred of infidels? Yes, of course, Danny answered. But not only that. You can't, you don't have the right, to pick out only the negative parts of a book like that. There is another Koran within the Koran, which is a message of mercy and peace.

And this beautiful scene, recounted by Robert Sam Anson in his pioneering report for *Vanity Fair* a few months after Danny's death: It's November 2001, just before the U.S. bombing of Kabul. There are more and more demonstrations throughout Pakistan. Danny is in Peshawar, caught up in a protest march where they're burning flags and effigies of Bush. Don't stay here, says Hamid Mir, the journalist who is with him. It's dangerous.... No, Danny replies. I'm here, I want to understand, and I want to see in these people's eyes why they hate us. The anecdote may not be true. A colleague who knew him well told me that it didn't seem very authentic to him. But that would be a shame. Because it illustrates so well the curiosity he had, the thirst to know the other, this radical non-hatred—the best of Americans?

There's the Danny—I've read his articles—who even if he is proud of America, thinks that America and, in general the West, has an obligation to the world, owes the world something.

There is the diehard humanist who, in spite of everything he sees and has seen in his life, continues to want to believe that man is not a predator to other men, but a brother, a kindred spirit.

There is the journalist who through his reporting goes unflaggingly towards the forgotten of the world, pays his debt, our debt, the debt of the hordes of smug and overfed Westerners who couldn't care less about world poverty and don't consider themselves "their brothers' keepers."

There is another debt, he's well aware. He's enough of a Jew to know that the problem is also those other hordes, the Muslims, who too often refuse to recognize their own debt towards a certain Book and the people who carried it. But he pays anyway. He pays in advance, in a way—without waiting and without assurance that he will be paid back. And that's admirable.

There's that face—there aren't that many—in which our era can see itself without shame.

Because in a certain way Daniel Pearl is still alive—because of the emotion his death has aroused, and also because of the values everyone can feel, indistinctly, he incarnated—he is this living antidote to all the modern stupidities about the war between civilizations and worlds.

Did they know what they were doing when they killed him?

Did they know what they were killing when they killed this journalist?

And is it for that reason that I became interested in him—is it for the same but inverted reason that I decided one day, and in fact immediately, to take on this investigation, to retrace his path, to write this book?

I don't know. It's always very difficult to trace the origin of a book. I'm in Kabul that morning. I have just arrived. It's the start of a "mission of reflection on the participation of France in the reconstruction of Afghanistan" that the French president and prime minister have entrusted me with, which kept me busy for part of the winter of 2002 and resulted in my *Rapport Afghan*. The previous evening when I was out after curfew, I'd had a small run-in with some members of the militia of Abdul Rasul Sayyaf, a neo-fundamentalist warlord and a former terrorist. And it was President Karzaï, who, that morning, gave me the news. We're in his office, with a few of his ministers. They bring him a piece of paper. He turns pale. And informs us, first in Persian for Mohammed Fahim and Yunous Qanouni, then in English for my benefit: We have received confirmation of the death—his throat was slit—of the American journalist Daniel Pearl.

Images, a little later. The shock of the video. Emotion. Compassion. Identification, naturally. Every journalist in the world must have identified, even briefly, with this man who suddenly resembled them like a brother. Their own death, the masked angel whose face they watch for in vain from one assignment to the next, and who is there suddenly in the devastated features of one of them. For me, the image, too, of a bright, personable American journalist I had bumped into during the summer of 1997 in Asmara, Eritrea, and who was trying, as I was, to make contact with John Garang, the Sudanese Christian fighting with the Khartoum Islamists. Was it really him? How can I remember? You don't know, do you, when you meet a journalist in Asmara who is trying on Panama hats in a store run by an Italian in the Piazza Centrale, that he's going to get his throat slit four years later, and that his image will pursue you for a year, probably longer? What I know is that for these reasons and others, for those which came to me immediately and for those I know now, because Pearl's story makes me afraid and prevents me from feeling fear, because of what it says about the horror of our times and equally about their share of greatness, because of what Pearl represented when he was alive and what he must continue to represent dead, because of the causes that were his and which remain essentially mine, because of all of that, his image is present now, and stays with me.

A kindred spirit. A brother. Dead and alive. A dead man that I must bring to life. And this pledge, this contract, first between him and me, then between me and myself: to contribute something. Usually you take out a contract on someone to kill him. Here it's the opposite: a contract out on Daniel Pearl, in order to resurrect him.

PART TWO
OMAR

CHAPTER 1   IN THE EYE OF THE ASSASSIN

I'm back in Europe.

Five months have passed since Daniel Pearl's murder and my decision to write this book.

I'm going over my notes on his life—and at the same time reading and rereading *At Home In the World,* the collection of his articles published by the *Wall Street Journal.*

And I confess that, the more time passes, the more I reflect on all this, the more I advance—if not in the investigation, then at least into the depth of Pearl's personality and the mystery of his assassination—the more I ask myself what could have led someone to designate such a man for a death so barbarous... and the more I am intrigued by the personality of his assassin.

Not that there was just one assassin, of course.

Not that one can say, "There, that's the assassin, the man who killed Daniel Pearl—the idea came from his mind, was carried out by his hand."

In fact, the little I know so far, the little anyone knows, is that, on the contrary, it was a complex crime in which many are implicated. The little that has been established so far is that it took not one but several men to ensnare Pearl—to disarm his vigilance, lure him into the trap at the Village Garden restaurant, drive him to Gulzar e-Hijri, sequester, kill, and bury him. I've cited the Yemenis... and Bukhari, the man who dictated the words to say to the camera... Fazal Karim, the man who held his head while another cut his throat... Saud Memon, owner of the property... Lahori... there are even more whom I have yet to clearly identify—but patience, it will come. It's not a crime, it's a puzzle. It's not an organization, it's an army. And nothing could be more simplistic in the face of this puzzle, this army, than to take this one or that one and declare: *"He's the assassin."*

But, at the same time, there undoubtedly had to be one person to recruit these men, one mind, having conceived of the crime, to channel their energies and distribute their assignments, an architect for such a pyramid, a conductor for this sinister orchestra, a director for this murder committed in unison, an *emir* who, though not necessarily present at Pearl's Gulzar e-Hijri jail, nor, as we shall see, at the Village Garden rendezvous, designated the target, defined the strategy, pulled the strings, and recruited Bukhari, Fazal Karim, Lahori and the others.

That man's name is Omar.

His exact name is Omar Sheikh—given name Omar, family name Sheikh (and not, as the Pakistanis often say, Sheikh Omar, in the same way they say Mullah Omar, for the Taliban leader).

He is the one I call "the assassin."

It is he who—arrested in the days following Pearl's death with three of his accomplices in Lahore—admitted to being the "mastermind" of the operation.

It is he who promptly declared to investigators, "I planned the kidnapping because I was sure I could negotiate with the

Americans for the release of one or two people, such as the former Taliban ambassador to Pakistan, Mullah Abdul Salam Zaeef."

It is he who, as his three accomplices (and others not yet judged) readily admitted, had called them one by one during the month of January, saying, "I've got a Jew, an American, a good target, not difficult, an excellent bargaining chip...."

It is he who, on 15 July 2002, at the conclusion of a three-month trial full of surprise developments—including three changes of judges, threats of terrorist attacks, numerous suspensions, adjournments, diverse pressures and blackmail—was condemned by a tribunal in Hyderabad to death by hanging.

And he is the one I'm thinking of when I write "the assassin," in the singular, intrigues me: his is the face I see when I tell myself that we must—without delaying or waiting to discover all the other pieces of the puzzle, the ramifications, the accomplices, and the people ultimately behind it all—regard, most closely, the assassin.

A portrait, therefore, of Omar.

Be careful, though, Mariane said in New York.

Keep yourself from personalizing too much, from delving too much into the psychology, both of Omar and his accomplices. Don't enter into their madness or, worse, their logic.

Don't give them, and especially him, the inestimable gift of celebrity, which is, deep down, all they dream of—the glory of the barbarian, the Warholian fifteen minutes against a background of cruelty and crime. Why not leave things as they are? Why not condemn this man to his essential insignificance? Why interest yourself in the soul of Omar?

In a way, of course, she's right.

It is, in fact, a precept that has long guided me whenever I have had to deal with figures of evil in this world. And so she is inviting me not to lose sight of a good and wise lesson—the snares of complacency, the risk of understanding so much you excuse it in the end. The risk that in telling how it was, in making it believable, little by little, by a gradual seduction of sense and reason, it becomes inevitable, almost natural, to conclude that things had to happen the way they did. "Enter not into the path of the wicked, and go not in the way of evil men," it says in Deuteronomy. Enter not into the mind of the perverse for fear of dulling the vital force of revolt, of anger, has been my own position, when I have written about the fascist figures of the 20th century.

And should I doubt or hesitate, for this particular crime, to follow the law that usually guides me, the strange attention this man has attracted in Karachi would end up convincing me.

The "moderate islamist" who in a letter to the editor of an English-language newspaper in Islamabad, explained in April, just before my trip, that Omar had at least the merit of "defending his ideas," of going "all the way with his principles," and for that he deserved the respect of "real Muslims."

Then there's Adnan Khan, a former member of Jaish e-Mohammed, one of the principle Islamist terrorist organizations, who served five years in prison between 1989 and 1994 for the murder of his landlord, and who, a few weeks after the death of Pearl, confessed to the crime in an attempt to clear his hero Omar. "My life had no meaning," he admitted to police in Sindh after they had verified that he had, in fact, nothing to do with the murder. "Always the same, the days, the seasons, the worries—but him, his life, at once just and glorious for Islam... God bless him... I wanted to help him—I wanted to save this great man...."

A letter addressed to Omar in early July in his Hyderabad prison, came to my knowledge through one of his lawyers: "My name is Sikander Ali Mirani. I live in Larkana. I admire your fight. You are in my eyes and in the eyes of all my friends a modern-day prophet of Islam. And to this prophet, this saint, I want to reveal my doubts, my difficulties and my sacrifices—and I want to ask also for his help. You are from a rich family, yes? Your father has business in England? Then please ask him to help me immigrate to London. Use your influence to help me to study, like you did." The young man attached a copy of his passport. Plus, as if for a casting call or a job application, a photo that looks as though it were taken for the occasion: an awkward young man, a little fat, looking tough. And on the back of the envelope, in the same careful handwriting, his address in Larkana.

Letters like this one, intercepted by prison officials, arrive by the dozen every week.

They testify to the resonance, not only in Pakistan but throughout the Arab-Muslim world, of Omar's act and the idea—present in Sikander Ali Mirani's letter—that a lesson was taught to Americans and Jews. The letters testify as well, it seems, to a resonance with his attitude during the trial, his defiant way of facing it, his arrogance and refusal to accept the rules of a legal system copied from the English.

And they make clear the need for extreme prudence when undertaking a portrait of this man and attempting to penetrate the mystery of his motives.

However...

I read the accounts of the trial appearing in the local press sent to me by my Pakistani interpreter and assistant—my *fixer*.

I note the strange way this man had of not really defending himself except on the finer points of certain details; how in the main, he stood by his deed.

I have before me a page from a major Karachi daily, from the time of the verdict.

There are two photos side by side.

That of Pearl's, face-front, with his sparkling expression, the dazzling glimmer in his eyes that made him seem curious about everything, his look of well-meaning irony, his sense of humor, his evident friendliness, and, on his lips, something like an old smile that hasn't worn off, caught by the photographer.

And that of Omar, in profile, handsome as well, his face well-constructed, high forehead, a look without vice or malice though somewhat veiled. His physiognomy appears intelligent and rather frank, tortoise-shell glasses, a strong chin under a well-trimmed beard, a good man it would seem, slightly tart smile, an intellectual demeanor, very Westernized—nothing, in any case, that signals the obtuse Islamist, the fanatic; nothing really that tells us, "Yes it is I, the assassin... it is from this head the plot to kill, then dismember, an exemplary American came...."

I have many other photos.

In addition to pictures e-mailed to me by my fixers, I brought back from Pakistan at least one photograph of each of the accomplices identified by the police: assassins plunged in their own vertigo, brutish, faces steeped in hate, death in their eyes, head down or demon laugh, hackles raised in vengeance or with the half-smile of the torturer awaiting his hour—they all give the same impression of criminality just below the surface.

But I admit that none of them affect me like Omar—none of them impress me like this strange man, apparently well-mannered and gentle, refined and subtle, and who, in the other pictures of him appearing in the Anglo-Saxon press taken at the very end of the trial, never veers from a confounding impassiveness that is rarely seen on the face of a condemned man.

This monster who is also a man like any other, this killer in whose face I fail to find any of the stigmata that, in the common imagination, signals the presence of absolute Evil; this manifestly astute man, this arrogant man who, after the pronouncing of his sentence, as he was being taken from the room, found nothing better to say to his judges than, "We will see who dies first—me or the authorities who arranged this death sentence for me"; this enigmatic character I read about in the *Guardian*'s brief—too brief—biography, in which the mixture of lucidity and blindness, of culture and brutal criminality reminds me of Ilich Ramirez Sanchez, alias the Jackal, alias Carlos, the Venezuelan terrorist who was all over the front pages in the '70s and '80s and whom I wrote about in my book *Diable en Tête*... it's not enough to say he interests me or intrigues me—he is clearly the second most important character of this book.

So who, then, is Omar?

Where does he come from and what do we know about him, his criminal career, his life, in the early summer of 2002?

We know, for one thing, that he is not quite thirty years old.

He is linked to Jaish e-Mohammed, one of the most extreme, the most violent and the most prominent Islamist groups in Pakistan—and it was the head of this group, Masood Azhar, a mixture of ideologue and brute, of saint and killer, who was Omar's master in terrorism, his mentor.

It is known as well that this is not his first such crime—he was arrested and condemned once before, in India, in 1994, for a kidnapping plot similar to that of Pearl's. The object then was to obtain the release of Masood Azhar, who had been imprisoned a few months earlier for anti-Indian terrorism in the disputed province of Kashmir. Omar's victims in that case—three English tourists and an American—were freed by the Indian police at the last minute. In the inexhaustible interviews those victims have been giving to the Anglo-Saxon press in light of recent events, they say things such as: "I saw the animal... I spent eight days, ten, fifteen, thirty-two in his company... this is what I know of him... this is the impression I had...." They tell of a paradoxical individual, at once totally unstable and intellectually coherent, who played chess and read *Mein Kampf,* hated Jews and skinheads, recited constantly from the Koran yet did not seem particularly pious, and who announced apologetically that, unless his demands were met, he would decapitate them.

We also know he served six years in prison for those kidnappings, first in Uttar Pradesh and then New Delhi, but that he recovered his freedom on 31 December 1999, thanks to a bloody and spectacular airline hijacking by a jihadist group to which he and Masood Azhar belonged: an Indian Airlines Katmandu to Delhi flight was hijacked to Kandahar airport at the height of the Taliban era. To demonstrate their determination to the

Indians and the world, in the front of the plane the hijackers staged a chilling scene in which one passenger was beheaded. After eight days of threats and bargaining, the 155 other passengers were freed in exchange for Omar and Masood.

And finally, it is known that this man—this madman, this hardened criminal, this zealot of kidnapping, this fanatic of God, this man whose hatred for the West brought him twice in eight years to violent crime —is not Pakistani but English; the reports I read make clear that he is, like all his comrades in Jaish-e-Mohammed, of Pakistani origin, but he was actually born in England, has an English passport, and spent his childhood and adolescence in England, that in England he was quite a brilliant student, that his family lives in London, his address is in London—that he is, in short, English.

Is this a monstrosity of an ordinary human, or the humanity of an extraordinary monster? That is the theme of this other investigation, as important to me as the first—into the mind of the Devil.

CHAPTER 2 A PERFECT ENGLISHMAN

I went to London, where Omar was born on 23 December 1973, to a family that had immigrated from Lahore in 1968.

I visited the maternity ward of Whips Cross Hospital, a large public hospital in London's eastern suburbs. It is a little shabby, as English public hospitals sometimes are, but it's prosperous, modern, medically reliable. This is where Qauissia, his mother, came to give birth. The family is liberal and broadminded, ostensibly not very particular in respect to Koranic laws regarding birth and delivery.

In nearby Wanstead, I found Perfect Fashions, the ready-to-wear import-export business that Omar's father established, and which he still runs with Omar's younger brother, Awais. It's a small store at 235 Commercial Road, on the corner of Myrdle Street. It's one long room filled with large, plastic-wrapped cartons piled on top of each other and marked either "made in Pakistan" or "Boston" (the name of another company?). On the day of my visit, stray open cartons and the few dresses displayed in the window on hangers or wax mannequins showed rather ordinary fabrics in garish colors and in cuts and styles destined for wholesalers. But business is prosperous. The balance sheets, available from the London Commerce Registry, indicate intense activity, a sound financial structure, and a pretax profit of hundreds of thousands of pounds per year over the last five years. The Sheikh family is well-off. Little Omar was raised in opulence. I imagine a happy childhood, an easy adolescence.

I found the house the family bought in 1977 and still owns, in Deyne Court Gardens, at the corner of Colvin Street, close to the Wanstead Bowls Club, and not far from the chess club which Omar frequented (because he was, it will be repeated to me at each step of my investigation, an excellent chess player). It's a residential street, lined with trees and gardens. It's a typical English cottage, with an attractive porch, arched windows, shingled roof, painted brick walls, a cluster of trees in front and, in back, an unfenced garden opening onto a common. I arrive early in the morning. It's the hour of the milk van and newspapers in the mailbox. The upstairs curtains are drawn shut. The family, because they stay late at the store, are probably sleeping. The shutters on one of the bedrooms are closed—Omar's room? Going around the back toward the common and looking through the ground-floor windows, I see a charming living room, an entrance where two men's coats and a hooded woman's raincoat hang, a well-equipped kitchen, an already set table, a pretty tablecloth, egg cups, boxes of cereal, a pitcher of milk, and flowered plates. All of which speaks of a close family, country living in the city, a carefree life, happiness. All of which tells a family story which must have been the same, even more peaceful, ten years ago, when Omar, the eldest son, was there. We are far, at any rate, from a setting of misery and oppression, of troubles and ruined lives, that we tend to associate with the genealogy of terrorism.

"I have nothing to say to you," Saeed Sheikh, the father, told me one evening, in a weary and constrained voice, when, after a long wait, I managed to catch him leaving his house, in a dark blue gabardine suit and felt hat. "No, I have nothing to say to you. Leave me alone." But I did have the time to make out, in the cold night air, his eyes like an aged child, the myopic look of his wan smile, his stiff, fan-shaped beard, the oddness of a drooping eyelid which gives him an air of perpetual irony. I had the time to observe in the lamplight what had struck me in a picture I had seen in the *Guardian*—he was the epitome of Commonwealth chic.

I met Awais Sheikh, the younger brother. He had also, over the telephone, after consulting with his father, refused to see me. But early one afternoon I surprised him in the store on Commercial Road. "I was passing by, Mr. Sheikh.... Just a little hello, to see if you've changed your mind, if your father still forbids you to talk to me? I'm writing a book on Daniel Pearl, it's true, but it's also about your brother, so, can't we talk? Why not tell what you know about the trial, and your brother? I think the trial was botched, a parody of justice—it's incredible, I've never seen anything like it... am I wrong?" And Mr. Awais Sheikh, twenty-five years old, in a T-shirt like a young Englishman on vacation, with an Oxford accent, an intelligent look, and a boyish handsomeness, offers me tea and a bit of conversation, which proceeds haphazardly among the cardboard boxes.

"No, no, my sister went to Oxford. I'm Cambridge. Law studies at Cambridge. For that reason, if we decide to talk, we won't need a lawyer to set the rules of the game. You and I will do it, it'll be like child's play for me. The problem, you understand, is the appeal. My brother has filed an appeal and our father insists that nothing be said that could interfere with the procedure. Have I always worked here? No. I first worked in the city. I was a stock broker. And then came this misfortune. My father was all alone. Completely alone with my mother and our lawyers. And I had to come help, join him at Perfect Fashions, comfort him. We're a close family. We've pulled together in this ordeal—and what an ordeal! What a disaster! Can you imagine having a brother condemned to death when he's innocent?"

The telephone never stops ringing. Mohammed, the employee, in Pakistani dress with the flowing pajamas and traditional white tunic, answers in perfect English. I notice that, contrary to Awais, he has a beard. I also notice, above his head, a poster resembling a calendar, with various "Words of the Prophet" for each of life's great moments: births, mourning, greetings, partings, condolences... Mohammed or Awais? Employee or boss?

"And you, Mr. Lévy—tell me a little about yourself. What do you think about Palestine? The war in Afghanistan? Chechnya? Iraq? Bosnia?" And after I established my credibility: "You say that my brother's trial was a travesty, that it was a parody of justice—OK! But don't say it's incredible, never before seen. Just look at Guantanamo. How do you explain Guantanamo? Isn't Bush's justice as bad as Musharraf's?"

We talk for half an hour. I sense the young intellectual, very concerned about what he calls the *massacre* of Moslems in Europe and the world. I also sense the little brother, fascinated, no matter what's been done, by the elder, whom he can't see as a criminal. In 1994, when Omar had organized, in India, his first hostage -taking, the English press descended on Awais to ask him about this big brother, who had cast his lot with jihadist groups fighting for the liberation of Kashmir, and was now rotting in the prisons of Uttar Pradesh. Awais confided: "Omar is a good man, a noble soul." And again today, even though his brother has committed a crime that has horrified the world and linked forever his image to the mutilated body of Daniel Pearl, Awais continues to see him only as a good boy, a defender of the widow and the orphan, always ready with passion for the noble cause. "The American journalist who was beheaded? Yes, of course, it's terrible. I feel the family's pain.... But it's not like my brother. I repeat that I don't believe he did it. Do you know he was such a gentle soul that he avoided reading about crimes in the newspapers for fear of becoming enraged, of taking up a victim's cause? Did you know that one time, in London, he jumped on the subway tracks just before the train arrived to rescue an old woman who had fallen off the platform?" But in the end, I don't sense an ideologue. I don't sense a fanatic. I have before me, in other words, a Moslem who is conscious of his identity and concerned—who can blame him?—for the fate of Chechens and Palestinians; but at no time do I have the feeling that he's a militant Islamist disguised as a Cambridge graduate.

I went from there to Leydenstone Station, which is an open air station not far from the family home. Too long ago, of course—no one among the employees could remember the event, but I tried to imagine this big, strapping and agile fellow jumping down, stopping the train, and extricating the old woman. Why not?

I went to the Nightingale Primary School, the pretty little school, typically English, close to home and almost like the country, where he spent his early years. No one there remembers him either, but I imagine him as a good pupil with no problems, the children's drawings on the walls the same as they are today, easy, happy school days.... It's so close, isn't it? The little boy can come home alone on foot, with his friends....

I went to the Forest School in Snaresbrook, a rather upscale private school—which counts among its former students the film director Peter Greenaway, the actor Adam Woodyatt, and the English cricket captain Nasser Hussain—where he completed the major part of his secondary studies. Georges Paynter, the headmaster, who was an economics professor at the time, still has very precise recollections of him. He remembers a bright student with exceptional grades. He remembers something in particular which attests to this: "School fees—the educational costs at the Forest School, at that time, must have been close to ten thousand pounds a year—well, we have a tradition of exempting each year a handful of particularly brilliant students. And Omar was among them. Let me turn on the computer... yes, here it is. The family had the means to pay but, because of his merit, we gave him a scholarship. So you see, that proves what I'm saying...." He remembers Omar in the first row, so attentive, so concentrated, setting the example. He remembers him as "head of house," helping the smaller boys, organizing theatrical evenings or the distribution of awards, assisting the cafeteria supervisors, polite with parents, good-natured with his classmates, charming with the teachers, blushing, helpful. Never unruly? Never. Never violent? Insolent? Never. Just an odd way, when I had finished my lecture and there was some point he thought remained obscure, of crossing his arms and leaning back in his chair and declaring in his loud, precocious adolescent's voice, "No Sir!" His voice was so sonorous, that the class, by now used to it, waited in anticipation, then burst into laughter. And when I had elucidated the point, he uncrossed his arms and, satisfied, in the same tone, said "Yes Sir!" which again made the class laugh. But would you call that insolence? He just wanted to understand! He didn't like not understanding. And I liked him very much, one of the students I was most attached to.

I took advantage, during a trip to Lahore, Pakistan, of the opportunity to visit Aitchinson College, where he spent a parenthetical two years, before returning to Forest School. Why these two years? Was it because Omar himself, as he later asserted, felt the need to reconnect with his Muslim "roots"? Or was it because his father, Saeed, had to return to Pakistan for business reasons? The question is not unimportant because its answer determines when he began his return to Islam and his future as a Kashmiri militant. What I do know, which supports the idea of a decision by the father, is that Saeed and a cousin created, in Lahore, a new company called Crystal Chemical Factories, and it was when this company failed that the family returned to London. Most important is my discovery that the Forest School (where he was a student from nine to thirteen years old, then again after Aitchinson, from fifteen to seventeen) is a school with a certain religious traditions. At least twice a week all the students have to assemble in the Anglican chapel—a practice that seems not to have posed a problem for the young Omar who, in his second enrollment as well as the first, if only because of his role as "head of house," was always present in the chapel, in the front row, seemingly unperturbed.

So, I visit Aitchinson College. I don't believe, then, that his reasons for being here were tied to his faith or his roots. But all the same, even if Pakistan corresponded, however little, to some desire to return to his ancestors, the reality is that the place would have been ill-chosen. With its perfect lawns, soccer and cricket fields, its beds of hibiscus from Bergerac and La Rochelle, its Olympic-sized pool, its colonnaded verandas, its bamboo screens and its rocking-chairs, with its strict hierarchy of the "lower boys" in short pants and the "grands" who had earned the right to "go into tails" and to wear at last a tail-coat, with its busts of Gladstone and Shelley in the classrooms, its illustrious parliamentarians present at award ceremonies, its soldiers at the entrance saluting in the purest Indian army style—Aitchinson is, in the heart of Pakistan, an enchanted place, an enclave, an aristocratic world preserved from the violence outside, a piece of England, congealed in its décor and conventions, a college more British than the most British of London colleges.

I met the headmaster. I found professors who had known Omar and agreed to share their memories. I was shown pictures of him where he still had that chubby-cheeks, good-boy look, cursed with thick glasses, and sideburns. In one, he is wearing the school uniform, navy blue vest and white, short-sleeved shirt with the V-shaped open collar of the school seniors; he is letting fall a stack of books held by an elastic band as he breaks into childish laughter. In another, he wears a colorful, shiny shirt and jeans with rolled cuffs, making his legs look a little short, and he dances a kind of twist or jerk. "He was a good young man," I'm told by the headmaster and former economics professor, who with his silvery hair is a very elegant double of a French poet friend of mine. Respectful of his "masters." Obliging with his "fellows." He loved poetry and flowers, and the sweetness of life. "Ah! the flowers.... Who remembers the beauty of the flowers and their perfumed mazes? Often, when my predecessor made his rounds and he came by here to check the color of his pansies"—he bends over a bed of blooming petunias, picks one, grimaces, signals to a gardener who rushes over, and says, simply, with slight disgust: "That's not it, too pink"—"yes, often he was among the pupils my predecessor found sensitive enough to take along. Do you know why he left the college? Because he systematically took sides with the weak, the scapegoats, and since he was a scrapper, it ended in blows. The Professors, who appreciated his mettle and considered him a gentleman, protected him. But, one day, he broke the nose of a nasty kid whose father was a tycoon from Lahore, and then nobody could do anything for him—what a pity! What heartbreak! I'm sure, if we had kept him, we could have prevented this accident. And his manners! What behavior! No Pakistani ever had such manners. No one was ever as faithful to the Aitchinson spirit as Omar Sheikh."

Forgive me, Ruth. Forgive me, Judea. I realize that, to evoke the Sheikh family and the London childhood and adolescence of their son, who became your son's assassin, I've used the same words, or almost, as those which were inspired, in Los Angeles, by the images from your shattered happiness. But what can I do? How can I rid myself of the feeling that these are parallel destinies? Is it my fault that Omar was, too, before dissolving into the quick-lime of perversion and murder, a kind of wonder child? I have a photo of him at the age of ten or twelve. He is wearing the pearl-gray school uniform. An escutcheon. A rose in the lapel. He is holding a trophy. And he has in his smile, in his look, at the same time shy and proud, and especially in his hair-cut, long and straight and falling in his eyes, something which truly and irresistibly reminds me of pictures of Danny with his football or his baseball bat.

I went to the London School of Economics where Omar enrolled, at the age of eighteen, in the Mathematics and Statistics Department which is, if not the most difficult, at least the one requiring the most assiduity. Attendance normal, there, as well. Grades normal and even brilliant. He who, according to George Paynter, didn't read much at the Forest School began to frequent the library and devour literature, politics, and eco-nomic treatises. According to those of his friends I managed to find, he was nice, hard working, obsessed by exams, a good friend, not particularly religious, still not Islamist. Saquib Qureshi, who is also of Pakistani origin and whose recollections are the most precise said: "No, I don't remember seeing him pray.... It's been a long time, but I think I would remember that.... He knew, we knew, that we were Muslim.... Maybe we had the idea that, in different parts of the world, Muslims were being attacked, but we were liberal, not at all proselytizing, we were moderate...."

In his spare time he plays chess. He plays better and better. (It occurs to me that Quaissia, his mother's name, is also, in Greek mythology, Caïssa, the name of the goddess of chess....) He is seen in the major London chess clubs where he gives the city's best professionals a run for their money. But it's especially at the Three Tuns Pub—a café in the heart of the little city that is the London School of Economics—that he is challenged to duels, which he always wins. He has a motto—which, in retrospect, doesn't lack piquancy—borrowed from one of the all time great players, his idol, Aaron Nimzovitch: "The threat is stronger than the execution."

He also boxes. A little karate. He becomes especially interested in arm wrestling, which, in London, seems to attract an impressive number of enthusiasts who, for the most part, remember him—and remember with the precision of people who haven't been overly interviewed and whose memories remain fresh. Frank Pittal, for example. Big Frank Pittal, an acquaintance of Omar's father, who sells womens' shoes at the Whitechapel market, near Wanstead, but whose real passion is organizing arm wrestling tournaments for money.

I find Pittal in his house in Wanstead, cluttered with cartons and dust, the smell of onions and cooking. He shows me pictures of his young self, tin trophies in imitation gold or silver. Together, we go through an old album full of yellowed press clippings about his big matches. Then, suddenly, in a page from the local Portsmouth newspaper, I recognize the young Omar, in an undershirt, his elbow on the table, his face strained, his opponent taller and larger than him, but whose respect Omar seems to hold.

"That's it—September 1993. I think it's his first tournament. He came to see me. 'Hey! Frankie! I want to be in it, I want you to take me into your stable, I'm the best in my college, but now I want to do it professionally." He had seen Sylvester Stallone's movie *Over the Top*, the story of an arm wrestling champion who, thanks to his arm wrestling skills, succeeds in getting his kid back from a rich, mean father-in-law, and that's what got him started. So I said, 'You don't say! Stallone's movie got me started, too! What a coincidence, it's incredible!' The next Sunday, I went to his house to pick him up in my van, and we went to this pub in the southern suburbs where he arrives with a carton of milk—what class! And a good wrestler to boot! I made a little money on him, believe me. Sometimes the tournaments are for money, sometimes for humanitarian causes. It lasted a year. We became damned good friends. I never would have thought he could do what he did to such a fine man as Daniel Pearl seemed to be. When I saw his face on the TV and the announcer said, 'This is Daniel Pearl's killer,' I swear to you, I didn't believe it! We had such good talks, the two of us, in the van, coming home from matches. We talked about everything. Everything. Except maybe one thing. And even there.... He was Muslim, I'm Jewish, and—"

"Jewish, really? Omar had a Jewish friend?"

"Of course," Pittal says with an enormous burst of laughter that pulls his head into his shoulders, like a chick. "Jewish or Muslim, it didn't count with him. He didn't see the difference. We were just two good buddies making the rounds of the London pubs. And even on Israel, we could disagree on this or that aspect of the politics, but he never denied Israel's right to exist. Was he religious? Not to my knowledge. He always said, 'I have a lot of respect for your people because, like us, you are merchants.'"

Chess, and arm wrestling. Strategic intelligence and muscle. The combination is uncommon. The young patricians of the London School of Economics observe this well-rounded young

Pakistani with astonishment. They come into the school cafeteria, where on certain evenings the left side of the room is arranged like a stage or theater, to admire this impressive man who nobody can beat in chess or in arm wrestling. And I can't help recalling the excitement my classmates and I felt twenty years earlier in Paris, over the performance of one of our fellows. I can't help recalling a television program called *Head and Legs* where, normally, we played on teams—an intellectual for the head and an athlete for the legs. Until one fine day one of our classmates decided, under the dumbfounded gaze of his comrades, that he would be the first to combine both roles, to form a team all by himself, to play the head, and since he was an equestrian champion, the legs too. Sorry, *petit camarade,* for the comparison. But in the way Omar's old friends evoke his double talent, in the amazed way they tell me about the chess champion and the muscle man, the ace of the Nimzovitch defense and the athlete, the only man in school who can delight you with a replay of a Kasparov pawn finale or a Spielman sacrifice attack, and the only one as well who can floor any bully looking for trouble, I can't keep from feeling the same emotion we felt, crowded around the few televisions at the École Normal Supérieure, waiting to see just how far your performance would take you.

"He'll end up a peer of the realm," Saeed Sheikh and Omar's mother Quaissia would say in the time of his glory. "Our son is a marvel, he'll end up knighted by the Queen of England, or become a banker in the city." And it certainly seems as if his teachers and the classmates who remember him did not find such ambition either unreasonable or absurd.

I remember an observation by Olivier Roy, the French specialist in radical Islamism, noting that jihadists who "graduate" from the Saudi or Pakistani *madrasas* are not that numerous. They pass through, granted. That's where they finish their training. Perhaps for these souls, corrupted by their commerce with the west, it's a kind of trial by fire, or an obligatory rite of passage. But Atta comes from Hamburg. The man with the shoe bomb on the Paris-Miami flight, Richard Colvin Reid, is English and started out in Catholic schools in London. Moussaoui is French, born in Saint-Jean-de-Luz, and studied at the university level in France. Khalid Sheikh Mohammed, bin Laden's lieutenant, arrested by the Pakistanis in February 2003 in Islamabad, was educated in the United States. Others are trained in Paris or Zurich, Brussels or Milan. All, or nearly all, come from well-to-do families and have done advanced studies in the major capitals of Europe, often brilliantly. And as for Omar....

Yes, Olivier Roy was right. At twenty years old, Omar's inner life is English. His friends are English. His frames of reference are English. The books he reads are in English. We can deplore it. We can try to forget it. We can respond as did the headmaster of the London School of Economics, Anthony Giddens (who, according to England's *Daily Telegraph* on 27 January 2002, has given, in recent years, three of his top students to al-Qaida) to a French writer asking for access to school or library records: "I don't want to see you or speak to you," said Giddens. "I don't want to know anything about this Omar Sheikh who is ruining my reputation. Let's just forget it happened."

The facts are there. And as always, they're stubborn. This enemy of the West is a product of the West. This fervent jihadist was formed in the school of enlightenment and progress. This raging Islamist who will shout out at his trial that he kidnapped

Daniel Pearl because he couldn't stand anymore to see the heads of Arab prisoners forcibly shaved in Guantánamo, this radical who will go berserk at the very idea of being judged not according to the *sharia* but British law, is a product of the very best English education. This character is both foreign and familiar to us. Here is the radical and banal nature of evil described by Hannah Arendt, which concerns us because it has the unsettling strangeness of mirrors.... Is terrorism the bastard child of a demonic couple: Islam and Europe?

CHAPTER 3 WHY BOSNIA?

But there is a second, more personal, reason that Omar fascinates me—and this second reason is Bosnia.

We are still in 1992.

Omar has just been accepted to the London School of Economics.

Physically, he's leaner. He's taken on the physique of an athlete and will keep it until the years of his incarceration in India. He looks older than his years. A young woman who knew him at the Forest School and who still sees him from time to time will tell me in all seriousness that his classmates had wondered "... is he older than he says? Maybe it has something to do with the difference between the Christian and Muslim calendars?"

Concerning his personality, all are in accord in praising his kindness, his cheerfulness, the disposition of a scion from a good family, confident, though a bit shy. And polite. There will be no one, among the people I meet in London, who fails to mention in the most glowing terms his modesty, his politeness, and his ability to pacify the tensest situations. "Violent, you say? Warrior? You must be joking! The contrary. Calm incarnate. Peace personified. All his aggression went into his arm wrestling matches. But, apart from that, an angel. The most gentle, the most delicate, the least bitter of young men. That's why we were so surprised when the news hit. We all telephoned each other— Have you seen? Have you heard? Omar? Really Omar? And yes, it was Omar, and we couldn't believe our eyes and ears."

The angel, too, sometimes has his peculiar side.

Inexplicable mood swings that worry his teachers.

Slightly weird laughter, a little too loud, which one of his friends tells me, seemed like "the laugh of a sleepwalker."

This same friend remembers the way Omar would say—he's only eighteen years old—that there is something spoiling in him, as if his mother had nursed him with poison instead of milk.

There are also surges of mythomania revolving around either the question of power ("I have friends in high places.... I am friend to the great of the world.... One phone call, just one, and I can have you hurt, or disowned, or fired...") or the question of origins (one time, he explains that his mother is Scottish; another, he pretends that his family has, for many generations, one of the great fortunes of the Commonwealth and that his father, Saeed Sheikh, started the career of Mohammed Al-Fayed, the owner of Harrod's; in still another, he fights with a classmate who doesn't believe him when he says he has Jewish blood).

There is the strangely excessive joy he derives from seeing himself, after his heroic act in Leydenstone Station, featured in the neighborhood press. "He danced for joy!" says the same schoolmate. "He said it was the best day of his life. He dreamed of glory, you understand—whatever glory, but glory! He would say—and this seemed bizarre—that nothing in this world seemed more enviable than to live in the limelight! He had one ambition, just one: to be one of the most high-profile figures of his time. And that story... he drove us crazy for months with that story of the old lady he saved in the subway...."

But that is all part of youth. He wasn't the first nor will he be the last young man thrilled to have his fifteen minutes of fame. And it would be too easy to play the prophet, with hindsight, and say: the claim of having Jewish blood, for example, this absurd mimetic delirium, the obsession with Jews so common in anti-Semitic genealogies—doesn't the criminal show through there? Isn't this a classic case of the neurotic who dreams of the election of the "chosen people," and feeling excluded, sinks into the assassin's delirium? Omar, at the time, is still a normal young Englishman. Still a model student. All his classmates vaunt, I repeat, his generosity, his zest for activity, his effort to give meaning to his existence. So, here in November of 1992, in the cushy but casually radical universe of the London School of Economics—was it not the center of London's Trotskyism and Maoism at the end of the sixties?—the Islamic Society, the largest student association present on campus, launches "Bosnia Week": an occasion, as with others staged by similar organizations throughout Europe, intended to alert public awareness to the fate of war-torn Bosnia.

The Islamic Society, of course, isn't quite like the other organizations.

There is a certain atmosphere around the conferences, debates, the film and slide shows it organizes—an atmosphere which didn't exist in what we were doing in France at the time.

Either because of the particular personalities of its leaders, or because they run the society—and therefore "Bosnia Week"—

in the name of inter-Muslim solidarity as much as in defense of human rights, their campaign has an orientation which, had our paths crossed, I imagine would have sparked debate between us.

But their tracts themselves are not so different, at least in their intention, and even sometimes in their words, from those we distributed in France.

They disseminate photographs of ethnic cleansing, portraits of raped women, images of the concentration camps at Omarska and Priedor, similar to photos I had found specimens of and which we had distributed ourselves at the time of the Sarajevo list and during our awareness campaigns.

Above all, they express views that are Muslim but not Islamist—as far as I can tell from the premier issue of *Islamica*, a journal created to mark the occasion and edited by the general secretary of the Islamic Society, Sohail Nakhooda (who has since become a brilliant Muslim theologian, passing through the universities of the Vatican, and now living in Amman). *Islamica* recounts, in detail, the coming together of "Bosnia Week" and the demonstrations that resulted, and shows the preoccupation with blocking the Islam-phobia mounting throughout Europe. However they are not using this banner to sneak in a fundamentalist hatred of the West. They express views which are, from the documents I was able to examine, not contrary to my own in the debate over the two Islams—the fundamentalist and the moderate—in which I was already participating at the time.

Of course, there are other branches of the Islamic Society, in London's universities—at Imperial College, Kings College and University College where the fundamentalist presence is strong and where the Hizb Ut-Tahrir is firmly established, and even in the majority. But that's not the case at the London School of Economics. I can't explain why, but it seems that the London School chapter was a center of opposition to the rise of fundamentalism in London at the time. So, when these other more militant chapters of the Society try to take over "Bosnia Week," to appropriate the whole project by announcing their intention to show up en masse, with their own speakers, at the London School campus on Saturday—the last day of "Bosnia Week"—the reaction is immediate: the local cell resists; the local cell revolts. On Friday night, Omar is among those who oppose the presence the next day of Omar Bakri and Yakoub Zaki, two fundamentalist preachers that he and his comrades categorically reject.

Omar, it becomes apparent, is at the heart of the whole affair.

Omar, nice, polite Omar, is at every demonstration organized by the committee.

Omar cuts classes. Omar slacks off in his reading. At the school library, Omar borrows only books on the Balkans or *The Clash of Civilizations and the Remaking of the World Order* by Samuel P. Huntington to which, in the coming months, he will not cease to refer. He doesn't miss a single television program on Bosnia. He doesn't miss a single article, and not infrequently, I'm told, Omar interrupts a class or a professor, even bounding up on the platform to shame him, and to shame the students for such terrible apathy in the face of the Bosnian tragedy: "No Sir!" he growls. "Yes Sir!"—except that he's come a long way since the Forest School and George Paynter's classes, and now his "No Sir! Yes Sir!" is pronounced in the name of an all-important solidarity with Europe's capital of suffering.

In a word, Omar is touched by the grace of Bosnia.

Omar has become, in a few weeks, enraged and obsessed by Sarajevo.

Omar tells anyone who will listen that he won't know a day, not an hour, of rest or peace as long as one man, woman, or child in Bosnia faces suffering.

Finally, for the last evening of "Bosnia Week," the committee has obtained the right from the school authorities to show a film of outrage, featuring testimonies on the horrors of the war. There are three, maybe four hundred people, crammed into a too-small room, to see the film and stay for the debate that follows. And Omar is there, in the first row, overwhelmed by what he sees, moved to his very depths, struck dumb. He relates in his journal, written during his Indian imprisonment, that it was the first, the strongest and the most durable political revelation of his life.

So much so that a few weeks later, when a London Pakistani, Asad Khan, holds another conference at the London School to declare that slogans no longer suffice, that now is the time to join words with action, and that a convoy will depart during Easter vacation with fresh supplies for the martyred city of Sarajevo, that a "Caravan of Mercy" will form to go into Bosnian territory to bring the besieged a modest but fervent expression of support (a few doing what, there again, is being done at the same time all over prosperous Europe), exactly seven volunteer to accompany three trucks loaded with food and clothing to bring relief to the city, and among the seven who, timidly, approach Asad Khan at the end of his conference to say that, yes, they are ready, but that it would help if Khan would talk to their parents and convince them, is young Omar Sheikh.

One film....

One humanitarian caravan proposing to challenge the blockade imposed by the Serbs and accepted by other nations....

As for the caravan, I'd have to be blind not to see the link with the reflex I myself had a few months earlier when gentle lunatics from Equilibre, a humanitarian association in Lyon, came to see me. They too, had it in their heads to force the Serbian blockade and get to Sarajevo.

As for the film, well I must confess that, the coincidence of the dates, the theme, what Omar himself said of the images that overwhelmed him and the way he described them in his diary, and what others who saw the screening told me—the image of the mutilated body of a young thirteen-year-old Bosnian, raped then killed by Serb militias; images of mass graves and concentration camps; sequences shot in a besieged quarter which, to me, sounded like Dobrinja—added up to my believing for a moment that the film, if not *Bosna!*, was my preceding film, the first one I dedicated to Bosnian martyrs, *One Day in the Death of Sarajevo*, made in late 1992 from images by Thierry Ravalet, and shown in Paris but also in London during the same weeks in November.

But it wasn't my film after all.

I succeeded, in a video store next to the Finsbury mosque, in getting my hands on one of the rare cassettes still in existence of the film that changed Omar's life.

It was a forty-five minute film, *Destruction of a Nation*, produced by the Islamic Relief, based in Moseley Road, Birmingham.

It was a good film.

It was a truthful film, put together with archival footage, some of which I would use in *Bosna!*

It was a film that, moreover, and to my great surprise, opens with an interview with Haris Silajzic, the social-democrat who was at the time the secular counterpart to the Muslim nationalist of Alija Izetbegovic.

It wasn't my film. But at the same time, it almost could have been. It was another film, written and edited by others, with intentions and ulterior motives that were not mine—but, made of images I know by heart and that mean a great deal to me.

I don't know if Daniel Pearl and I crossed paths or not in Asmara. But I know that his killer was roused by scenes I could have filmed. And I know that he arrived in Sarajevo in March or April 1993, which is to say—the notes in my book *Le Lys et la Cendre* are proof—at the precise moment I was there myself.

When the Pearl affair broke, certain people would try to explain it in terms of the rancor of a little Pakistani humiliated by the English.

They would serve up the old story of a child who is different, persecuted because he's different, champing at the bit, waiting for the hour of revenge.

Notably, Peter Gee, the English musician who served a sentence for cannabis smuggling in Tihar Jail in Delhi, from 1997 to 2000, and who knew Omar during his first incarceration for the kidnapping in New Delhi. He freely talks about the Omar whom he knows better than anyone—they spent hours discussing philosophy and life, they played chess and Scrabble, sang, talked of Islam, evoked their respective adolescences (one at the London School, the other at Sussex University), they gave their fellow prisoners courses in general culture and geography, and thanks to the destiny imposed by alphabetical order (Mr. O. as in Omar; Mr. P. as in Peter) they slept side by side for months in the terrible dormitory of Prison Number 4 where more than a hundred were packed. "Well," says Peter Gee, "Omar became what he is because of a childhood wound. Omar kidnapped, then killed Daniel Pearl because England is a racist country and throughout his childhood he was called a 'Pakistani bastard.'"

There is no need for me to challenge a testimony, the accuracy of which I will have occasion to verify at other points in this investigation.

But I don't believe this theory.

I don't much believe, in general, explanations of the type: childhood humiliation, rejection, desire for revenge, etcetera.

And it seems to me that here the idea is particularly absurd.

First of all it flouts what we are told, not by the diviners of what has come, nor those obsessed by premonitions, nor those who picture the monster-already-peeking-out-from-behind-the-good-boy, but by the actual witnesses to Omar's adolescence, those who knew him and report: a perfect Englishman, I repeat, integrated without problems into an England that he never experienced as hostile to who he was.

It minimizes what we know of the London School of Economics in those years, when it was a model of liberalism, open to the world and its cultures, cosmopolitan in word and deed, and tolerant: Did it not have, in 1992–1993, according to the Islamic Society archives, more than one hundred Muslim students? How could Omar have felt himself different, ostracized, when we know that over half of these students, all religions and nationalities taken together, were born outside of England?

But the idea is absurd above all because the facts are there and even if they are embarrassing or shocking, even if I was the first, once aware of them, to have taken them as very bad news, they are, alas, undeniable. If we must put a date on the turning point, designate precisely the moment that saw Omar's life diverge, if we must put a name on the event that led this secular and moderate Muslim to understand his membership in the Muslim world and his ties to the Occident as antagonistic, if we want to mark with a black stone the event that caused him to think that an inexorable war opposed, from now on, the two worlds and that it was his duty to take part in this war, if we want to make the effort to listen to what he himself said and wrote incessantly, and initially in a passage in his diary where he explains that just the mere thought of the raped adolescent in *Destruction of a Nation* is enough, years later, to put him into quasi-convulsions—that event is the war in Bosnia.

The instant he decides to go, Omar is no longer quite the same. He still plays chess.

He continues his arm wrestling tournaments and is even on the British national team that in December, in Geneva, will compete in the world championships.

But his heart is no longer in it.

His mind, Pittal and Saquib tell me, is elsewhere, over there, in Sarajevo which, according to them, preoccupies him completely.

And now, when he plays in a public chess match or accepts a challenge to arm wrestle on the stage of the cafeteria, it's under the double condition that those in attendance bet big and that the money goes to Bosnia.

He, who dedicated himself, without qualms, to the study of finance and who had already created, as early as his last year at the Forest School, a small amateur stock market company, now starts introducing to his friends new theories of Islamic finance, Mohammed's prohibition of interest on loans, and finance mechanisms that can be used as alternatives.

He, who according to his friends knew nothing more of the Koran than what is known in assimilated English families, which is to say very little, starts to quote it all the time, to ask and to ask out loud questions as decisive as, has a good Muslim the right to enrich himself during the time of his pilgrimage? He is heard wondering how can one be a banker without betraying the *sharia*, how does this or that *sura* help distinguish good finance from impious finance, or how another *sura* justifies opposing the trendy futures market sweeping the City, fascinating his fellows preparing for their careers.

He reads *Islam and the Economic Challenge* by a certain Umer Chapra.

He reads a compendium of texts—Abu Yusuf, Abu Ubaid, Ibn Taimiyya, Al-Mawardi—entitled *Origin of Islam Economics*.

He watches a documentary on the BBC, titled *The Invitation*, about Muslim integration in Great Britain, and it infuriates him.

But the truth is that his energy is concentrated only on the journey to Bosnia. He thinks only of that, he occupies himself with only that. He comes to classes only to talk about his precious journey, to promote the idea of the "Convoy of Mercy," convince his friends, collect money, blankets, foodstuffs. The real truth is that once he leaves, he never comes back.

He is still enrolled at the London School, but he doesn't return after Easter.

He re-enrolls, or his family re-enrolls him, in September, for a new year, but again he doesn't appear.

Where is Omar? What's become of him? Is it true that Omar joined the Bosnian army? Is he dead? Wounded? Taken prisoner by the Serbs? By a war lord? The rumors, at school, are flying fast. The legend swells. Muslims and non-Muslims alike, all are fascinated by the strange destiny of this polite young man, so nice, so perfectly English, who seems to have lost himself, like a new T. E. Lawrence, or Kurtz from *Heart of Darkness*, in a distant theater.

Only Saquib Qureshi sees him again. One time. In September 1993. Maybe October, he's not sure. Omar arrived without warning one afternoon in the Three Tuns Pub where he used to come for arm wrestling matches. Except that he's not the same Omar. "I have never seen," Saquib tells me, "a man change so much, in so little time. Physically, to begin with, he's changed. The beard. He's wearing the mujahideen beard now, just the size of a hand. He wears the traditional Pakistani pajamas. He doesn't have the same look. And not quite the same voice." "What are you still doing here?" he says to Saquib, as they go arm in arm, like before, walking on Houghton Street. "How can you continue courses with Fred Halliday, while so many Bosnians are dying?" And when Saquib asks, "What's the alternative? What do you propose in place of Halliday?" the new Omar gives him an answer that, at the time, surprises him, yes, but in retrospect, chills his blood: "Kidnappings. Kidnap people and exchange them for actions by the international community in favor of Bosnia, that's what I propose. There, for example"—he points toward the Indian embassy across the street—"there, you see, we could kidnap the Indian ambassador." Then he gestures toward the school. "Or, even simpler, the son of a Pakistani minister—I've made inquiries, he's arriving this year."

CHAPTER 4 RETURN TO SARAJEVO

I went to Sarajevo.

I took advantage of a literary symposium organised by the Centre André Malraux to return to the Bosnia Omar and I have in common.

With my friend Semprun, I debated the identity and the future of Europe. I discovered the island of Hvar, in Croatia, where I went with my old friend, Samir Landzo. He'd gotten thin, Samir, and melancholy. People are ill-disposed towards veterans in Bosnia today, he tells me. It's no longer an advantage, but rather a disadvantage. It's no longer a safe-conduct, but something that makes people look at you askance. "Oh! Sarajevo's changed, you know. You won't recognize anything any more! The shirkers, the people from the outside, the profiteers have the advantage now. The people who didn't fight are in power now, and they resent us, the combatants of the first hour. At court, it was very clear. My lawyer tried to use my past as an argument, to say, 'A résistant, a hero, cannot have done what he is charged with.' He tried to find witnesses to say, 'Samir L. was one of the first defenders of the city. This very young man was one of those who had the right reflex. It is to people like him that Sarajevo today owes, etcetera.' Well, bad idea, that was almost worse."

He laughs. We laugh. With Suzanne, his wife, whenever we get together we talk about the bad times, that were, in a way, also the good times—days passed with only the flame of cigarette lighters for light, the trenches, the night before the victorious offensive of Donji Vakuf, when three or four of us amused ourselves by guessing in what order the stars would come out. Sort of ah, Bosnia, that we know so well, *doobeedoobeedoo.*

But the truth is—during the symposium, with Samir, on the hills around the city where I always go in pilgrimage, in the old city and the new, at the phone building that's been completely rebuilt and at the ruins that remain of the library, where till the end of my days I'll see, roaming through the rubble in his Ray Bans, his earrings, his brown fedora pushed back off his forehead, his gold vest, Ismet Bajramovic, known as Celo, the chief of the hoodlums of Sarajevo, at the Holiday Inn, in front of a bar in the rue Marsala Tita where a man just started barking one morning, and as I cross the paths of all these men and women who have gotten used to their crutches—I'm thinking of only one thing: I'm not in the Bosnia of today, but of yesterday. I'm not even in my own yesterday, but in *his* yesterday, that of Omar, in those days of April or May 1993 when I could have, or I should have, run into him. What does he do? What does he see? The town of Split, OK, in Croatia—but after that? Mostar? Sarajevo? What does the model student do when he arrives? Does he meet Kemal? The president? Does he witness, as I do, the startled moral and military reaction of the Bosnians? Does he see the lambs become wolves, the victims change themselves into fighters who render blow for blow on the two fronts—fascist Serbs on one side, Croatian paramilitaries on the other—where now, the war has spread?

I went to the Bosnian outpost of the French secret services, but there were no archives predating 1994.

I saw Amir, the man from the Bosnian services with whom I had concocted some still-born projects to transport arms across Turkey in that same year of 1993: He has a file on a Pakistani named Sheikh Omar, but who was born five years before the one I'm looking for, and who arrived in February. Is it the same one?

I went back to see Izetbegovic, retired to his home in the Sarajevo suburbs. A modest house, with only a guard at the street entrance. A Twingo parked in front serves as a staff car. Worn furniture. Medicines on one table. Books. *Le Lys et la Cendre* in a Bosnian translation. A satchel of black skaï that he says, with a smile, I gave him—I can't remember when, but I don't dare ask. Where is Gilles? He seems surprised and disappointed that Gilles Herzog, the companion of my Bosnian adventures, isn't there. He has heart trouble. You look better, Mr. President. You don't look the way you did the last time, as if you were going down slow, à la Mitterrand. Aha! But you should see a doctor all the same, come to Paris and see my friend Professor C. Oh, no, he says. But his daughter Sabrina appears ready to say yes. It obviously scares her to see him so pale, so tired, his large blue eyes taking up his whole face now, and I sense that she wouldn't be against his contacting Professor C. But no, he says with a smile, that would be silly, there is a moment when a man has lived his time and must put himself in the hands of God.

"But you? What did you come to talk to me about? You didn't just come back to talk about my heart and my health? Omar, you say? Omar Sheikh? Oh, all that is far away, so far away. Why dig up all those old stories? I know the international community attached a lot of importance to the foreign fighters who came here during the first two years of the war. But you, you know the truth. You know there was just a handful, and I did everything to stop them. And frankly, you who know the situation—Bosnia, of course, has no access to the sea, so where did they come from, these fighters? Who brought them here? Do people know, for example, that there were training camps in Slovenia? Can you explain to them that the grand mosque of Zagreb, under the authority of Sefko Omerbasic, regularly sent us recruits for jihad?"

And then, since I insist, since I tell him I'm writing a book and it's important for me to know, he searches his memory, turns to Kemal, his wartime advisor, and then his son, who are both sitting in on the interview and who, so far, have said nothing. He remembers, yes, he has a very vague memory.... Perhaps not the Omar I'm looking for, but a group of young Pakistanis who came from London and proposed the formation of a foreign brigade of fighters. It was in the Tuzla region. But he has the impression they were Shiites—is that possible? Could my Omar have been a Shiite?

No, I tell him. Absolutely not. On the contrary, he was adamantly anti-Shiite. But wait one second—fighters? A brigade? At the same time I came to you in Geneva, with others, to propose the formation of an international brigade—remember?

He nods then, the gesture of one who was right before you were and would like it to be recognized. "Now maybe you understand why I wasn't wild about the idea. But rest assured, the speech I gave you was the same I gave them. I told them, too, no, thank you, that's very kind, but we have our fighters—Bosnia needs arms, it's true, but she does not lack young men ready to give their lives for the defense of their country."

The president is tired. He's not breathing so much as panting. Again he has taken on the same translucent mask that
Mitterrand had at the end. The thought crosses my mind, as it
always does, that this admirable man, this Bosnian De Gaulle,
the man who, for four years, struggled to keep Bosnia and the
cadaver of his idea alive, could have been playing a duplicitous
game and making fun of me a little. Isn't that what my friend
Robbe-Grillet said, right from the start?

"Izetbegovic? Aha! What a great joke! Did you ask him to
explain his Islamic declaration? "

Isn't that the opinion as well of Jovan Divjak, the Serb general who defended Sarajevo? Wasn't that why, in the last year of
the presidency of the "old man," he refused to attend the cere-
mony where I was awarded the *Blason*, the Bosnian legion of
honor I'm so proud of, the only decoration I've ever accepted. I
leave him. He hasn't told me anything.

I went to Bocinja Donja, an old Serbian village 100 kilometers north of Sarajevo that they say Izetbegovic gave as a fief to a
hundred veterans of the 7th Muslim brigade, from the Middle
East. There, in this village where women wear black burqas and
the men long beards, where it is forbidden to speak to strangers
and, of course, to drink alcohol, in this village that greets the
outsider with a sign at the entry reading, "Be afraid of Allah,"
where life comes to a standstill for prayers five times a day, I
finally found a man willing to talk to "the friend of Alija" and
maker of *Bosna!* He is a veteran, now a schoolteacher, and willing
to recall a young, exceptionally brave Pakistani, dedicated, solid
as a bull, excelling in hand-to-hand combat and knife fights but
nonetheless willing to pick up a shovel to dig a trench or do
other menial labor. Nice boy, in other words, of above-average

intelligence... although with a laugh that made his comrades' blood run cold. He said Europe was dead and there was nothing to expect of it. He explained that ammunition didn't grow on trees and should be used sparingly, which was why the knife was preferable. He was—and the schoolteacher remembers this, for the young man bragged a lot and liked to flaunt his exploits—a chess champion in England, and in the evening, around the fire, while the others watched, fascinated, he ran through all the battles, all the deployment strategies, as if they were huge chess games. He was obsessed with Bosnia's lack of access to the sea and said it was hemmed in, that Croatia was the enemy because only through Croatia could the Muslim nation secure a sea port. Any pictures of those days? Photos? You'd have to go to the military archives. There were some photos taken at Gradacac, he's sure of that. The problem was that Omar was out of control, a little loony, and the military police finally had to expel him because one day, in a fit of anger, he profaned a Chechnik tomb. What an extraordinary man! What a loss! Except.... Again, is this really my Omar? Or is it still another with the same name? How is it that no one ever spoke of Omar's expulsion, for example? And why is it that this man, too, remembers him as a Shiite?

And so I went to Solin, near Split, in Croatia. There, in this lovely city on the Dalmatian coast, I went back to the two-story building that was the stopover, the logistical base, and the depot for the Convoy of Mercy. I found the trace of a Muslim NGO, the Third World Relief Agency (TWRA), involved in the financing of fundamentalist groups in central Bosnia, with which Omar would have been in touch. I learned that he spent time with a dozen or so Arab fighters who had trained in the

Afghanistan war and were on their way to Sarajevo, as well as with a certain Abdul Rauf, also a veteran, but Pakistani, a member of Harkat ul-Mujahideen, just arrived from Kashmir, who gave him a letter of recommendation for the Harkat representatives in London and Lahore.

"You're strong," he had said. "You're motivated. You speak any number of languages. You know modern techniques. Why don't you get the appropriate military training? Why not go first to Afghanistan, where there are excellent camps, and you'll come back trained for combat against the Serbs?"

Omar protests that he's still young, he has to finish his studies, only with great difficulty did he convince his father to let him leave on this Bosnian expedition and, for now, his father is still the one who decides everything.

"We'll talk to your father," says Rauf. "I'll organise a meeting for him with Maulana Ismail, imam of the Clifton mosque, a holy man, who is experienced at guiding young English Muslims to our places in Afghanistan and who will find the words to convince him, I'm sure. It's an honor for a family to have a son who abandons his useless studies to consecrate himself to the life of jihad."

Here, at Solin, Omar decides to wear a beard.

The vagueness, the contradictions, the lack of substance of these bits of information may be due to a number of things.

The first might be that Omar, at this time, is not yet the person he will become. He has a negligible existence. And so, he leaves behind him equally negligible traces. No records, it's normal. Past history rewritten, it's classic. Omar went to Sarajevo and fought there. But at the time he was far too insignificant to have made much of an impact.

The second might be found in the explanation of Asad Khan, the Convoy of Mercy organiser, whose address I found in London and who has become, a decade later, the head of a sort of all-purpose NGO that sends its "convoys" not only to Bosnia, but to all theatres of "Muslim misery." He receives me one evening in his office in the east of London, the office that dates from Omar's time. He tells me about his combat for the Chechens, and the other contemporary martyrs of the war of civilizations. He also says it's rotten luck for him to see the name of his dear association systematically linked to the itinerary of a terrorist.

"Did you know that for ten years, I haven't been able to set foot on Pakistani soil for fear of being arrested in connexion with Omar?" he says. "Did you know my name was even in the police report of the interrogation by the Indian police, in 1994? And can you imagine that in this police report, I am at the head of a list that includes the most important terrorists of Pakistan and Kashmir, noted as an 'associate of Omar in England'?"

But he has a theory, Asad, an explanation he begs me to listen to and to tell others, because, really, he is sick to death of the misrepresentations on the part of the press.

"Omar accompanied us as far as Solin, near Split, in Croatia, where the Convoy had its base. But he became ill during the trip. Not the flu, a sort of seasickness, with vomiting and diarrhea. He comes to aid Bosnia, he wants to play tough guy, but he's all soft inside, like Jello, and it's a burden. And if they have such great difficulty remembering him in Sarajevo, if you haven't found a trace of his presence in the field, it's because, the morning we left

Solin, this valliant being, this hero, this jihadist-in-the-making who dreamed of exploits, of blood spilled, of martyrdom, quite simply didn't wake up in time, and he let us finish our mission without him. Omar never entered Bosnia, that's the truth. Never. We went there, to Jablanica, near Mostar, to distribute our truckloads of food and clothing. And we picked him up at the base in Solin on the way back, and took him home, sick, to London. Subconsciously deliberate mistake. Shame. I've rarely seen a man who felt quite as ridiculous. But that's how it happened. So he came by to see me three or four times in the next few months, here, in this office. He felt so guilty! He always came with a little cheque, fifty pounds, sixty—here, it's for the Convoy, I'm so sorry, excuse me...."

Of course I understand the interest Asad Khan may have in telling me all this. I sense that it is vital for him to separate his own destiny from that of Omar and to squelch the rumors that, since 1994, say that everything started with him, during that trip. But there's something that has a ring of truth in his tale, a real sincerity. And I have to admit that, despite its overall implausibility, I find my assumptions shaken. A detail, for example. A tiny detail: A few months later, passing through Split, I discovered while combing through the Croat papers of the period that during those weeks, perhaps even that day in Solin when Asad Khan says Omar stayed behind, there was a chess match between two international masters, Ivan Ljubicic and Slobodan Kovacevic. Does one in fact confirm the other? Could it be that Omar preferred chess to Bosnia? That he put on this phoney display of illness so he could watch a bold and magnificent gambit? That would be enormous. But after all....

The third explanation is that of Saquib, his friend from the London School of Economics, who is visibly very surprised when I tell him Asad Khan's story.

"I can't believe it," he says. "I can see him, so clearly, in October, going along the walkways of the London School, and then walking down Houghton Street, when he proposed kidnapping the Indian ambassador and the son of a Pakistani minister. I can hear him as if it were yesterday, telling me about how he fought in Bosnia."

"He really said fought?"

"Yes, he said fought, there's absolutely no doubt that that's what he said. I can't believe he lied."

"And so?"

"And so, I can only find one explanation," Saquib concludes. "There were two trips to Bosnia, not one."

The one, in other words, that may have ended at the gates of the promised land, the way Asad Khan described it. And another, soon after, without Khan, without the Convoy of Mercy, just him, just little Omar, erasing the failure of the first journey and, this time, going all the way. I'll come back, of course, to Asad.

"What do you think?" I ask. "What do you think of the possibility of Omar returning, without you, to Bosnia?"

Asad thinks about it. Nods his head. And replies, confirming Saquib's words, "Yes, why not? Omar wouldn't have lied about it. Perhaps there was a second trip, without me."

And then, there's a last hypothesis, a sort of a middle-ground theory, between one extreme and the other. There is one hypothesis, ultimately, that is the most plausible, and that both the supporters of the golden legend and those of the lamentable, subconsciously deliberate mistake can agree upon. But no—I'll wait and reveal this last theory in due time, at the moment during the investigation when it actually occurred to me. . . .

For the time being, what matters is this fact, and this fact alone: Whatever Omar may have accomplished, whether or not he went to Mostar or Sarajevo, whether or not he saw combat, whether or not the man at Bocinja Donja is telling stories or if it is Asad Khan who's rewriting history to disengage himself from responsibility, what is important in any case, then, is that the Bosnian affair, in Omar's own, never-varying words, decided everything. In other words, we can assume that this sudden consciousness of a world where it's a crime to be a Muslim, and where another destiny seems possible for European Islam, profoundly shakes the happy Englishman he was. Here, without the shadow of a doubt, is a model student, an Englishman, a cosmopolitan adolescent who, everything seems to indicate, has never thought that his belonging to the world of Islam and to that of the West were in the least bit contradictory, and who topples over the edge into madness in a very precise place.

And that, this obvious fact, I find profoundly disturbing.

Let me be clear.

Basically, I'm not surprised.

I always knew there were foreign fighters in Bosnia.

I saw them in Donji Vakuf, strange, haggard, marching like robots, without apparent fear, along the Serbian lines.

I saw them at Mehuric, near Travnik, Ivo Andrik's city; at Zivinice, Bistricak and Zeljezno Polje in the Zenica region; at Igman where, on 23 August 1994, during one of my last trips, an "international brigade" liberated the village of Babin Do; and even on the Dobrinjna outskirts of Sarajevo itself, where the 50-man "Suleiman Fatah" unit took part in defending the area during the darkest hours of the siege, in April and May 1993.

And I learned from Izetbegovic himself—who had received the information when the little plane taking us to see the Pope in April 1993, when the war with the Croats was at its fiercest, landed in Rome—that a brigade of foreign combatants (the 7th, linked to the 3rd Corps of the official Bosnia-Herzegovina army) had been discovered to have committed heinous acts of violence in the towns of Dusina, Vitez, Busovaca and Miletici, in the Croat zone. I myself wrote the draft of a communiqué, to be sent to the chief of staff and the press agencies, disowning irrevocably the "handful of lost soldiers" who had committed these horrors and dishonoured the Bosnian cause.

I quickly learned, as well, of the questionable role played by the Muslim NGOs—for example, supposedly charitable organizations like "Muassasat al-Haramain al-Khairiya," or the "Charitable Establishment of the Two Holy Mosques." I contacted them in Zagreb in the spring of 1993 before learning they were channeling money to the dreaded "mujahid battalion" of Zenica, and that their operations were a secret to no one, including the Croat authorities. (It should be remarked in passing that President Izetbegovic is not entirely wrong in saying these foreign fighters did not fall from the sky, and that to get to Sarajevo, they had to have strong non-Bosnian—in other words, Croat—accomplices.)

One day at staff headquarters in Travnik, when I was looking at some archived video images I was thinking of using in

Bosna!, I came across footage the archives service of the 7th Corps had inadvertently left on the cassette, where one could see Arab mujahideen, their long hair dyed with henna and tied with a green band, playing soccer with the heads of Serbian soldiers.

And, concerning the mere presence of foreign fighters, I'm not mentioning all the things I heard but did not personally see, yet, given the sources, feel compelled to grant a certain credibility: another detachment, linked, again, to the 7th Corps, in the Mount Vlasic region; a unit of Tunisians and Iranians in the Bistricak village area, not far from the headquarters of the 33rd Division of the regular army; another in the Banovici sector that reportedly took part in the Vozuca offensive; the seventy Pakistani and Kuwaiti "Shiite mercenaries" of Tuzla; the detachment of the Revolutionary Guards from Iran, who arrived in May 1994 to act as "religious police" in the ranks of the mujahideen battalions. For further evidence there's the interview of Abu Abdel Aziz, the Kashmir-trained war lord who became inter-army commander of all the foreigners stationed in Bosnia, that ran in *Time* and in the Saudi London daily *Al-Sharq al-Awsat*.

To say nothing of after the war, when all these "foreigners," contravening the conditions of the Dayton Accords requiring them to leave the country, remained in Bosnia, married, had children and obtained Bosnian nationality, and might have made Sarajevo the center of international Islamic terrorism in Europe, had society not resisted. Their projects were many: a plan, in liaison with the Algerian GIA, to assassinate the Pope, in September 1997; two years before that, a plan for a car-bomb, in revenge for the condemnation to death of Sheik Omar Abdel Rahman, mastermind of the first World Trade Center attack; the

1998 affair of Algerian Bensayeh Belkacem, which imagined a simultaneous attack on the American embassy at Sarajevo and the bases of the international forces stationed in Bosnia; the case of Imad el-Misri, an Egyptian close to Osama bin Laden, who was arrested in July 2001 in the Sarajevo suburb of Ilidza, carrying a Bosnian passport; and finally, the case of the Bosnian veterans—such as Jasin el-Bosnevi of Sarajevo, and Almir Tahirovic of Novi Travnik in central Bosnia—who went to Chechnya to fill out the meagre ranks of the fundamentalist brigades and, more often than not, lost their lives.

In short, the case of the foreign fighters has always been an open secret for the handful of intellectuals, journalists, and humanitarians who pleaded for Western military action from the very first day.

But the foreign fighters' presence had no influence upon what those cognescenti observed in Sarajevo, and in central Bosnia as well, of the profoundly tolerant, moderate, and, to sum it up, European nature of Bosnian Islam itself—women without veils, alcohol served in the cafés, secular habits. And when confronted by these foreigners with their ridiculous rules, their sermons, their empty pharaonic mosques, Bosnians showed the solid cynicism of those who have no desire to die and who, abandoned by all and dependent solely on their own forces, took what little help was offered to them.

Better still, no matter what one may say, the albeit shocking presence of these combatants remained marginal, circumscribed to certain regions of the country and in no way contaminating (or at least less than has been said) the morale, the culture, or the

functioning practices of the army of Bosnia-Herzegovina: soldiers of three nationalities with Serbian and Croatian officers in
some cases commanding troops made up of a majority of
Muslims. Of course there were imams, but they were no more
than chaplains in a French regiment. And there was the 7th
Regiment, to which many of these units were attached, which
was commanded by General Alagic, who, in that capacity, covered up their war crimes—but I observed them enough in action
to be able to attest to the fact that they were not, in any case, a
fundamentalist or Islamist corps.

As for Izetbegovic himself, I knew his past. I could see that,
like all the Bosnians, he used the support of these "Arabs"—
whom he disliked and feared—without scruple. But I also saw
that I could talk to him without difficulty about Salman Rushdie
and his support for the Bosnian cause. I saw that Gilles Herzog
and I had no trouble convincing him, the pious Muslim just
returned that day from Ryad, to come to Europe to meet
Margaret Thatcher, and the King of Spain, and, especially, the
Pope. I can see him still, strangely pensive after his meeting with
John Paul II, in the *Mystère 20* François Mitterrand—either
clever or a good sport—had sent to Rome to bring us back to
France, and then to Sarajevo. Could it be that the holy man had
unsettled him? What kind of an Islamic fundamentalist could be
so moved, so shaken by the head of the Catholic church? When I
had doubts, when people in France jeered at my support for the
author of the "Islamist Declaration," I remembered how uncomfortable everyone was following the screening of *Bosna!* in his
honor at a cinema in the Latin Quarter in Paris. *"BHL!"* the
Bosnians of Paris chanted, *"BHL! Bosnia-Herzegovina Libre!"*

No, no, some of his counsellors grumbled, we don't like the "secular Islam" mentioned in the film's commentary, we really don't like that. But this led to Izetbegovic's typical style of arbitrating: "BHL is right. Maybe we should think this idea of 'secular Islam' through." A conservative. Perhaps a nationalist. But one who never gave in when it came to the essential, the multicultural dimension of Bosnia that he had defended and whose cause brought us together—he, the Muslim man of letters, astute reader of the Koran; and I, a Frenchman and a Jew, a friend of Israel, who never, in any circumstance, failed to say who I was and what I believed. How many discussions between us, but peaceful ones, about Jewish destiny, the mystery and the question of Israel.... And as for his Bosnia—*our* Bosnia, I should say—how many times did he tell me, with the touch of melancholy that appeared every time he found a moment's respite from his role as commander-in-chief to reflect and talk: "I could be happy with a little Bosnia. I could consent to the partition that everyone, from the West to Milosevic, seems to desire and whose first effect would be peace. I could build a refugee state for all the persecuted Muslims of the region. Well, maybe I'm wrong. I know I'm considered a stubborn old man, a dreamer, but you see, that's not my idea. I cannot say good-bye to the beautiful dream of a multicultural, cosmospolitan Bosnia!"

Even if I think that at the time I should have brought up the issue of the Islamists' presence more clearly, denounced it more loudly, devoted more than just allusions to it in *Le Lys et la Cendre*, even if I say that I gave in, at the time, to the classic syndrome (whose effects I have often pointed out in others) of the intellectual who fears he will harm the cause he stands by in telling the whole truth, I still think, today, that I was—that *we* were—right to respect this simple theorem. Not: "The fact that there are Islamists in Bosnia should dissuade us from intervening." Rather: "The longer we wait to intervene, the more Islamists may rush in. It is because we do not intervene that, politics by nature detesting a void, Islamists utterly foreign to this Bosnian civilization may assume our role and profit from the despair of an abandoned population, to take root in the Balkans."

The new element, then, is, as always, the appearance of an individual, of a singular destiny, of a discreet body.

The new—and terribly troubling—element is this idea of a man, one man alone, who plunges towards the worst in the very location that was, in my eyes, the center of honor and courage.

Here is a man who arrives in the European capital of sorrow. Here is a course of action that follows motives initially not all that different from those at the very same moment inspiring French human rights militants, as well as others who see, in the situation in Bosnia, the great test of late 20th century Europe— the advent of fascism, the Spanish civil war of our generation, etcetera. Except that, since noble causes sometimes produce dissimilar effects, his conversion to Islamism and to crime dates exactly from this point.

The Devil is not in the details, but in the great causes, and in History.

CHAPTER 5 FROM ONE PORTRAIT, ANOTHER

In Pakistan, I did all I could to meet Omar.

I contacted his family, who referred me to his lawyers.

The lawyers advised me to consult the President of the Supreme Court.

In November 2002, I went to see the police, who said, "Yes, why not? You just have to go to Hyderabad and negotiate with the warden of the prison." So I went to see the warden of the prison who said, "It's not as simple as all that. Omar has just been transferred to the prison's maximum security sector, the Mansoor Ward, and only the minister, Moinuddin Haider, can authorize you to see him."

I requested an appointment with the minister.

"They tell me you are a lover of literature. Well, I am an novelist. I am writing a novel whose main characters are based on Pearl and Omar, and so I need to meet Omar," I told him, using my good old cover.

The minister listened to me. He had a strange, old-fashioned face, a mixture of Paul Claudel and Saint-John Perse, with an amazing capacity to change expressions instantly. He would be amiable in the extreme, excessively so. And then, when he thought I wasn't looking, a gleam of murderous ferociousness would shine through. I read in his eyes that he dreamed of someone ridding him of these foreigners who incessantly bugged him with this goddamn Pearl affair.

And in fact, he told me clearly, "What? A novel about Pearl and Omar? Since when does one write novels about such characters? Has the French literature I so love and respect fallen so low as to find its sustenance in such appalling affairs?"

Well, at least he listened to me. He saw I was persistent, and that I seemed to really believe that the nobility of literature could lie in creating a story out of an actual fact. He even pretended to take notes. But I had come at the wrong time, he said. They had just had elections, and the government was resigning in an hour. So I would have to introduce myself to Brigadier Javed Iqbal Cheema, the spokesman for the Ministry of the Interior, who was really in charge here. Yes, I can assure you, he is the boss now. I'm leaving, it's over, you're my last appointment as minister, but he, on the contrary, is staying on. He'll take care of this for you, you'll see.

Now it was Brigadier Javed Iqbal Cheema's turn to give me a lecture.

His hair and moustache were colored with henna, and he wore a green, houndstooth suit that complimented his tall figure. With a steely look that expressed an absence of affability, he began by asking me, "But what are you all coming to this country to look for? In every society, there are areas it's not a good idea to walk through. What would you say if I, Brigadier Javed Iqbal Cheema, started messing around in the underworld of Paris or Chicago? That's what this American Jewish journalist did, he went outside the boundaries. Be careful not to make the same mistake."

And then, "Besides, why did he rent a house? Doesn't it seem suspect that a Jewish journalist, based in India, would rent a house for 40,000 rupees a month? Suppose I want to see someone in France. I get a room in a hotel and I sit down with him in my room, I'm not going to rent a house. The fact that he did proves that he intended to stay, and that, you see—let's not tell any tales—is no longer journalism! That is why he is suspected of having worked for a foreign power."

And then, as to Omar, "As for Sheikh, you who are a writer, don't you find him strange, Omar? Look at the photos of him when he left prison in India. He seems to be in good health, he doesn't look like someone who just got out of prison. And that's why sometimes I have the feeling this whole thing could have been fabricated, from beginning to end, by the Indian secret services. Did you know that this Sheikh made at least 24 calls to India on his mobile phone? And did you know that at least two of them were to close aides of a minister?"

Nothing happened there either. He took note, he promised, he gave me all the numbers, including his mobile phone number, where I could reach him "at any time." But that request, like the official requests I made to return to the place where Pearl was held so I could take photos, or to interview the famous Gilani he thought he was going to see the day of his kidnapping, remained a dead letter.

I couldn't see Omar.

Everything seemed to be organized so I would never have any contact with him.

To give some substance to my imagination of what he was like physically, I had to settle for a fleeting glimpse of him in May, as he was being transferred from the Hyderabad prison.

As in Karachi, the police had had the courtroom evacuated, with the exception, for reasons unknown, of two foreign journalists. All of us, Pakistanis and foreigners, were stuck a hundred yards beyond, at the entrance to the street, behind metal barriers and sandbags guarded by teams of over-equipped commandos. Sharpshooters kept an eye out for any signs of disorder from the rooftops of a nearby hotel and some apartment buildings. Immediately surrounding the prison, troop transports and tanks appeared ready to move every time one of the protagonists of the trial or the judge or the prosecuting attorney appeared, escorted by his own armored car. There were incredibly nervous men in uniform everywhere, eyeing each other as much as they were watching for any potential assailant. Had the police gotten word that Omar had devised a plan to escape, with the help of the secret service, during his transfer? Were intelligence services persuaded, on the contrary, that the police had put together this scenario, to saddle them with the responsibility? In this state-of-siege atmosphere, behind the bullet-proof window of a paddy wagon with its escort of armed vehicles, I saw the figure of Omar Sheikh, caged like a wild beast. The lower half of his face was hidden by a scarf. And then, as he was crossing the barrier that blocked our entry to the other side, the commanding officer of the detachment threw a white blanket over his head. But I just had the time to see a tall figure in a traditional white *shalwar kameez* flash by. His hands were tied in front of him, his face was a bit thick, and in his eyes was an expression of triumph.

And then, like a painter, I had to work at length with photos of him. In London and Karachi, I had to multiply the images, collect all the portraits of him I could find, unpublished or in the press, like the two prints from *The Guardian* and *Dawn* that had struck me so the first day. I had to thoroughly and intently examine his features on paper to try to pierce the mystery, or the glimmer of the mystery that transformed the model Englishman into such a murderer.

There is first of all the black-and-white photo everyone is familiar with, probably a school photo, where he looks like a nice, chunky boy, kind, affable and well-behaved. A pouting mouth, chubby cheeks, soft features, normal for his young age. There is, just barely, something troubling in the eyes, a sort of a cold vibration that is frightening. Then again, that may be just the quality of the photo, or something I'm reading in to it myself.

There's another photo, perhaps taken a little later, when he was at the London School of Economics. Dark suit. Black tie. Thick forelock primly combed down over the forehead. A greediness about the mouth, a new firmness of the chin. The photo is fuzzy, especially around the eyes, that seem to have been gobbled up by the light. Except, it's bizarre—the eyes are nonetheless the most expressive part of his face, with their strange stare, pitiless and sad, the pupils bottomless pools that suddenly make him look older.

Grenville Lloyd, known as "the Panther," a referee of the arm wrestling matches Omar loved to fight in during his last London period, gave me two astonishing, unpublished photos taken at about that time. Decor of a pub, with a television suspended from the wall on a moveable arm, a blackboard with "Today's Special" written on it in the background. A referee in a white T-shirt and a navy blue baseball cap and a gold badge, wearing an intense expression, almost frightened, as though he were going to yell. And standing in the foreground, separated by a table that comes up to their waists where plastic-covered foam cushions have been placed to break the fall of the arm on the wood, two very young men locked in a struggle. Omar is the bigger of the two, wearing a sweat-soaked, light-colored undershirt and navy blue wool pants with a brown leather belt. You can tell he has a hairy chest. His arm, also hairy, is swollen with the effort of making his adversary give. The other hand, closed around a wooden post, is holding on so tightly not just his knuckles but his entire phalanxes are white, the small, mobile bones seeming ready to pierce the skin. But what is the most striking is his expression—his eyes lowered, features tense and deformed with effort, the nose pinched, as though he were compelled to stop breathing, and something at once childish and concentrated, wild, pitiless, in the lower part of the face... Omar Sheikh isn't playing, he hates.

There is an extraordinary document dating from the same time that Leecent Thomas, known as "The Force," his Jamaican buddy and sporting partner from arm wrestling days, brought me one evening at my hotel in London. Not a photo, but a video—and what a video! Several hours, continuously filmed, on June 18, 1992, in a London pub, where we see, all at once alive, full of strength and action, the very young Omar Sheikh, contending for a championship. Omar appears eleven times. With eleven different opponents. But it's always the same situation. The pub, the crowd yelling and applauding. Young people with close-cropped hair and tattoos, muscle-bound torsos, sitting on the floor with pints of beer. Bad music in the background, smoke. An atmosphere at once rough and good-humored, very 1960s Teddy Boys. A referee. And Omar who, each time, walks into the frame, positions himself at the table and confronts a new adversary.

The video is of poor quality. The color is off. Depending on the light, Omar's pants, filmed the same day, look either green or brown. The sound, especially, is non-existent—a hubbub, with bits and pieces of indistinct voices, the television braying in the background, almost covering the sound of the music. But what stands out is the little number he does, the game of his character.

The way he walks into the scene, for example: without a glance towards the camera, nor towards his opponent; the others look at him, exchange looks among themselves, wink at the public, mess around. He is completely serious, concentrating, barely blinking. He's chewing gum.

His rapport with the referee: The referee is a constant presence. He corrects positions, gives final advice, encourages, rectifies—"sit up straight, elbow right on the table... not like that, the grip, like that, the wrist... relax...." But while the others listen, sometimes talk or joke with him, and the last-minute tips always produce a certain familiarity, a nod of the head, a complicity, Omar never once glances at the damned referee. Tight-lipped still, he does what he's told, of course, but his attention is always elsewhere. Cut the crap—are you done with the useless advice now?

His very strange way of warming up, too: He stamps, taps his foot and nods his head as though he were searching for the beat. He takes his opponent's hand, does it again several times to get the right grip, and when he has, he paws it, shakes it, still chewing his gum, and always rhythmically, as though he were jacking him off, shakes it gently. Finally he presses up against the table, rubs against it. With his chest projected, his stomach glued to the wood of the table, nostrils flaring, fixed stare, he's the one who looks like he's having a wank now. Once, the situation is so obscene the referee intervenes—I can't hear what he's saying, but he shoves Omar a little and unglues his pelvis from the table.

His tricks—for he is really the craftiest of all. Against a colossus with a shaved head, for example—the double of Gregorious, the wrestler in Jules Dassin's *Forbans de la Nuit*—a mountain of muscle and fat, with arms like thighs, hands like shovels, twice the weight of Omar and almost twice his size. And we see Omar, tiny and thin, his hand drowned in the huge paw of the other, flexing his muscles, mobilizing his entire body to resist, but then weakening, bending his arm a little... that's it, he can't take any more, he's obviously lost... except that, when the colossus is sure of it and, thinking he's won, eases up on the pressure, Omar suddenly marshals his muscles, reverses the movement and, with one thrust, just one, plasters the wrestler's arm on the table to the cheers of the crowd.

His air of indescribable pride, finally, as when he wins the point against Gregorious—head thrown back, a slight smile, the only time he brightens up, that expresses either pride, or regret, or even, bitterness, I can't tell which. It's all there, on this video, beneath the mask—his secret face of a brute.

And then, dating from the same period, a last unpublished photo found at Frank Pittal's, the Jewish friend of the family, organizer of the arm wrestling tournaments, the man who paraded his Omar through all the pubs of England, like a circus owner showing off his bearded lady. It's a group photo that resembles a class picture. But no. It's in Geneva. And it's much more important than a school picture—it's the family photo of the English arm wrestling team at the December, 1992, World Championship. Omar is not in the front row with the two kneeling heavyweights, nor in the second or third row, both standing. He is, bizarrely, between the two back rows, the only one who is out of line, with a big smile on his face. Of the nineteen boys and two girls his smile is the broadest. Because he has won? Because he's just glad to be there, when his actual record, his official victories, his own merit, wouldn't have been sufficient in itself? (I heard repeatedly that the federation was poor and couldn't reimburse travel expenses, so they needed champions who could also pay their own airfare.) He looks happy, yes. Carefree. No longer the slightest trace, suddenly, of either rancor or hatred. This is just weeks before his departure for Bosnia. A few months before his conversion. And he looks like a happy child again.

There are more recent photos, after the crime, after the *crimes*—ten years have passed, the conversion has taken place. He has gone to Bosnia, and from Bosnia to Afghanistan, and from Afghanistan to India where he organized his first kidnappings before serving his first prison term. Young Omar Sheikh has become, before as well as after the kidnapping of Daniel Pearl, one of the most prominent jihadists of Pakistan. The former student of the London School of Economics, the arm wrestling champ, the nice teenager whose old friends all praise his kindness, his politeness—is one of the most hunted terrorists on earth.

There is the famous photo, taken around 2000–2001 in Lahore, where he is dressed entirely in white and wears red flowers, the color of jam, around his neck. He is an adult now. He is arrogant. Flamboyant. He has massive shoulders and a sculpted torso. He wears the medium-long beard of the Taliban and a large, white turban, wound around his head several times. I suppose the photo must have been taken at about the time he returned from India, at one of those receptions he wouldn't miss for the world, where he rubbed elbows, it is said, with the Punjabi elite of the city—"May I introduce Omar, a man of principles and convictions... our hero, our star, the man who expresses our feelings and wears our colors... the Indians tortured him, he withstood it." He looks happy. There is something peaceful, fulfilled, in his expression. It's a three-quarter view, but you can see his man-eating smile, and behind his tinted glasses, the look of a watchful wildcat. To me, this photo gives him a false resemblance—less a few pounds—to Masood Azhar, his mentor and guru, the man who has impressed him more than anyone in the world and with whom he is now in competition.

There is a picture of him, taken two years later in front of the prison at Hyderabad, during his trial, maybe on the day he received the death sentence. His head is bare this time. He wears a shirt. His beard is shorter. He is surrounded by a crowd of policemen in their navy blue caps and Rangers in black berets. In the foreground is a raised hand, but it's impossible to tell if it is there to strike someone, or to stop someone or something. One can guess that, beyond the frame, there was a good deal of agitation, probably the reason for this strong military presence. In fact, everyone seems nervous. Everyone is anticipating an incident, perhaps even a riot. But he, Omar, is calm. His eyes are lowered. He is facing the camera, his torso leaning slightly backward, as though the pressures of the crowd, the cameras, the police, disgusted him a bit or irritated him. And in this slight movement of recoil, the refusal to look directly into the camera while everyone is swarming around him, is the black insolence that reminds me of the days of his arm wrestling tournaments in London.

There's another photo taken then, but more cropped, framing only his face which he has raised to the light now. His head is thrown back as if he were listening to a distant sound or taking a deep breath of the cool air. The face is pale and stony, with a slightly mocking expression, like the remains of a smile. (Did the photographer catch him at the end of one of those diabolical laughs that made the blood of his friends in London and that of his hostages in New Delhi turn to ice?) This time we see his eyes. And in those eyes we feel an utter contempt for everything that has just happened—the sorrow of Pearl's loved ones, the Court's severity, its legalism, hearing himself condemned to death by hanging and knowing, or feigning to know, that no one believes it and it's all a vast sham, and now all this fuss around him and for him.... The truth is, one senses in this photo that he doesn't believe what is happening to him. He seems to be saying to himself, "What does it matter, after all? Why are all these people getting so excited? I know that within a year, maybe two, I'll be out of this grotesque hell. And in the meantime, I will have become a great, a very great, jihadist, the equal of Masood Azhar, my old patron, may the Devil take him. Now I'm the one who will be the symbol of the movement...."

And another shot from the same day, in fact, the same situation, the same Rangers surrounding him, his hands bound across his stomach—except that now, it's all over. He is ready to get into the blue armored vehicle waiting for him. He seems sober. Perhaps the crowd around him has dispersed. Perhaps he has realized the enormity of his situation. And in his face, there is suddenly, curiously, something lost and defeated. The eyes seem dazzled. The smile is prudent, a little silly. He must be trembling a bit, shivering. I even get the impression I can see a drop of sweat standing out on his forehead. The arrogant man, the hero, the successor of Masood Azhar who envisioned himself entering the pantheon of combatants in his lifetime, has become again a sort of a debutant—with something of the weakness, the softness, the childish indecisiveness in his features that was there in the very first photos dating from the time when he was only a child looking for his identity and destiny.

The mobility of his face, the malleability of his expressions, this incredible capacity, in photos taken in the same period and even, as here, almost at the same instant, to change expressions and become, suddenly, another person—they said the same of Carlos the Jackal, it has been said of bin Laden. Do they all have this diabolical aptitude to be, truly, several people—this name, and these faces that are legion?

The photos missing are those of the interim period: Bosnia, the Afghan and Pakistani training camps, India, the hostage takings, prison. Do they exist? Are there images of that Omar, and if so, where?

Actually, I do have one extraordinary photo, one that is, I think, unpublished. He is lying bare-chested on a hospital bed, no doubt at the hospital in Ghaziabad, in India, where he was cared for in 1994 after the assault of the police to liberate the hostages. An I.V. feed is visible at his left. His right arm is bent and his hand is touching his forehead. He is very pale. His beard is very black. His features are emaciated. He looks almost as if he were posing in imitation of the famous photo by Freddy Alborta of the dead Ché Guevara. The annoying thing is that it's the only such photo. And it's taken from too far away to say much more about it. So, for that period, I had to rely almost entirely on the oral testimony of Peter Gee, the Englishman who was Omar's cellmate in New Delhi for over a year and who is thus one of the people in the world who knows him best.

The shady Gee, who was in prison for trafficking in cannabis, was released in March 2000, three months after Omar. He did not stay in England. He went to live in Spain, in Centenera, a secluded village in the heart of the mountains, between Huesca and Barbastro, without electricity, without phone, a general delivery address, and the e-mail address of a friend he checks in with once or twice a month. A real treasure hunt to track him down. I met him for dinner in a hotel in San Sebastian where I went for something else entirely (to preside over a meeting of solidarity with the victims of E.T.A. Basque terrorism with Fernando Savater and his friends of "Ya Basta").

He looks a worn-out thirty, short, blond hair, with a touch of the burned-out hippie who lives on music, hash, yoga, and never sees the papers or the television, who takes his doses of the world with an eye-dropper. An old Dutch companion, even further gone than he, drove him here and views him much as one views stars or great men because of his time in India and his ties to a celebrated terrorist. Why did Gee come? Why did he accept, not just to talk to me, but to drive all this way? Friendship, he says,

Omar was a friend. He liked his honesty, his idealism, his gaiety. And just because Omar's in deep shit he's not going to change his opinion. If he popped up here, at the next table, he'd just say to him, "Hey, man, how you doing? Sit down, let's talk!" Other reasons for talking to me? I don't know, nor am I looking to know. I'm too happy for the windfall of his appearance to waste my time in conjectures and not take advantage of this miraculous opportunity to raise some questions I've been dying to ask.

The Omar he remembers is a pious man, truly pious, who believes in the immortality of the soul and the existence of paradise "like he believes an egg is an egg and two plus two make four."

He's a fundamentalist, without a doubt. For a whole year, Gee can't remember having seen him read anything other than the Koran, or commentaries on the Koran. "I tried Daniel Defoe's *Robinson Crusoe* on him, or Dostoyevski, but he couldn't understand how they could be of any use to him."

That said, he was open. He wasn't the kind to think there were only Muslims in this world. Once, for example, two non-Muslim Nigerians had been punished because tobacco was found in their cell. In such cases, the practice was to attach them to a bar and have their fellow inmates come by and whip them with a bamboo switch. Well, Omar refused to do it and started a hunger strike in solidarity with the Nigerians. OK, so it didn't work. People reported sick so they could go to the infirmary and eat. But it gives you an idea of the state of mind of Omar, of his humanism.

Gee remembers his charisma as well. The power he had over others. Was it his voice? His unblinking, unwavering stare? His high intelligence? The fact that he had been to Bosnia,

Afghanistan? His exploits? In any case, he reigned. He bewitched people. He lived—he was—like a sort of Don, the godfather of all the Pakistanis and Bengalis in the prison. Sometimes it even bothered him. He didn't approve of behaving like a mafia chief. He'd say, out loud, "Beware the intoxication of power! The important thing is ideas, not power! Ideas!"

Was he violent? Does Gee remember conversations, scenes, where he sensed this taste for violence that led Omar to assassinate Pearl or, before that, to threaten his previous hostages— Nuss, Croston, Partridge and Rideout—with decapitation? Peter Gee hesitates. He realizes that his friend's skin could be at stake in his answers. On the one hand, he admits, there were signs. The fact that Omar struck the director of the prison at Meerut, in Uttar Pradesh, where he served the first part of his sentence. Or the day in the Tihar jail, where he had organised a boycott of the *Jai Hind*—the Indian patriotic prayer all the inmates, Muslims included, were obliged to recite every morning—when, faced with the administration's reprisals, he spoke of killing one of the head guards. But on the other hand no, signs are just signs, not acts, and he thinks deep down, Omar was basically good and pacifistic. He can't believe he could have killed Daniel Pearl. And as for the other affair, the threats towards the hostages in New Delhi, he has only one thing to tell me: "At the time when we thought I was getting out of prison before him, he gave me the address of those people and asked me to go see them, to tell them for him that he regretted his duplicity, that he was sorry he had lied to trap them. Isn't that proof of his goodness?"

Women. This is a mystery to me, Omar and women—does Gee have any ideas? Hypotheses? Did they ever talk about women, during their long conversations in the cell? It's simple, Gee said. It's his obsession with purity. He puts them up too high on a pedestal. And so he didn't dare. He was twenty-five at the time, and deep down, Gee's not certain Omar had ever made love with a woman, or even seen a woman nude.

"I remember a conversation," he says. "We were in the prison refectory and we were talking about what it is to be courageous. His theory was that real courage isn't necessarily risking death, because all you need is to be a believer like him, and then it no longer holds any fear and there's no merit in facing it. Facing a woman, on the other hand—now that's true courage. To walk up to the girl he found attractive at the London School and, rather than talking through go-betweens, ask her out for a coffee—it's something he had never done, and he suddenly regretted it."

Islamism and women, this depth of panic and terror, this fear and, sometimes, this dizziness in front of the feminine sex I've always thought was the real foundation of the fundamentalist urge. Is Omar proof?

Omar's secret, Gee tells me, is lack of belonging or, the same thing, the fervent desire to belong. A double culture. Pakistan in England. England in Pakistan. It was Omar's idea to leave the Forest School in 1998 and go to Lahore. What? No, you say? You found out that it was his parents' decision, and it's when Crystal Chemical Factories Ltd. stopped that they returned to London? All right, maybe. After all, you're the one who's done the investigating. All I know is that, it didn't work that way either. He realized that not belonging works both ways and that he wasn't any more at home at Aitchison than he was at the Forest School. So, in your opinion, when you get to that point, when you're split this way, what do you do? What solution is left you? The loony Dutch friend, who has been drawing circles and saying nothing since the beginning of our talk, suddenly and vigorously agrees. More than ever, he admires his friend Peter Gee.

I remember what one of the New Delhi hostages, Rhys Patridge, said a few weeks ago. He recalled Omar's terrible outbursts of verbal violence against the Jews. He remembered a thorough and radical hatred for England. Was this a recent hatred, or an old one? Dating from his terrorist period, or before? The happy student, the polite child, was he keeping it a secret, waiting for his time to come?

"I have a theory," Patridge told me. "I thought about these famous arm wrestling tournaments, and I have a theory. Deep down inside, he hated them. He had only contempt for those fat Englishmen bursting with beer, tattooed, obscene, propping up the bar. Just that—he learned to know them and to hate them. He was like a double agent in contact with the enemy. That's what arm wrestling did for him."

A phallic challenge then—yes. Homoerotic jousting in an atmosphere seeking annihilation of the *other*—who, of the two of us, has the biggest arm? Patridge vs. Gee—the thesis of the grand phallic merry-go-round, homosexual and mimetic, as opposed to the thesis of the outsider.

Who is Omar, really?

Are there two Omars? A wolf and a lamb in the same cage? The perfect Englishman and the ultimate enemy?

Are there more than two—protagonists of even more contradictory scenarios? A truly diabolical Omar?

Or is there only one Omar; but one who must have always been cheating and who, already in London, acted like a good boy but nonetheless had a sinister double, a shadow, that was about to swallow him?

I reflect, one last time, upon all the bizarre things his friends have told me about him—I think about his phobia about pigeons, or of the period that went on for months when he told his friends, "I smell like a dead rat! Stay away from me, I smell like a dead rat! Once a rat died in my room, and he stank it up and I've never been able to get rid of the smell."

I think about his terrible laugh, more menacing than joyous, enraged, that everyone mentioned—his friends, the school-teacher in Sarajevo, Rhys Partridge.

It's the eternal enigma of this kind of individual and of his visible metamorphosis.

It's *the* great question we always come up against, and that, once again, stops me cold.

Either he's the character from the theory of two-lives-in-one, of discord, of heartbreak, and, basically, of conversion—someone who "changed their souls," as it is said of great converts, the elected, the chosen, who wake up one morning and see the veil lifted and turn from their errant ways. Why shouldn't what applies to those who are called to turn from errant ways also apply to those who are not? Why not the same law for saints as well as great criminals, the damned, the monsters, the counter-converted?

Or, he's like the character in Roger Vailland's *Un Jeune Homme Seul* who says, in essence, that there are no "dissonances" in a man's life. "I operate on the principle that apparent clashes are the intermittent fragments of a counterpoint that I've missed or that is hidden from me." So, "I play," he says, to whomever he has before him, "I grope," and "when I've found the counterpoint that makes sense of all the dissonances, I know all I want to know about the past and the present" of this person. He can even "predict his future." All he needs to do is to "continue to play in the same key. . . ."

I don't know.

CHAPTER 6 RECONSTITUTION OF A CRIME

I have a clearer idea, though, of how Omar Sheikh spent his time in the days and weeks leading up to the crime.

I saw one of his close friends.

I read some of the Sindh police reports.

I walked in his footsteps and followed his tracks, whenever I could, as I would soon do for Daniel Pearl.

My aim was to cull through the evidence, for the most factual account possible. By gathering the myriad of information that is available I hoped to etch a portrait of that which is unknown, the way negative space can define an object. And my object was to use the known facts to give an accurate reconstruction of the crime.

And when the tracks were missing, when the witnesses fled, or when there was no actual information because I was dealing with his inner existence or scenes in which he was the sole actor, I used the methods of investigation that had allowed me once before to reconstitute the last days of the poet Charles Baudelaire within the limits of my perspective—never give in to the imagination when reality is there and direct investigation should be able to find it, but give it a role when reality eludes you and circumstances are such that you are compelled to speculation.

Everything counts, in that case. The most infinitely tiny details. The most apparently useless information. As Leonardo Sciascia writes, again in *Affaire Moro*, "The most minute, almost imperceptible events contribute to the construction of every event which, then, is displayed in all its grandeur, rushing in a movement of attraction and aggregation towards an obscure center, an empty magnetic field where they take form and are, together, precisely the great event." And then—and how can one not agree?—"In this form, in the ensemble they create, no small event is accidental, incidental, fortuitous. The parts, even if they are molecular, find necessity and thus explanation in the whole, and the whole in the parts."

To begin at the beginning, it's the 11th of January, 2002, in Rawalpindi, in the Hotel Akbar, a modern place facing Liaquat Bagh Park, right at the top of Murree Road. Pearl's fixer, Asif Farooqui, has arranged a meeting there with Omar and it's the first contact, the first encounter, between the two men.

Omar has shaved.

He is wearing western clothes.

He was seen the day before, buying Ray Bans in an Islamabad store. They're like the ones he wore day and night last year in London, the ones his father had said made him look like a Bombay mafioso.

He was also seen at Mr. Books, the big Islamabad book store, right near the buildings of the Presidency and the Supreme Court of Pakistan. He was spotted chatting with Mohammed Eusoph, the proprietor, who had ordered a book in English for him a few months earlier. Omar was more or less the hero of the book, since it told the story of the Indian Airlines hijacking that led to his liberation from prison in India at Christmas, 1999. This time he was looking for a 1991 book on the war in Iraq and another on American Special Forces training, as well as Montgomery Watt's 1988 book *Islamic Fundamentalism and Modernity*, which Eusoph had to order, and a fourth by a certain Abu Saoud, "Muslim economist" and "Arab League counselor."

When Pearl arrives at the Akbar, Omar is already there, sitting at a table with three bearded men in the hotel restaurant, a small, ill-lit room across from the reception desk. He had cut off his beard and so reassumed his air of the perfect Westerner. That morning he had spent two hours doing his "accent exercises"— slipping from the most caricatured Punjabi into the most distinguished British accent in a second, a talent that always made his friends at Aitchinson College laugh. He would be in dire need of it today. Now he is going to pass two hours, maybe three, in a room on the fourth floor, doing his "Englishman" number for the journalist, answering his questions, providing all the clarifications he likes about the complex relations between various Pakistani jihadist groups, and promising to do everything possible to set up the interview he's dying to do with Sheikh Mubarak Ali Shah Gilani, head of the sect Pearl thinks "shoe bomber" Richard Colvin Reid belonged to.

The chase is on—the terrible ballet, that will last twelve days, of the hunter and his prey.

The next day, considering Pearl hooked, Omar goes home to Lahore, to Sadia, the young scholar of English with a Master's from the University of Punjab, the first woman ever in his life and his wife for the past year, who has just given him a child.

I wasn't able to meet her. She was locked away, invisible, when Omar was free, and she still is now that he is back in prison. But I know that she is intelligent and pretty. I know that under her *burqua* she now has the pale but luminous complexion of newly secluded women who lived in the sun as teenagers. I believe, also, that she shares Omar's ideas and that she was "proud," like most Pakistanis I met, that he had "followed his ideas through."

After meeting Pearl he stays at home with her for two days.

He spends these two days establishing two new mobile phone contracts and developing his relationship with Naseem and Saquib, two Afghanistan war veterans who are members of the Harkat ul-Mujahideen, a group he has close ties to. After the abduction, they will be responsible for sending out press communiqués by e-mail. He also devotes some time to perfecting his disguise of a young Pakistani, friend of the West. In a downtown boutique he buys some Gucci loafers, a signet ring, a Breitling wrist watch, a navy blue rain coat he will sleep in so it won't look new, a suede jacket, a pair of jeans, another pair of Ray Bans (prescription), a pair of tortoiseshell glasses without smoked lenses, so that he'll look like the London School of Economics student he once was before plunging into the world of fanaticism and crime.

Is all this necessary for only the operation, or does he take some secret pleasure in it? In any case, he accumulates the signs of belonging to the West he has severed his ties with, that he is supposed to hate, and one of whose more successful representatives he is preparing to kill. He is, in this, like the September 11 terrorists, Atta, Majes Moqed, Alhazmi, and Khalid Almihdhar, whose last pleasures in this world, the FBI discovered to their astonishment, were a trip to Las Vegas, a fling with a Mexican whore, ten minutes in a sex shop, and an hour in one of the main streets of Beltsville, window-shopping for lingerie.

He goes to a garage to buy a Toyota, then thinks better of it and rents one instead.

It's the 15th.

He takes the rental car to Dokha Mandi, his father's birthplace and the village of his family's roots.

The next day, on his return to Lahore, he plays a game of chess, has lunch at the Liberty Lions Club, the watering-hole of the city's Punjabi elite, and goes to the dentist. He prowls around the area of Aitchinson College, but without making his presence known. He goes by the Anarkali bazaar, stops briefly to pray at the Sonehri mosque in the heart of the old city, and walks all the way to the Shalimar gardens, in the east, at the end of the Grand Trunk Road, where he strolls for a few hours between the fountains and the lanes of hibiscus and bougainvillea and the rose gardens.

His last moments of peace?

Ultimate tactical adjustments before the operation?

He apparently also makes contact with the people of Lashkar e-Janghvi, a group he does not belong to but hopes will assist with the operation.

At Badshahi, the old, red sand mosque near the Fort, he encounters a man who is in contact with Maulana Masood Azhar, Omar's old mentor, the chief of the Jaish e-Mohammed, who is now in prison, where Musharraf had him thrown.

And finally, he writes to Pearl. Five days have passed since their meeting in Rawalpindi and Omar sends him an e-mail from an address not, in retrospect, entirely devoid of humor: Nobadmashi@yahoo.com—in Urdu, "no rascality." He tells Pearl, in essence: My wife is ill and has had to be "hospitalized".... That's why I'm a little late in responding in regard to this "meeting" with Gilani we discussed at the Hotel Akbar.... But I've talked to the office of "Shah Sahab" and I "conveyed" to him the articles you mailed me; "I am sure that when he returns we can go and see him".... Please "pray for my wife's health," would you?

The machine is in motion.

The countdown has begun.

People who cross his path at this time are struck by his calm and determined demeanor... and sometimes, in his eyes, a sudden, instantaneous flicker of helplessness.

On the 17th he leaves the house on Mohni Road with Sadia and the baby and they get on the train for Karachi, one of the long Pakistani trains crowded to overflowing, without numbered seats, that passengers storm rather than board. He has had the strange good fortune to find a compartment that's nearly empty—just three passengers, no doubt merchants, apparently intimidated, who leave him one of the banquettes.

During the journey, he says his prayers on a rug in the corridor. He has donned his new look—clean-shaven, a twill jacket over his *shalwar kameez*—but he misses none of the day's prayers.

The rest of the time he reads, meditates, sleeps. Sadia, veiled from head to toe, wearing uncomfortable shoes with low heels, is in the part of the compartment reserved for women, separated by a curtain, with the baby.

When they arrive at the Karachi train station, a place of intensely concentrated poverty, a strange incident occurs: Omar is shoved, almost accosted, by a beggar, one of the hundreds that sleep there on the ground, wrapped in moth-eaten blankets and stinking of old filth. What's going on? Did he bump into him without noticing? Did the beggar take him for a foreign businessman, an infidel? Or is this all an act, designating a message, and if so, what and why and to whom? A few heated words are exchanged, a policeman appears and Omar hands him a few rupees as if to say, I can handle this myself. Other beggars crowd around the first one, grumbling and threatening, appearing to challenge him. But either Omar's stature or his athletic build intimidates them, or else it's all an act, and they soon disperse. The spent traveller rushes for the nearest taxi, his wife following him with some difficulty, the squalling baby in her arms, and they head for the home of a beloved aunt, where he plans on staying until the kidnapping.

So now, he is in Karachi, ready to get down to work, in this city he doesn't know well, where he is scarcely known in turn, and where he can't go 'round boasting of his deeds as in Lahore—and it's all a little disconcerting.

The next day—the 18th of January, five days before the kidnapping—he spends the day at the famous and mysterious Binori Town Mosque, a place that has taken on cult status amongst Pakistani fundamentalists and where it is said the Taliban elite received their religious training.

He is alone, at first, concentrating intensely in the half-light of a study hall of the adjoining *madrasa*, separated from the pilgrims who have come from all over the country and all over the world—he speaks little, eats next to nothing, stops only to spend an hour at a nearby gym late in the afternoon, then returns to sit on his heels, hands at the nape of his neck like a prisoner, listening with a fixed stare to a preacher who has come into the room during his absence and is calling for a holy war.

In the evening though, four men come to see him—three of them are from Karachi and thus familiar with the city, its secret networks, its seedy quarters. According to the information I obtained, they are the men from Harkat ul-Mujahideen handling the electronic communiqués, Fahad Naseem and his accomplices Salman Saquib and Sheikh Mohammed Adeel, and a certain Syed Hashim Qadeer Shah, alias Arif, who lives in Bahawalpur. Does Omar also see the others? Will he meet Bukhari, the man who will dictate to Pearl the things he must say in the video? Fazal Karim, the caretaker, who will hold Pearl's head at the instant the Yemeni decapitates him? The Yemeni executioner himself? The other Yemenis? It's an essential question, for the answer determines not only the degree of Omar's implication, but of his control and mastery of the entire plan.

Two indications lead me to believe that Omar did meet the others that night: Mobile phone calls traced by the police and by Jamil Yusuf, the former businessman who is now director of Karachi's Citizen-Police Liaison Committee, which specializes in the investigation of kidnapping cases; and a statement by the owner of a restaurant in Karachi's squalid Little Bangladesh neighborhood, who insists he saw Omar that night accompanied by a man in an Afghan hat whose description matches that of Bukhari.

The day after going to Binori Town, the 19th, Omar has lunch with Faheem and Saquib at the Village Garden, near the Hotel Metropole, where he plans to stage the kidnapping.

He spends the afternoon not far away, alone at the bar of the Marriott, adding up long columns of figures—the state of his finances? The estimated cost of the operation?

He meets Naseem again, in front of the Village Garden, both of them standing in the cold, whispering, discussing, walking to the Marriott to warm up, returning, then retracing their footsteps, perhaps to count how many, to measure and note the time it takes. Omar writes everything down. In fact, ever since the countdown started, he has been scribbling brief notes incessantly in a brown note pad he carries in the front pocket of his tunic. Where are these notes? What happened to them after his arrest?

Still together, they walk to a neighboring cybercafé. (By coincidence, it is the same café where Pearl had gone to wrap up his investigation of the "shoe bomber," looking for the place where Reid had received his final instructions to take the Paris-Miami flight.) There, Omar sends a second e-mail to Pearl: Sorry, he says, to have taken so much time in getting back to you... but I mislaid your number.... My wife... the hospitals, in Pakistan, are so "miserable and harassing" for "poor people"... it "made me realize once again that our family has a lot to be grateful for".... But "I have good news"... I spoke to "the Sheikh's secretary yesterday" and "he told me that the Sheikh Sahab has read your articles and that you are welcome to meet him".... He is in Karachi for the moment.... Do you wish to wait until he returns to Rawalpindi? Do you want to "put some questions to him," to "mail them to me" and "I will pass the printout to his secretary"? Or else, "if Karachi is on your program" you may also "see him there."

Then they wait in front of the computer screen. Five minutes... ten.... Questions by e-mail, what a great idea! Omar tells his companion. He thinks it the mark of a professional to act as if he's asking for nothing and to appear indifferent about the meeting with Gilani! And, sure enough, in barely the time it takes for the message to route through the *Journal*'s network, Pearl replies yes, of course, with pleasure—he has another good reason to come, with his wife, to Karachi, and he readily opts for the meeting. Are you in Karachi yourself? Will you be at the meeting?

Omar jumps for joy.

The bait has been taken.

Afterward, without Naseem, he goes to a general store in the old city and comes out with a package wrapped in newsprint under his arm, which he takes back to his aunt's house—a gun?

That evening, he is seen near the Marriott again, buying a set of slides from a street vendor. (Scenes of Kashmir? Crimes of Americans and Russians in Afghanistan? Bosnia?)

He is seen as well in the hotel cafeteria, relaxed and seemingly carefree, writing postcards to his little sister, Hajira Sheikh, and his brother Awais, and a third to an Indian doctor, perhaps the head of the Ghaziabad hospital in the state of Uttar Pradesh, where he was taken in 1994 after being arrested by the New Delhi police, the setting of the pseudo-Guevara photo.

That evening he returns to Binori Town but only for an hour. A final contact? With whom?

Finally, I imagine him afterwards mailing a letter that evening, a real letter, addressed to a lawyer or a journalist or a friend—I can't believe there doesn't exist somewhere, in a strong box, in some safe place, a hand-written document detailing, just in case, the origins of the operation, the number of accomplices, his own role, as well as the network of complicity ultimately reaching to the high places he will have needed to successfully accomplish his task.

Sunday the 20th he sends another message to Pearl, a third one, from another cybercafé. "Gilani can see you Tuesday, maybe Wednesday. His secretary is still in Rawalpindi and will give me the phone number of one of his followers you will call when you arrive and who will take you to him. Give the sheikh my best, tell him not to forget me in his prayers, and tell him we miss him a lot here in Rawalpindi and wait impatiently for his return. What a shame you have to leave Pakistan so soon! I hope you have enjoyed your stay."

Monday the 21st he meets two of his accomplices in an apartment in the upscale Defence Society neighborhood, and he gives them money to buy a camcorder, a scanner, and a camera. When Naseem returns with the camera, a little Olympus, they go to Clifton Beach, a stretch of gray sand in the middle of the city where the sewers empty out. Omar takes the pictures: A 4x4 Rodeo, a group of silent women hobbled by their burquas, in stockings, getting their feet soaked as they try to avoid the gobs of tar. Another woman, unveiled, with the waxy, anemic complexion of those who have been shut away too long, who cries "rape" when he snaps the photo. A child on a camel. A snake fight. A sign reading, "No photos allowed." He finds all this highly amusing. He exults. At the end of the afternoon, he walks through the change stalls of Jinnah Road and then back to Binori Town for a meeting with an unknown person, perhaps one of the Yemenis.

On Tuesday, the 22nd of January, he sends a last message to Pearl confirming an appointment for tomorrow, Wednesday, around seven. It's certain, Gilani has decided; they'll have half an hour for the interview and then an hour, if he likes, with the followers who live with him. Omar gives Pearl the phone number—00 2170244—of one of the young disciples who will be in charge of driving him there: His name is Imtiaz Siddique. "He will arrange to meet you." I am "sure you will gain a lot from the meeting." Don't forget to tell me "all the details." After that he goes, ironically, to the Pearl Continental Hotel to change another bunch of dollars, makes a call from the lobby, another from his mobile phone, leaves, notices a storm drain, and throws the mobile phone away.

He sleeps badly that night.

He sleeps alone in a tiny room at the back of his aunt's apartment. In spite of the raincoat, in spite of the relatively mild climate, he shivers with cold—and he sleeps badly.

He spends the night wide awake, alert, his lips moving as though he were praying. As soon as he tries to shut his eyes, images loom in his mind, like nails driven into his soul—his kind aunt tried everything yesterday to lighten the bad atmosphere, but no, the thoughts are still there.... A puddle of congealed blood in the Sarajevo snow. A wounded man he saw at Zenica, in the throes of death. Another near Thathri, in Kashmir, whose head and face had been bashed in with blows from rifle butts and boot heels—all he could remember was a wound, a pulp, with one ferocious, suffering, gaping eye still shining. The shrieks of a comrade in a neighboring cell, one night at Tihar Jail. Pearl's face the other night at the

Hotel Akbar, less disgusting than he had expected, rather frank for a Jew, and clever for an American... strangely curious, too, about what a sincere jihadist could be thinking. Unless he was pulling a number, an American Jew trick—play it sly, lull your vigilance, all the better, then, to betray you. He dreams about Pearl, with his skull smashed in, his brains coming out his ears.... He dreams of Pearl dead before even killing him and can't tell if the idea pleases or scares him.... Sometimes he has the impression of feeling pain in Pearl's place.... Then he finds the idea absurd and curses him.... Sometimes, on the contrary, he is jubilant, and his jubilation makes him shiver....

He is groggy, his head heavy when he rises on the morning of the 23rd of January.

He drinks three cups of coffee, one after another, but he still cannot seem to warm up or clear his head.

He tries to eat something, but everything he puts in his mouth tastes like cardboard.

He shaves, and notices that the mirror is cracked—he's sure it wasn't that way last night.... And this shadow on my face, it's the first time I've seen that, too.... And what if the son of a bitch had understood everything? What if that was the explanation for his unbelievable gullibility? And what if he were an agent, really a cop, and he came with other cops to the appointment at the Village Garden? What if he's the one, smarter by half, who is setting a trap for us?

The day has come, and he's worried.

Is Omar there at the actual time of the kidnapping? Is he at the Village Garden with the others when Pearl arrives at seven p.m. and gets into the red Suzuki Alto? Or has he invented a last-minute alibi? Has he taken the train back to Lahore in the afternoon, as he stated at the trial, and as his wife confirmed?

I don't know for certain.

On one hand, there's the statement of Nasir Abbas, the taxi driver who picked Pearl up at the Sheraton, drove him to the Village Garden and who, in his second deposition, declared that yes, of course, Sheikh was there. With his own eyes, he saw Sheikh get out of the Suzuki that drove up in front of his cab just as Pearl was paying. He saw them shake hands, and saw Omar open the rear door for Pearl to get in. Moreover, says the prosecutor, how could it be otherwise? How would Pearl have gotten into the car had he not seen the now familiar face of Omar? Would he have been foolish enough to get into an unfamiliar car, with a driver he did not know?

But on the other hand, apart from the Omar's own statements and those of his wife, there is defense lawyer Abdul Waheed Katpur's objection, expressed at the trial and in an interview with *The Guardian*, that Nasir Abbas is a cop, and in Pakistan you can't send a man to the gallows on the sole strength of testimony from a cop. All the more so because—and this is the major argument—Omar had more or less announced in his last two e-mails that he would not be there ("my best to the Sheikh, don't forget to tell me the details of the interview"). Unless there was a counter-order that day, or if Pearl himself thought better of it at the last minute and requested, in one of his two phone conversations with Imtiaz Siddiqui on the afternoon of the 23rd, that Omar be present, it is not absurd to suppose that the American came to the appointment knowing full well that Omar would not be there.

Or did Pearl think better of it?

Did he demand expressly that Omar be there?

To know, you would have had to meet Nasir Abbas, the driver.

And in order to judge whether it was materially possible for Nasir Abbas, cop or not, to recognize Omar at fifty feet, you would have to know what the weather was like that evening, when the sun set, the quality of the light, whether there was any haze. I know it was nice out. The day's weather report announced sunny, dry skies, and I even found a waiter at the Village Garden who says he remembers "it was like summer in January, that's what we all said that day, and since that doesn't happen very often, it stood out in our minds." Summer weather until the end, all the way up until the evening?

How can one know if Omar was there?

The truth is, I have no idea and on this point I am, more than ever, reduced to conjectures.

My guess, then?

My bet, since I am condemned to bet?

My bet is that Omar was there and not there *at the same time.*

Not there, because he said it was agreed upon with Pearl and I have no reason to believe that either he or Pearl changed their minds.

But there, at the same time, inevitably there, at a distance, where he could see and make sure that the operation was going smoothly as planned, but without being seen, because, after all, he's risking everything! His freedom! Perhaps even his life! Faced with all this and the anxiety that's eating at him, how could he calmly buy a ticket for Lahore and wash his hands of the whole thing? Moreover, how could this kidnapping zealot, this ace, this artist, not be tempted to supervise, right to the very end, the scenario he crafted and that he's certainly not going to leave in the hands of a Siddiqui or a Bukhari?

There are two possible positions for this.

After several scouting sessions, simulations, and reconstitutions, I found two places he could have hidden so as to observe the entire operation without actually participating in it.

A half-demolished wall, opposite the restaurant, where a man can easily stand and watch the entire area where the cars stop.

Or else, inside the restaurant itself, behind the door to the garage, a recess that lends a better perspective of the avenue but has the drawback of affording a view of only half the broad parking lane, since it follows a curve.

I picture him behind the wall.

I imagine him standing there, his face turned toward the sun setting over the city, watching the taxis, thinking, "That's it, he can't be far off now," or, "What if he doesn't come? What if he gets scared at the last minute and decides not to come?" I suppose that part of him, at this instant, is surprised to find himself hoping that Pearl will not come, or that he'll come with Mariane, or with his fixer, or with a someone from the American consulate. But if this is what I suppose, I also know that it's just a fleeting thought and that, deep down, he realizes that the die is cast and it's a good thing.

Things don't happen, he thinks, they wait for you. And this instant, and all the rest to follow, is waiting, as it has been since the time, such a long time ago, when I was a good old "Paki bastard" who smelled like a rat, aped the little Englishmen, and made such pathetic efforts to please them and become one of them.

"Salvation lies in disaster," Convoy of Mercy organizer Asad Khan used to say, when he would urge his young comrades on to action by describing the apocalypse awaiting the Western world. At the time, Omar didn't really understand what his new friend meant. Now he sees, and he understands. He knows he is on the road to ruin, but that ruin will save him. He senses that, one way or another, something will go wrong with this affair—but how can he not, at the same time, feel God's finger upon his forehead?

He isn't cold any more.

He's not even really afraid.

He feels as light as a feather, relieved of his own self.

I was, he tells his wife, like a new mother who sees her baby.

What is the meaning of a life? Well, this is it. He has the feeling, even more than in India, of having fulfilled his mission. He is bursting with joy. He exults.

PART THREE
CRIME OF STATE

CHAPTER 1 MYSTERIES OF KARACHI

19 September 2002.

Second trip to Karachi.

Once again, I use my old diplomatic passport to facilitate my entry into Pakistani territory.

No stopping by the embassy.

No grand hotel, where you're instantly spotted.

Instead, a little guest house on the road to the airport, right near the place where the cab was pulled over and I was forced to pay a bribe to the policeman during my first visit.

And, in case of questions or trouble, a brand new story: Quite apart from my "novel" on Daniel Pearl, I've come looking for a printing press and paper supplies for the new Afghan newspaper *Nouvelles de Kaboul*, since those things are not available in Afghanistan.

"Don't kid yourself," says Gul, my fixer from last spring who came to meet me in the lobby of the guest house, a small, smoke-filled room with cushions lining the walls, samovars of tea with milk on the center table, and the stuffed head of an animal on the wall. "Don't think they believe a word about your novel and, now, your paper for Afghanistan. They came to my place last June, after you left. They questioned my wife. Shut my kid in his room. Searched the whole house. They wanted to know what you did, what you were looking for, what I had told you, what you'd seen. They had me summoned by an old *uléma* at the other end of Rawalpindi, who gave me fair warning. You've got to be careful. They're everywhere."

The "they" he is talking about is the dreaded ISI, the Interservices Intelligence Agency, the Pakistani secret service that, in principle, as in every country in the world, should be concerned with gathering foreign intelligence. But since the Bangladesh war and the nationalist uprising in Baluchistan under Bhutto, and since the Afghanistan war and the Shiite upsurge resulting from the Iranian revolution, the ISI is increasingly inclined to expand its activities. In internal matters, it has an increasing tendency to substitute itself for the Intelligence Bureau, suspected of separatist sympathies. But Gul does not say "ISI." No one in Karachi ever says "ISI." They just say "they," or "the agencies," or "the invisible government," or even "the three letters," just "the three letters." Or even, when they can, they gesture with three raised fingers—as though the simple fact of saying those three cursed letters out loud was dangerous.

"Don't hold it against me," he says, glancing nervously at the man behind the reception desk, a timid, toothless, little old man with a round face who cannot possibly hear us at this distance. "I can't go on working for you under these conditions. It's not just a question of their visits, you know.... I had weird phone calls, incessantly, after you left, which, given the circumstances, is perhaps even more worrisome than all the rest. Here in Pakistan, when you get a call on your mobile phone, the caller is always identified. Except...."

The man from the reception desk walks over to us. He pretends to be arranging the cushions and asks us, in broken English, if we need anything. All of a sudden, Gul looks scared. His nostrils start to tremble, as if he were going to cry. What a new, strange way of talking to me without making eye contact! And now, while I answer the man from the reception desk, he stares at me, but surreptitiously, in fleeting, panicky glances. Clearly, something must have happened. This is not the same Gul I saw in the spring, cheerful and daring, casual and confident, ready to try anything, asking me about Reporters Without Borders, ready to be their correspondent if they asked him, making fun of paranoid journalists who saw bin Laden sneaking around every corner in Islamabad. The man from the reception desk returns to his post, and Gul continues.

"...Except when it's people from the army or the services. I got several calls this morning, and there was never anyone on the other end of the line, just breathing. And the number wasn't on the screen. That's why we must part ways. It's better for me. But I think it will be better for you, too. Would you like me to find someone to replace me? I've got an idea. His name is Asif. You'll see, he's a good man."

I'm thinking that Asif was the name of Daniel Pearl's fixer, and for some reason, that bothers me.

I'm thinking as well that Gul is probably right, and that the people from the ISI, if they are as well organised as everyone says, will probably think there's something fishy about my story of paper for the *Nouvelles de Kaboul.*

And then I think again about the two e-mails I received from him and from Salman, another one of my connections, this summer. In my absence, I had asked each of them to look for information on the bank accounts of the "jihadist" organisations outlawed by President Musharraf that Danny had been investigating when he was kidnapped. Salman had found me an informer who had immediately begun working on it, and Gul had recruited another. And then, an e-mail from Salman on July 25th: "My Karachi source has disappeared, I found out yesterday. He has been out of touch for several days. His family is very concerned, and so am I. I'll let you know when I have any news." And then an e-mail from Gul, on August 13th: "I was on vacation. Before leaving, I had given your e-mail to the journalist and asked him to send the material to you directly. When I returned, I learned he had a serious accident and so could not accomplish his mission. I am really sorry for this loss of time. Would you authorize me to deal with someone else? It will take me another ten days or so. Best."

It didn't register immediately; I didn't make the connection then, not between the two informers, and especially, not between them and me. But what if it was all related? What if someone was trying to prevent me from tracing Danny's path? What if, in other words, my story about a novel didn't fool anyone?

"No, no," I said, "not Asif. It's better in this case to be really careful and avoid someone they can eventually trace back to you. I know of someone, an old friend from the days when I was reporting about Bangladesh. He's not exactly a Bengali, he lives in Peshawar. I never really lost contact with him. He's one of those extraordinary fellows who, like you, saves the honor of this country. I'll call him."

Gul, both sorry and relieved, gets up and leaves. I watch him as he walks out to the street and melts into a crowd of pilgrims approaching a neighboring mosque, a head taller than all of them. Is it my imagination, or did I really see two men get up and follow him, the ones I had taken for passing shopkeepers who had come in to sit down at the far end of the room while we were talking?

I call my old friend Abdul, who works for a western NGO in Baluchistan and who, amazingly, is free for the next few weeks.

"Such a long time later," he says, in the same deadpan tone I remember, pretending not to be surprised at my call and taking up our conversation as if we had seen each other only yesterday instead of 30 years ago. "It's funny. What do you look like, after all these years? With me, it's my hair, you'll see. Give me two days to get there."

And so here I am alone, idle, wandering around to kill time, in chaotic, feverish Karachi, with its wet, smoky autumn sky, its rainy light, humming with rumors of last night's crimes or the latest adventures of the war between the Haji Ibrahim Bholoo and the Shoaib Khan gangs. Karachi is one of the only cities in the world where the mafia are so much a part of the mainstream of life in the city that their clashes, their incessant split-ups, their compromises, have the same importance as episodes of political life back home in the West.

Here I am in the *souk* of Lea Market in the north of the city; in the market of Little Bangladesh, in Ziaul Hoque Colony, where you can buy an adolescent Bengali girl for seventy thousand rupees (ten percent for the police). I'm in Sainab

Bazar, the great cotton market, the best echo chamber, the best source, if you want to know what's going on and what's being said in Karachi.

Three hundred virgins arrived last night, via India, to be sold in Dubai....

The nocturnal fantasies of the "gunmen," the private security agents in orange caps you can hire for the day and who sometimes fight among themselves at night....

The results of a gangland killing they found this morning in the Karachi boat graveyard at Gadani: an entire family, father, mother, two grandmothers, three children including a baby, all dead, undoubtedly for weeks. The baby had been skinned and one of the old ladies quartered, the others crucified. The corpses had been left to rot in the hold of an abandoned and stripped tanker....

Danny again, still Danny, the invisible trace of Danny every moment, with every step—did he come by here? Or here? Or why not here, in front of this fishmonger who gives me pleading looks, like a beggar? Or here, on Jinnah Road, before Binori Town, the grand mosque where Omar spent so many long hours in the days before the kidnapping and that I cannot imagine escaped Danny's radar.

And then this other bit of news I don't imagine attracted much attention in France but that everyone is talking about here—last week, on the night of 10 to 11 September, the Pakistani police, backed up by the Americans, raided an apartment building in the residential neighborhood of Defence. They found computers with maps of American cities stored on their hard drives, and piloting manuals; some documents proving the presence, at the heart of command structure of al-Qaida, of three of bin Laden's sons, Saad, Mohammed, and Ahmed; they found and arrested ten Yemenis who had entered Pakistan illegally; and among them was Ramzi bin al-Shibh, Mohammed Atta's roommate in Hamburg, who had planned on being the twentieth World Trade Center highjacker, but whose entry visa to the United States, like Zacariya Essabar, had been refused at the last minute. . . .

"A victory for democracy!" says a rickshaw driver.

It's a defeat for the "dogs of al-Qaida," repeats the pistachio vendor before the Jinnah mausoleum, wagging his finger.

And the press, even if they're incapable of finding out whether bin al-Shibh has been sent to the United States to go to Guantanamo or if he is temporarily being held at the base at Begram in Afghan territory, call him "the first high official of the Organisation to have been neutralized since the arrest of Abu Zubaydah, at Faisalbad, in March."

I go there, to 63C 15th Commercial Street, in the middle of Defence, the residential area in the middle of the city where I remember—because it seemed strange to me—that immediately after independence, fifty years ago, most of the apartments were allotted to military personnel.

I don't really know what I'll find there.

For the moment, I don't see any connection with my investigation.

But I'm all alone, I have two days to kill while I wait for my new fixer, and so I decide to go see the neighborhood where the Pakistani police raided an al-Qaida hideout.

There is still a certain amount of activity there.

There are still a handful of journalists and onlookers, a squad of "gunmen" wearing black T-shirts marked "No Fear" in English, and a cordon of policemen guarding a metal barrier.

But life goes on. The Igloo ice cream shop across the street has reopened, and so has the real estate agency. Three men, naked from the waist up, white loin cloths floating on their skinny hips, their ribs and bony backbones showing under the skin, with long hair pulled back in pony tails—probably Christians or Hindus—are busy working on the sewer pipes that were damaged during the raid. A gang of children who are playing around the site hang on to me and ask if I know Leonardo DiCaprio. A teenager is filming me with an video camera. Another one asks if I want some black-market cigarettes. No doubt about it, a nice area. This is not one of those fleabag suburbs where I could imagine al-Qaida fugitives hiding. Approaching the apartment building where it all happened, recognizable because of the hundreds of bullet and grenade holes that have pockmarked the façade, I see a handsome, proper, four-story building with a rather well-to-do air, standing next to the local electricity company.

"Would you like a cup of tea?" an employee from the real estate agency asks, obviously happy to meet and talk with a foreigner.

The police, he tells me, started blocking off the neighborhood around three in the morning.

About twenty ISI agents positioned themselves around the building.

A little before nine, they arrested two Afghans who came out placidly to go to breakfast and they started yelling to alert their comrades who were still on the fourth floor.

At midday, after a fierce gun battle three hours long, with a hundred police reinforcements arriving throughout the morning, we saw a woman, two children, and ten men come out with their hands on their heads, all of them yelling "Allah Akbar" as loud as they could.

"How did we react?" he says with a guffaw. "Were we surprised? Oh, not at all, it wasn't a surprise to anyone. We saw them coming and going, and the lights on day and night. Everyone, starting with the police, knew that Arabs—well, in any case, people who did not speak Urdu—lived here in the neighborhood. There are embassy employees, and students of the *madrasas*. Why should we be suspicious of people who come to study here, friends, who do not make any trouble? How can you expect good Muslims to refuse hospitality to other good, God-fearing Muslims who do no wrong? So this place, like so many others, was known. We saw them going out to do errands every morning. Even the television came to see them two months ago, and the police were aware of it...."

Television? It turns out that he is talking about Yosri Fouda, star of Al-Jazeera, the Arab Bob Woodward, who last summmer came to this apartment to interview not only Ramzi bin al-Shibh but Khalid Sheikh Mohammed, bin Laden's right hand man. Khalid Sheikh Mohammed: the shining star of the al-Qaida galaxy, a lover of the good life who, they say in Karachi, often travels by helicopter and makes a point of staying in only 5-star hotels, the mastermind of September 11, the inventor, a decade ago in Manila, of the genius idea to turn airplanes into flying bombs, the man to whom one of the kamikazes of the synagogue at Djerba would make his last phone call, just before going into action—in a word, the man whose capture American intelligence services said, six months before his arrest, they would prefer to that of bin Laden if given a choice, because he, and he alone, has "all the pieces of the puzzle."

Does one have anything to do with the other? Was the Al-Jazeera interview the provocation that set everything in motion? The man from the real estate agency doesn't know. He doesn't seem to think that receiving a leading journalist from Al-Jazeera is any more serious and compromising than going down to the street to buy milk and the morning newspaper, but in the end he doesn't know. Since then, I have verified that the interview, scheduled for 12 September, hadn't yet been broadcast when the Rangers stormed the building. But there were leaks. Al-Jazeera announced it. *The Sunday Times* of London had run some long extracts, as teasers. Fouda himself had talked about it. Here and there, he told how he got the scoop. He spoke about messages he had received in London, secret emissaries, clandestine meetings to plan things, Islamabad, Karachi, pass words, car changes and stealthy exits, a thousand and one details, each more fascinating than the last, leading up to the scoop—and how, finally, one finds oneself face to face in a big, empty apartment with two of the most hunted terrorists on the planet, who tell you, two days running, the real story of September 11, radical Islam's "Holy Tuesday."

In short, I do not believe the two events are unrelated, nor do I think they are automatically linked. And I can well imagine the Pakistani powers-that-be panicking when they suddenly realized that this damned interview was going to be broadcast in a few hours, and expose the fact that an al-Quaida cell (and what a cell!) was functioning with impunity in the heart of Karachi and known openly to the press—and deciding to take the initiative by staging a spectacular operation on the eve of the broadcast.

Fouda said it all, after his scoop: "If, as a journalist, I am able to reach these people, then why the devil don't the Pakistanis do so?"

But there are other strange details about this affair.

I hang around the Igloo ice cream shop and the real estate agency for another hour or two. I talk a while longer to the real estate agent, who is still fascinated by what's happened. I listen and observe, and I realize that there are a few more peculiarities that reinforce my feeling of unease and that fail to corroborate the ministry's communiqué about its grand antiterrorist operation, heroic and valiant and ultimately dangerous, that led to the pitched battle.

The fact, for example, that from what I can see, there seemed to be, coming from the fourth floor, little fire in return: a few bullet holes in the wall of the ice cream store, and signs of one grenade, maybe two, that seem to have exploded where the Hindus are now busy working. That's not much for the ferocious battle the police and the Rangers supposedly encountered.

Seeming to confirm this observation is the fact that, when the Rangers broke into the apartment, they found prayer books, documents, radios, computer equipment, blank computer discs, everything necessary for forging fake passports, and gigantic *Allah Akbar*s written on the walls in blood. But instead of the expected weapons cache, instead of the arsenal described in this morning's edition of *Dawn*: one Kalashnikov. Only one. The man from the real estate agency is adamant. He spoke with the police, and then he spoke with the people responsible for putting the police seals on the building, and he can certify that they found, in all, one Kalashnikov—not much for the den of the Devil.

Mohammed—the fearsome and mysterious Khalid Sheikh Mohammed. He was the one they were looking for, the big fish. I repeat that the entire FBI believed that if they could only interrogate one person from bin Laden's inner circle, or only put away one al-Qaida leader, including bin Laden himself, it would be Mohammed. But he's not there on that day. Usually, he was there, the real estate agency employee told me, he was there every evening, like the others, and we'd see him come and go, because it was his place. But, as if by chance, he is the only one who did not come home the previous night—and so he escaped. Was that really by chance? Indiscretion? A leak?

The children. Among those arrested were two children. But I discover—it's in the papers—first of all, that they are Khalid Sheikh Mohammed's children. Secondly, it's obvious the police know this because General Moinuddin Haider, Minister of the Interior, announced it to the press right after the operation, adding, in a burst of lyricism: "We are holding them. We are not turning them over to anyone. And we will get Khalid." And thirdly, today's news—the police released the children yesterday morning, supposedly for "humanitarian reasons," thereby giving up their only apparent means of tracking down the architect of September 11.

The date. The operation takes place on the date of September 11. The eve of the Al-Jazeera broadcast of an interview that's no longer a secret and is obviously going to make a huge splash. But really, one cannot help but think that it is also *the* September 11, and that to launch such an operation against the brains behind the September 11 attacks on the very anniversary of those attacks is something of a miraculous coincidence. If they had chosen this date, if they had known that an al-Qaida cell was there, if they had decided to wait before revealing it, and dismantling it, until this symbolically and politically significant and media-tailored day, they could not have done better. It was as though the Pakistani authorities, once again, had arranged and calculated everything. As though they wanted to send a very clear, strong message to their American ally. Happy Birthday, Mr. President! What do you think of this thoughtful and subtly planned anniversary present?

And then finally, the essential, not only the most bizarre, but the most incredible and, for me, the most dramatic turn of events that will relaunch my entire investigation: among the "Yemenis" arrested (whether or not they have been turned over to the Americans I have been unable to determine), among the "Arabs" who walked out in single file shouting "Allah Akbar" (in reality, only eight Yemenis, since there was an Egyptian and a Saudi), among these ten "terrorists" (a man from the electricity company is talking now, as the ice cream seller watches and the real estate agent nods his head solemnly) "was the American journalist's assassin," the real one, the one who held the knife.

I ask him to say that over again.

What journalist? I ask.

I press him: "You're talking about the *Wall Street Journal* reporter, the man whose throat was slit at Gulzar e-Hijri, Daniel Pearl?"

Yes, that's who he's talking about.

He seems to be saying, I don't see what you're getting so excited about. Other people in this world have had their throats slit! Other journalists have died. Do they have to be Americans for the West to take an interest? Does he have to be a Jew to suddenly become more important than thousands of

Kashmiris, of Palestinians, who die every day from Indian or Israeli bullets? A double standard.... You are hopeless....

He takes a key out from under the counter, opens a cupboard behind him and takes out a photo of a charred little body, hunched over and curled up, lying in a green, green field. "My cousin, in Kashmir, the war against the Indians. Did the Zionist newspapers print this photo of my cousin?"

In any case, the fact of the assassin's presence is there.

It is, indeed, what these men are talking about.

I've been here for three days. Every day I read the Pakistani press and listen to the radio and watch the television, but nowhere and at no time have I heard this story mentioned. I had to come and hang out here, between an ice cream shop and a real estate agency, to learn this astounding piece of news.

If they are telling the truth, it means that: 1. for the past week the authorities have had in custody the man who held the knife that killed Daniel Pearl; 2. rather than boasting about it, as one might expect, rather than crowing from the rooftops the great news of a political victory, as well as a victory for the police, they say nothing about it—nothing spectacular, a news story like any other, no reason to put it on the front page; 3. the man, in any case, lived here for at least a month, if not two months, in this neighborhood infested with former military men and crawling with police—this mysterious criminal, this killer the police scoured the country to find, was quietly going about his business in one of the residential quarters of the city.

Three pieces of information in one.

Three odd facts that, to put it mildly, leave me perplexed.

That's enough to make me want to rethink the whole affair, but this time, starting from the other end—that of Omar's accomplices, those other actors in the drama who were as responsible as he was for bringing this crime to its dénouement and who, until now, I have neglected.

CHAPTER 2 PRESS REVIEW

The first thing I do, as soon as Abdul arrives, is to hurry to the nearest library's reference room.

No matter which one.

No matter, either, the real name of Abdul, the old, former journalist converted to rights-of-man advocate whom I picked up at the train station early in the morning and who, from now on, is my companion. Ah yes, the old former journalist... thirty-two years have passed since the time of our red India... thirty-two years since our good-byes on the last line of the front, at the very end of the Indo-Pakistani war—the trucks of Yahya Khan's army took him back to Pakistan, and I rode on to Dacca in those of the Indian army. I left a Maoist who had given me the opportunity to encounter the loony Indian pro-Chinese known as "naxalists." What remains of that young man, the joyous internationalist, impassioned and ingenuous, whose determination to question himself and his side became a ruling principal, leading to a lasting commitment to those "enemies of the country," those "traitors," the oppressed Bengalis? A voice, a flicker of regret in his eyes, a few familiar gestures, and beyond that, the old former journalist who, as he warned me, has lost his hair....

What's important now is that we shut ourselves up in this room panelled in wood like a terribly British club, with polished woodwork, threadbare carpet, and a long, oval table in the center.

Without revealing what we are actually looking for, but using the pretext of a study of sanitation in Pakistan's northern provinces, we have them haul out all the major newspapers from the last week, and then, week by week, all the way back until mid-May. English for me, Urdu for him.

And, gradually, painstakingly, we go over everything, down to the local news and the human-interest stories, looking for the unnoticed wire service dispatch, or the unsigned paragraph, giggling like children at the outlandish story about a fight between two fake doctors in Sadiq Town, near Quetta, or exclaiming over an absurd photo. We stop, tears in our eyes, and remember a similar scene thirty years ago in the library of *The Times of India* in Calcutta, where we used to go, like modern Fabrices at Waterloo, to look at the map and trace the battles we had watched but of which we understood very little. It brought to mind as well the paragons of those days, Jean Vincent, and Bernard Ullman, and Lucien Bodard, a mountain of a man, a little shy, standing in his underwear, in the hotel room at the Intercontinental at Calcutta, providing a continuous spectacle with his perpetual speeches and his magnificent volubility.... We start from the top, taking into account every small detail: a proven method that has never failed me in all the stories I have covered over the past thirty years, including and especially in countries where the press cannot be considered entirely free. I've never encountered an enigma, or any extreme confusion, that attentive, critical reading of local newspapers, provided it is timely, failed to clarify to some degree....

First, the organization chart of the crime.

Up until now, I haven't given it much thought.

So I profit from this plunge into the archives, because it enables me to clearly identify the different cells among which Omar Sheikh divvied up the tasks of his crime.

The first cell's assignment was to arouse the journalist's professional curiosity and, on the pretext of leading him to Mubarak Ali Shah Gilani, to persuade him to come to the Village Garden. That was Omar, of course. But it was also Arif, alias Syed Hashim Qadeer, director of a small madrasa in Ahmadpur East, already wanted for his alleged role in the murder of at least seven people in the Pakistani Punjab and known to have close ties to Harkat ul-Mujahideen. It was Arif whom Pearl initially contacted; according to Pearl's fixer in Islamabad, Arif was to lead him to Gilani, and he was also the one responsible for the liaison with Omar since he organised the meeting at the Hotel Akbar. The third member of this contact cell is Hyder, alias Imtiaz Siddiqui, a.k.a. Amjad Hussain Farooqi, real name: Mansur Hasnain, a veteran of the Afghan wars and a member of Harkat ul-Jihad-i-Islami, the other extremist group that, under a hail of American bombs and in armed combat against the Northern Alliance, paid the heaviest tribute of solidarity with the Taliban. In some wire stories from February, I read that, a year ago, using the pseudonym of Sunny Ahmed Qazi, he was the organizer of the plane hijacking of Kandahar. ("I owe him my life," Omar reportedly said after he was freed.) I read as well that he is the one Omar asked to make the last two phone calls to Danny on the afternoon of the 23 January to confirm the date at the Village Garden. He'll come up again in a moment in my research on cell number 3. But one of Hyder's neighbors told investigators he saw him returning to his village one day at the beginning of January, long before the kidnapping, accompanied by an Arab and a Pakistani who resembled Omar, which indicates that he was already in this first cell and a very early participant in the plot.

Second cell. This is the cell that helped Omar address the series of e-mails to Pearl to inspire his confidence and lure him into the trap. This is also the cell that scanned the photos of the journalist in chains, and sent them, along with the communiqués claiming credit for the kidnapping, to the major national and international news agencies—the cell in charge of exterior relations. Three men, again. Three men to send two series of e-mails from one or two of the city's cyber cafés: Adil Mohammad Sheikh, policeman, member of an elite anti-terrorist unit and probably leader of the group; his cousins, Salman Saquib and Fahad Nasim, specialists—especially Fahad—in computer science. All three were veterans of the Afghanistan war and linked to Jaish e-Mohammed, the "Army of the Prophet"— the group that was outlawed by the Paistani government just days before the kidnapping on January 12. And Pearl's decapitation, according to the police, bears the group's signature. In 1999, the founders of the group killed poor Ripen Katyal in the same way, bleeding him like a pig in front of his fellow passengers in the forward cabin on the Indian Airlines plane that was hijacked to buy the liberation of Omar Sheikh and Masood Azhar. They're "brave," Omar said during their common trial, alluding to Salman Saquib's scar-covered body. They are "true fighters of Islam," he insisted: I knew them in the field, and, in lending their competence to the army of redemption I had raised, they accomplished a deed that pleased Allah.

Third cell. The largest. The one at the rendezvous at the Village Garden, that stayed with Danny right up until his execution. Seven men, eight if you count Hussain Farooqi, alias Mansur, who, apart from his role in cell number 1, was asked to stay with the other jailers and Danny for the duration of his captivity. There is Akram Lahori, the *salar*, or supreme commander, of Lashkar I-Janghvi, the fanatic Sunni group whose original leader, Riaz Basra, died in the first days of 2002, in circumstances that remain unclear. And Asif Ramzi, Lahori's right hand man and the head of the Qari Hye, a subfaction of Lashkar, that takes care of Arab fighters who came for the Afghanistan jihad and ended up in Pakistan after the fall of the Taliban. And Naeem Bukhari, a.k.a. Atta ur-Rehman, another one of the directors of Lashkar and the real boss in the Karachi area. He was at the Village Garden, too. He was the one on the moped leading the car with Danny in it, and the one who forced Danny to read the text for the video. Since Lahori, technically his superior, came and went from Gulzar e-Hijri, Bukhari took over as acting head of the operation, along with Hyder. And Fazal Karim, who fought with Bukhari in Kashmir and in Afghanistan and, during the kidnapping, chauffeur for Saud Memon, the proprietor of the house and the land. He also stayed until the very end and, in fact, he may be the only witness besides the executioners to the execution. Interrogated following his arrest in mid-May, he said in his deposition to the police, "I would go out and do it again; he was a Jew, an American; I feel great to be a part of the revenge against America." And Faisal, alias Zobair Chishti, Lahori's and Bukhari's enforcer, involved under their aegis in the most murderous operations of Lashkar i-Janghvi and brought into the plot

at the last minute as a sort of strong man, in charge of close surveillance of the victim (the escape attempt by the window of the
toilet, shot in the shins with the pistol, etc.). And then there are
two more of whom I know nothing, except their first or last
names: Mussadiq, a caretaker; and Abdul Samat, a student or former student suspected as one of the participant in the suicide
bombing against the French engineers at the Sheraton on 8 May
2002, who seems, for the time being, to have been a sort of assistant to Hyder in charge of supervision of the cell.

And then, finally, the fourth cell. The actual killers. Those
who, arriving at the last moment, held the knife and filmed the
throat-slitting. Perhaps, as well, whoever called them on this last
day with the order to carry out the execution and thus took
responsibility for the dénouement. Of him I know little, except, if
he exists, his name, Saud Memon, and the fact that he is a rich and
powerful Karachi businessman, landlord of the house in Gulzar e-
Hijri. (I say "if he exists," because, according to another hypotheses, nobody made the call from inside the compound: rather, on
the morning of the 30th, someone called from outside, announcing the arrival of the three killers and giving orders to allow them
to "operate as they wish.") As for the killers, if they exist as well, I
read that they are "Arabs" or "Yemenis" or "Yemeni-Baluchis,"
with the father from Yemen, the mother from Baluchistan, or the
inverse. (And I say, "if they exist," because, according to another
hypothesis, "the Yemenis" may have been invented out of thin air
to confuse the investigators and hide the identity of the true per-
petrators from cell 1 to cell 4, all actually Pakistanis.) I read that
one of them, probably their leader, was walking through the village south of Islamabad with Omar and Amjad Farooqi at the
beginning of January. I read also that an employee of a telephone

shop, Ehsan, heard this person make a mysterious phone call to Canada, and say, "I will complete the mission." Who was the Canadian? Another sponsor besides Omar? One of Omar's clients? A financier? None of the articles say. And none of them say exactly what the Arabs looked like, or what organisation they belonged to. For one: the Jaish e-Mohammed of Masood Azhar.... For another: the Jaish Aden Aben al-Islami, the Islamic army of Aden, based at Sanaa and directly linked to al-Qaida.... And for a third, a group with ties to the Americans of Yemeni origin arrested in a Buffalo suburb at the beginning of January, a dormant al-Qaida cell in the heart of the United States....

This isn't an organisational chart any more, it's a labyrinth. One with signs sticking out everywhere, with Pashtun and Punjabi names, people with double, triple, quadruple identities, all of them like hedges barring entry into the heart of this shadowy world where Westerners have such difficulty identifying the different characters in the maze but where one senses, all the same, that something essential is being plotted. And enthroned in the middle, Omar, the poor man's Minotaur, planted behind a series of obstacles he has placed between himself and the truth.

And then, the September 11th arrest.

The man who may have been Pearl's executioner—one of the three Yemenis captured with bin al-Shibh in the anti-terrorist raid at Defence.

And, apart from the Yemeni, the exact status of the investigation, a rundown of all the arrests by the police or the FBI to date, seven months after the death of Daniel Pearl, and the question, in other words, of the effectiveness of anti-terrorist operations in Pakistan.

I follow the barely perceptible trace of the alleged Yemeni assasin and the confirmation of his arrest through numerous obscure corner-of-the page news articles. His name is not mentioned. But Fazal Karim, taken by the police to the secret prison where the ten who were arrested at Defence are incarcerated, is reported to have positively identified him. Plausible. Who better than Karim, whose duty it was to control the victim during the execution, to tie his hands and then hold his head, could identify the face of the man who held the knife?

Of course I knew of the existence of Fazal Karim. During my first trip here, I had heard he was the one who, in May, had led the police and the press to the place at Gulzar e-Hijri where they found Danny's remains. But I had never really understood just when and under what circumstances he had been arrested. The answer is in an article in the 19 May edition of *Dawn*. Well, article is saying a lot, more like a filler piece. It revealed that he had been denounced by a certain "Mazharul Islam, alias Mohammad Omar Choto, alias Dhobi," whose name I had never run across before, and who was nowhere to be found in my organisation chart of the crime. This Dhobi was arrested in April in a shakedown in the Sunni underworld related to "sectarian" anti-Shiite murders of recent months. He had in his possession video cassettes dealing with run-of-the-mill criminal activities of Lashkar I-Janghvi, or so the police thought. Except that, on viewing the videos, they realized one was footage of Danny's decapitation, and that the man they had just arrested was in charge of distributing it to foreign press agencies.

In a 19 June edition of *Dawn*, and in the *News* of the following day and the day after that, I find reports that another group of men suspected of being involved in the car bomb attack in front of the Sheraton Hotel that killed eleven French engineers of the Direction des Constructions Navales of Cherbourg were arrested on 16 June. How many were arrested? How were they treated? What court tried them? The article doesn't say. But it does mention two familiar names among the group of "terrorists" and "gangsters" caught in the Sindh police "dragnet"— Naeem Bukhari, alias Atta ur-Rehmann, the man behind the camera who dictated to Danny what phrases he should say, and Faisal, alias Zobair Chishti, his accomplice, the man who accompanied the prisoner to the toilet and shot him in the leg when he tried to escape.

In a longer article published a week later in an Urdu weekly Abdul translates for me, I learn that, during an interrogation by Pakistani police who put aside the kid gloves (allegedly in concert with an FBI team), Bukhari and Chishti fingered Akram Lahori, their chief, who was immediately arrested. Of course, the article refers to the anti-French operation at the Sheraton and the June 14 attack on the American consulate, both Lashkar sponsored. And, of course, it doesn't mention the Pearl case. But we know Lahori was present at the scene of the murder and that, as Bukhari's "supreme commander," he may well have been at the top of the chain of command and consequently the one who took the ultimate responsibility, with Saud Memon, of calling the Yemenis and ordering the execution. So another important piece of the puzzle falls into place.

Omar himself must be added to the list.

One should also remember that the three members of Cell 2, the weak link of the chain, were arrested at the beginning of

February when the FBI traced their e-mail address, antiamericanimperialism@hotmail.com, to a cybercafé in Gulistan e-Jahaur, a suburb of Karachi, from which most of the messages were sent, and then on to Fahad Naseem, who had made the mistake of operating from the hard drive of his own computer.

It's a good idea to be wary.

One must, as with the organizational chart, be extremely cautious about jumping to conclusions.

All the more so because, in addition to the vagueness of these reports and the problems of the press—its way of providing information without actually providing any, or of providing it only in dribs and drabs—you run up against the eternal problem of any investigation into Islamist groups or al-Qaida in particular: the extreme difficulty of identifying, just identifying, these masters of disguise, one of whose techniques is to multiply names, false identities, and faces.

Sometimes you think you're dealing with two men when, in reality, you're dealing with one who has two names.

Sometimes you think you're dealing with one man when, in reality, there are two using one name. Asif Ramzi, for example, is also the pseudonym of another terrorist, a resident of Muhammad Nagar in Karachi, who is also known as Hafiz or Chotto, Chotto being one of the pseudonyms of Mazhurul Islam as well, the latter also known as Dhobi, the man who had the cassette and led the police to Karim!

Someone like Khalid Sheikh Mohammed, who has a mania about fake identities, has at least a dozen known aliases.

We know of half a dozen pseudonyms for Zakarias Moussaoui, the Franco-Moroccan who was Mohammed Atta's roommate and would have been the 20th hijacker in the September 11 attacks had he not been arrested in Minnesota a month earlier.

In addition to five credit cards, three passports, three social security numbers and birth dates, two addresses in London and another two in the United States, a plethora of e-mail connections, cell phone numbers, and bank accounts, Omar himself has at least seventeen aliases—and these are only the ones I am aware of: Mustafa Ahmad, Mustafa Ahmed al-Hawsawi, Mustafa Muhammed Ahmed, Sheik Syed, Mustafa Sheikh Saeed, Omar Saiid Sheikh, Shaykh Saiid, Chaudhry Bashir, Rohit Sharma, Amir Sohail, Arvindam, Ajay Gupra, Raj Kumar, R. Verma, Khalid, P. Singh, and Wasim!

That said, I nonetheless now have a clear idea of the state of the investigation.

In short, three waves of arrests: one in February, the result of tracing the e-mail addresses; a second three months later at the beginning of May, following the attack at the Sheraton; and the most recent, in the Defence neighborhood.

Eight conspirators out of seventeen behind bars, among them the mastermind of the crime, the Yemini assassin, the boss of the team guarding Pearl at the house, the man in charge of shooting the video, and the one who had it in his possession.

And still at large, the two other Yemenis. Mussadiq and Abdul Samat, the two as yet not clearly identified members of the third cell. Ramzi (who will end up dying, at least officially, on 19 December 2002, with six other terrorists in the explosion of an apartment house in the east Karachi suburbs, where the Lashkar produced explosives in a clandestine workshop). At large as well is Mansur, the man who made the last two phone calls to Danny. (According to one report, when the Pakistani police turn up at his home, on 15 February, they find only his brothers, his wife, his son and two friends. "Mansur's not here," they say. "Mansur just infiltrated the Jammu Kashmir"—a way of saying, in code, that he is under ISI control, according to Abdul.) Also at large, Arif: According to another report, the police, at about the same time, went to arrest him at his home in Bahawalapur, in the south. The whole family is there, in tears and formal mourning. "Hashim Qadeer is dead," they say. "Hashim Qadeer left for the Afghan front and Allah the Merciful called him to his bosom... the tomb? no tomb... the body? no body.... Hashim died a hero, no, better, a martyr, and everyone knows martyrs don't necessarily have a grave on earth, because they go directly to Heaven, between the angels and the virgins...." At large also, of course, is Saud Memon, the proprietor of the land.

And that's when I arrive at the last, and most fruitful, observation.

Every time one of the newspapers, having released some information and so dropped a morsel of truth our way, asks the authorities for a confirmation or at least a commentary, every time you ask a cop, or a high-ranking civil servant, or even the governor of the province, if it is true that Fazal, or Bukhari, or Akram Lahori have been found and put behind bars, interrogated, you are regularly treated to obfuscations that vary only depending on the circumstances.

Thus: "Fazal Karim, don't know him.... Bukhari, never heard of him.... Zobair Chishti, the accomplice, never seen nor heard anything about him.... We demand you tell your readers it is by error, a very gross and regrettable error, that your newspaper, in the editions of such and such dates, found it necessary to write that we are holding Mr. X, Y, or Z, in one way or another involved in the kidnapping of the journalist Daniel Pearl...."

Or: "Yes, of course, we know who he is.... But, just a minute here! MPO! Maintenance of Public Order! this preventive law that grants us, as policemen, the power to incarcerate antigovernment elements without telling anyone! Perhaps the people you are alluding to are in our custody... or in the custody of another agency.... But we have nothing to say regarding your question.... We have the right—indeed, the right—to make no comment on this information...."

Or, even more subtle: "Yes, of course we know them.... Yes, of course they are suspects.... But this trial is complicated enough without introducing new suspects who can only hold up the process of arriving at the truth.... So, for these suspects allegedly, but only allegedly, guilty, we have a legal status which is a Pakistani specialty: detained but not charged, in prison but not indicted, identified, if you like, but officially unknown.... We realize they may bear some responsibility for this affair.... The press is entitled, within limits and because we are indulgent, to report this possibility. But we refuse to confirm it.... In fact, we refuse to confirm anything.... And even this declaration that we're making to you at present, we're making it without making it and insist you record it as coming from an 'anonymous source.' Understand?"

And the result is this Associated Press dispatch of 18 August, concerning Lahori and Bukhari: "The Pakistani authorities are not aware of their detention."

Or this declaration given by Manzoor Mughal, "chief investigator" of the Pearl case, to the Agence France Presse the following day when asked if there had been any arrests after those of Omar and the three members of the first cell: "We have arrested no one, apart from the four who have appeared before the Court and been judged. And as for this story about the 'Yemenis,' I say, and I repeat, no Arab has been implicated, much less arrested in the context of this case."

Or this, a filler from the 15 July *News:* "The authorities deny that Fazal Karim is being detained in their hands."

This note, in the following day's *Dawn,* concerning Fazal Karim and Chishti: "The decision not to announce the arrest of other suspects was made at the highest level, as early as 16 May, by the police and the Minister of the Interior of Sindh."

Kamran Khan's 15 July citation in the *Washington Post* of a high official who said that the arrest of Lahori, however "crucial," had occurred too late, during the "last phase" of the trial, well into the pleadings. Any official confirmation of the arrest would risk derailing the entire proceeding, and that is why it was out of the question to "make it public."

Or: The citation of still another official, cited "anonymously" in a *Dawn* article by editorialist Anwar Iqbal, who declared, "We know who killed Pearl, but we don't want to reveal it. The trial is already a nightmare, the suspects are forever threatening officials. We don't want to go through all this again."

No need to go into the perverse effect this sort of declaration has on the trial proceedings.

No need—or is there?—to delve into the case of this man, Omar Sheikh, who, we can assume, would not have been convicted on the same charges and might have pleaded extenuating circumstances if the arrest of accomplices—such as those who had been in charge of the guards, or had called the Yemenis, or physically held Danny while the Yemeni slit his throat—had been taken into consideration.

No matter, then, because it is not my intention to pardon the mastermind of the crime, and I don't think the presence, or absence, of a Lahori, of a Bukhari, of a Chishti, would exonerate Omar in the least of the immense responsibility of having concieved and planned the kidnapping of Daniel Pearl. No matter, then, the—to say the least—bizarre course of a trial that was, on many counts, an onslaught of formalities where they nonetheless chose to ignore essential witnesses, major protagonists of the crime, even though they were under arrest and had in most cases confessed, and one needed only to cite their confessions.

What interests me for the time being is the strange, almost rhetorical, system for the treatment of information that results, every time, not in clarification but in even greater vagueness and mystery.

What bothers me is that at the very moment when the affair is being treated by process of law, every effort seems to be made to render it perfectly unintelligible. (The best observers, the most moderate and the most critical politicians, all end up no longer knowing themselves if there were actually any Yemenis; whether Lahori is dead or alive; and if the story of Fazal Karim leading the investigators to the spot where Danny was buried isn't ultimately a piece of disinformation reworked and repeated three or four times.) It's all the same, making the whole case extremely simple. (We have a culprit, and he's a good culprit; we have an assassin who is a perfect assassin; we don't want to introduce any new elements into the trial that would oblige us to stop everything: And after the trial, we don't want to take any new elements into consideration, because then we would have to start all over again.)

As though—right from the start—everyone had the same objective in mind: make the nightmare, not of the death of Danny but of the trial of his murderers, as brief as possible.

As though everyone—judges, police, political powers as well as, with very few exceptions, the press and public opinion—had tacitly agreed to get rid of the Pearl affair as rapidly as possible.

As though this affair contained a secret, a heavy and terrible secret, and that every means had to be employed to prevent this secret from being revealed.

CHAPTER 3 A SHADOWY AFFAIR

I contact one of the lawyers for the defense.

His name is Khawaja Naveed Ahmed.

He's defending, not Omar, but Sheikh Adil and Fahad Naseem, his accomplices in Cell no. 2, the only ones tried at the same time as Omar, in the same batch, so to speak—receiving twenty five years imprisonment each.

He pleads extenuating circumstances.

Like me, he has a list of all the "new elements," the "detained but not indicted" suspects, Bukhari, Karim and, now, this Yemeni executioner, whose legal status is so unclear. All of them are reasons, for him as for Omar's lawyer, Abdul Waheed Katpar, to protest a parody of justice: "How can you judge one without judging the others? How can you get to the bottom of a crime when the man who held the weapon (the Yemeni), the one who assisted him (Fazal Karim), and the one who gave the order (Bukhari) are not even involved in the procedure? Is the fact of having bought a camera, or scanned a shot, or sent an e-mail, is this really more important than having decapitated a man or having forcefully immobilized him while doing so? This trial doesn't make any sense!"

I understand, from another source, that Khawaja is a militant lawyer, tending to sympathize with the cause of the jihadists he defends.

I'd heard about his declarations, fulminating against Musharraf's alignment with the United States and the human rights violations of the combined forces of the Pakistani Rangers and the FBI inspectors.

I know he protested a police raid during which "foreign" policemen forced the sister of one alleged terrorist—as it turns out, Kulsum Bano, Bukhari's sister—to open the door, thereby allowing them to look at her: how dare they! How could someone so flout another's faith and modesty? Is there a cause in this world that authorizes men to so violate a woman, if only with their eyes?

We've seen lawyers like this in Europe, in the days of the Baader-Meinhof gang and the Red Brigades in Italy.

I knew some of them a little—such as Klaus Croissant in Germany, whom I met with Michel Foucault—these specialists of the defense of breaking ranks, of the diversion against the bourgeoisie by the bourgeois law itself.

And in this case, there are elements that make me suspect Khawaja was the source of the hunger strike his two clients and Omar Sheikh undertook when rumors of new arrests in April and May began to circulate.

However, it's not because of this that I decide to seek him out.

Although.... A voice, in this country smothering under the unspoken, that presumes to break the omerta.... A voice of one who, for whatever reason, stops behaving as though the murder of Danny were a simple affair ending in a show trial.... Why not?

He receives me in his smart, well-kept office in the Sharah e-Faisal area, in the heart of modern Karachi.

Bearded men in the stairwell. In the waiting room, bearded men. Along the wall, in the hallway, around a large color photo of Srinagar, the capital of "occupied" Kashmir, more bearded men, but they're more elegant—reminding me of Saeed Sheikh, Omar's father, the evening I caught him in front of his home in London: the portraits of the senior Khawajas, father and grandfather no doubt, the founders of the firm.

Khawaja Naveed Ahmed is a modern lawyer. His English is perfect. Like all of his colleagues bustling around him, he has the look of a young New York attorney: tie undone, shirt sleeves rolled up, a confident and forthright countenance, the smile and the laugh of a friendly fellow. He's welcoming to the French writer working on a novel about Pakistan. But his firm obviously specializes in the defense of Islamists.

"Of course all these people are in the custody of the authorities," he begins. "They can deny it all they want. This summer, we heard again the 'force's law officer,' Anwar Alam Subhani, who denied that the Sindh police had ever heard of the arrest of Karim and Bukhari. But there's no doubt about it. And here's proof—this is a document concerning Karim that I give you permission to publish. I'm sure you'll find it interesting."

And over his desk, piled high with faxes, e-mails, and cardboard case files overflowing with papers, he hands me an amazing document: it's a sheet of notebook paper, covered on both sides with minuscule writing in a cramped hand, signed—in Urdu and, below that, using the Latin alphabet—by "Mazharul Hasan, son of Mohammed Sadiq, Security Cell 19." Khawaja starts to translate and I take notes.

"I was arrested at my residence on the night of 30 April 2002 by Inspectors Hafiz Junejo and Fayaz Junejo from the Civil Lines police station in Karachi. The two inspectors were following orders from Police Superintendent Zulfiqar Junejo. I was detained for ten days in a cell on the third floor of the CID, the Central Investigations Department."

The CID, Khawaja informs me, is a state agency, although it's related to the police. This man, whose confession we have before our eyes, though it doesn't say what crime he was detained for, nonetheless makes it clear that he is in the hands of the true invisible power of this country. Khawaja returns to reading the statement.

"After ten days of detention, I saw a husky individual with a beard and a swarthy complexion in the cell next to mine. He had a blindfold over his eyes. When they took it off, I immediately recognized Fazal Karim, Omar's chauffeur, an employee of the Al-Rashid Trust."

The attorney then explains: Fazal is Saud Memon's chauffeur, not Omar's. Memon is one of the administrators of the Al-Rashid Trust, which is a Muslim charity organisation whose offices are near the Super Highway, close to the farm where Daniel Pearl was buried. But no matter, you already know that. Let's continue:

"Fazal Karim is a Mujahid, a holy warrior, a veteran. I immediately saw that he had been brutally tortured."

In Karachi, terrible stories circulate about the gamut of tortures practiced by certain branches of the ISI. They talk about sophisticated variations on the bathtub suffocation torture. They talk about men who have been hung by their hands, a funnel placed between their teeth to force them to drink water until their stomach explodes. There's talk about electrodes attached to the toes, genitals burned or squeezed with copper wire, eyes gouged out or burned with a hot poker, heads plunged in bathtubs of boiling water, testicles squashed in a door and then cut. Is this the kind of treatment to which Saud Memon's chauffeur was subjected? Is that why he talked? Is it he, rather than the brilliant intelligence of the Sindh police investigating the attack at the Sheraton, who is responsible for the arrest of Bukhari and Chishti?

"I learned he was betrayed by Javed, the brother of Shireen Gul, the Madrasa Iqra's chauffeur who lives in the area known as Metroville. The police made a raid on Javed's place and he wasn't there, so they arrested his brother Shireen. After two days, the superintendent of the Nazimabad police station took Javed to the station and released his brother, Shireen Gul. After that, from the information they got from Javed, the police arrested Fazal Karim."

This scenario makes me wonder. Why did this man Javed talk to the police? Under what circumstances? Under what kind of pressure? I imagine the terrible *danse macabre* of those tortured, and those threatened with torture. I picture all these men secretly incarcerated, just like modern versions of the Man in the Iron Mask while Omar, the only one accused, parades before the cameras at his trial. I can imagine the sweating faces in the cellars, blood flowing from wounds or spurting from between teeth, the bandaged heads, the cries and the moans, the shouts of the torturers and the trickle of confessions that, sooner or later, emerge.

"Fazal Karim, then, was held at the CID station for ten days. During his detention, he indicated where Daniel Pearl's body was buried. The CID agents handcuffed Fazal Karim and Javed. At night, they kept them in a pickup truck. They were afraid of a raid by the agents of the High Court, looking for Fazal Karim. After ten days, another agency took Fazal Karim away."

The High Court against the ISI.... One branch of the police against another.... Better still, the courts against all the police.... If the man from "Security Cell 19" is telling the truth, it confirms that there are two antagonistic forces in Musharraf's Pakistan. And moreover, it confirms my hypothesis: there are those who want the truth about the kidnapping, and those who do not; there are those who are ready to see justice done, and those who prefer that important secrets be silenced. The author of the letter drives the point home.

"On 22 May, CID Inspectors Mazhar and Fayaz came to get me. I was detained at the Saddar police station. I saw Fazal there too. His hands and feet were handcuffed. On 25 May, I was sent to the Orangi Town police station, in the district of Karachi, and from there they sent me to prison. For thirteen days, I saw Fazal Karim, we ate together and I talked to him. He told me many things. I can share this information with you."

This gets more and more interesting.... Here is a man who knows some "things." He even knows "many" things. And he is willing to tell anyone about these "things." But apparently, nobody wants him to. The letter made the rounds, Khawaja says. All the legal, military and police authorities in the country were aware of it, in one way or another. The judge even had it in his file several weeks before the verdict of 15 July. But nobody had the idea to go see Mazharul Hasan, son of Mohammed Sadiq, to listen to what Fazal Karim told him in the cell they shared.

"A police commissioner and Inspector Fayaz (the one who, with agent Hafiz, discovered Daniel Pearl's body and was promoted after Fazal Karim's arrest) told me they had encountered Faiz Bhatti and Rehman Bukhari."

Who is Faiz Bhatti? Khawaja has no idea. But he knows, as we all do, who Bukhari is—the Yemeni's man, the one who ordered Karim to hold Pearl's head and who was present, then, at the execution....

"What do you think of this document?" Khawaja concludes. "What do you think of our methods of justice? And do you have any doubts left about how bizarre this trial is?"

I spend about two hours discussing the whole thing with Khawaja.

He gives me a piece of information that I remember already having read, but that was immediately buried, as usual, beneath a cascade of denials: Omar, realizing that things were going badly, called Hyder, the chief of cell 3, the detention cell, at the last minute, to tell him to free the prisoner (in the coded language they had agreed on, "shift the patient to the doctor"). But Hyder allegedly told him it was too late, that Danny was already dead, filmed, and buried (in code, "Dad has expired; we have done the scan and completed the X-rays and the postmortem").

"Don't you find that astounding?" Khawaja rages. "Don't you think that changes everything? I'm not Omar's lawyer, but all the same, isn't that one hell of an extenuating circumstance? And if it isn't Omar any more, who made the decision about the execution? Huh, who? And why? All of this is much, much less simple than the way the papers tell it."

He also talks about the more general problems of Pakistani justice, as he sees it: ignoring habeas corpus, lack of respect for human rights in prisons, persistent rumors of the presence of FBI agents in the Pakistani antiterrorist units. "No, no, there's no doubt about it. We have very precise reports. They were there, for example, when they arrested Bukhari—and by the way, no one has seen him alive since Mazharul Hasan wrote that letter I read to you.... The Americans shouldn't—they signed the 1984 treaty abolishing torture, they're a country that supports human rights. How can they be accomplices of these commando operations, all these things that are offensive to democracy? Tell them: Through this policy they're feeding the growing hatred against them...."

He's passionate. Voluble. He has an air of the plump and prosperous about him, at odds with the image he'd like to project of the advocate of the poor and the oppressed. But he's likable, open. Once we get to talking, establishing some confidence, I find he has a side that's almost more aesthetic than militant—an artist of law, an acrobat of procedure and hypothesis, juggling texts and presumptions. And the truth is, I rapidly realize, his suspicions go beyond the question of "detained but not indicted." The truth is, he finds the whole story, from day one, bizarre, even more bizarre, he finally confides in me, more complex, more confusing than both the newspaper articles I've found and the statement of the man in cell 19 would lead one to believe.

So let's go back to the statement, he says.

Without a doubt, the man saw Fazal, and Fazal is in prison.

"The police are saying: 'Fazal doesn't exist. The man who took us to the grave of Daniel Pearl on 17 May was a special informer.' Fine. I'm all for it. The only problem—you don't know it, but I'm telling you now—is that Fazal is the one who, the day he took them to the grave, gave them the chip from Daniel Pearl's mobile phone. And there's something else that casts doubt on this story about a 'special informer.' Let's assume for a moment that he indeed exists. Why would he have waited this long to come forward? And especially, why wouldn't he have gone to the Americans, who, remember, were offering five million dollars and safe conduct to the United States for the information? No, it doesn't hold water. The story about the 'special informer' doesn't make any sense. So we have to take it as an established fact that it was, actually, Fazal who, once arrested, took the police to the burial place."

However, there's room for uncertainty about what happened next, continues Khawaja, and we can imagine some contradictory hypotheses. Especially, he suggests, leaning towards me, eyes shining, like a sly, mischievous conspirator, if we consider the point that seems to have intrigued you the most just now when I was translating the document, and which is, in fact, the most problematic. Which one? Can't you tell? The point that isn't all that certain, the one I take with a good deal of caution, the one that makes me wonder if this could be a source of misinformation, is—he gestures like a magician taking a rabbit out of a top hat—torture!

"What do you mean, torture?" I say. "Karim wasn't tortured?"

"I don't know," he says, suddenly embarrassed, as though the fact that he doesn't know is a real problem for him. "I'm not saying he wasn't. But I'm saying I don't know, that I haven't found any evidence or rather, if he really was, it was in a strange place, by strange people, not the usual ones. I looked into things, you know, I did my own investigation. Fazal was arrested and interrogated in a mosque in Nazimabad, a fundamentalist part of town, which is already out of the ordinary. And, as for torture, there are as many signs indicating that it has occurred as not. If you like, I'm not excluding the possibility that this document was partially manipulated, that an entire scenario was worked out to convince the man in cell 19 that Fazal had been tortured when, in fact, he had not."

"Why?" I say, stunned. "Manipulated? To what end?"

He hesitates, looks at me as though he were sizing up my capacity to comprehend the extremely subtle things he is about to tell me—and starts to sketch a theory that I summarize here.

We can imagine anything, he begins, a crafty expression in his eyes.

We can say: Fazal was atrociously tortured so that he would confess to a crime he really committed and take the police to the grave, etc. Except, the argument that is valid for the "special informer" is equally valid for him—why would he wait until he was arrested? In his place, wouldn't you or I have gone directly to the Americans? Double play! You avoid torture, and you end up with five million dollars in your pocket!

Or, we can try a slightly different version: Yes, Fazal was tortured. The man in cell 19 saw what he saw. But all that was to make him confess to a crime that, on the contrary, he had not committed. And it is precisely for that reason, because he did not commit the crime, that they had to torture him so. The point of the maneuver was to cover and exonerate far more important people than Fazal. The whole operation consisted of making him, voluntarily or by force, take the responsibility for someone else's crime.

And then, finally, we can also theorize that he was not tortured at all, that the man in cell 19 was deceived about this, and that the entire scenario was concocted to cover for the fact that they had withheld information that was actually in their possession from the very beginning. You have to recall the atmosphere at the time, he insists. The Pearl family protests. International pressure mounts. One way or another, they had to make some concessions. And they just wanted a way to get out of the situation and say, "That's it! Eureka! We found the body!" When in reality, they had always known where it was.

Khawaja stops. All of a sudden, he's somewhere else. I'm worn out, almost out of breath from the flurry of his hypotheses. But he is calm. Thoughtful. He seems to be questioning his files, gazing at them, the way others might consult the stars.

"There's something else," he begins again. "The Lashkar.... The fact that Fazal, Bukhari, Chishti, Lahori, in fact, all those rounded up in the latest arrests belonged to the Lashkar.... The fact that, all of a sudden, everyone mentions only the Lashkar.... And why do you suppose that is, hmm? Why this sudden wish to take the spotlight off Harkat ul-Mujahideen and Harkat ul-Jihad and shine it on Lashkar i-Janghvi, the party of Fazal and Bukhari? For you Westerners, they're all one and the same. It's all the same big, nebulous, Islamic terrorist network, and you don't see any point in differentiating between one and another. But there is a difference...."

He clicks on the mouse of his computer to print out a page, which he hands to me: it's a chart, with squares and arrows and different colors, outlining the topology of jihadist groups in

Pakistan. Who's who? Who's tied to whom? How are they influenced, controlled, financed?

"For a Pakistani, there's a decisive difference. Some of them—the HUM and the HUJI, the Harkat ul-Mujahideen and the Harkat ul-Jihad-al-Islami—have in common that they are notoriously linked to the army and the secret services. You see, here on my chart, the arrow runs towards the top, meaning Islamabad. Whereas the Lashkar is a relatively free electron that nobody minds using as a cover. That's what its being on the left margin of the page signifies."

He bursts out laughing.

"It looks complicated to you? No, no, in every hypothesis, there's a very simple constant. You have, there"—he stops and points to the ceiling, snatching the sheet back from me at the same time and quickly putting it under a stack of papers, "people who have known everything and supervised everything, right from the start. People in high places who have always known where the body was and who decided, at a given time, to release the information by playing the Fazal card. The rest, all the rest, would be, if this is right, just an act."

He says much more, of course. I am oversimplifying. But as I listen to him, I'm thinking about the very strange story of the death of Riaz Basra, who was chief of the Lashkar i-Janghvi before Akram Lahori, and who died in an ambush last May, two days, as if by a coincidence, before the names of Fazal and Bukhari were put into circulation. Abdul explained to me that there never was any ambush. In reality, Basra was already in the hands of the services, and had been for several months, for reasons that had nothing to do with the Pearl affair. Materially speaking, there couldn't have been an ambush, and the man could only have been cold-bloodedly executed: because, in fact, he was being held as Fazal and Bukhari are held today; and they suddenly decided—two days, I repeat, before the arrest of Fazal and Bukhari—that it would be better to make him disappear. Why? What were they afraid to see him do or hear him say? Were they afraid he would protest that they were flattering his group by attributing to it a role in the kidnapping of Daniel Pearl? Were they afraid Basra would say: "Look here, I'm the chief and until you hear otherwise, I am aware of what people in my group are doing and not doing! What is this cock-and-bull tale about Fazal and Bukhari being involved at the heart of an affair that's either none of our business or in which we were mere subcontractors?" In other words, was there a risk that Basra would blow the whole operation that Khawaja had just described and thereby make it obvious that the responsibility for the crime rested squarely on the shoulders of the HUM and the HUJI— the two groups they were trying to extricate from the game?

I'm thinking of another friend, a journalist at a Karachi daily, who told me that, at around the same time, the 18 or 20 of May, which was also the time of Fazal's arrest and when Lashkar was put in the forefront, he and many of his colleagues received a strange phone call from an organization that none of them could quite catch the name of. Maybe the "Hezbullah Alami".... Or the "al-Saiqua".... Or maybe "al Saiqua" renamed "Hezbullah Alami".... The caller claimed triple responsibility for the 17 March attack on the Protestant church of Islamabad, the 8 May suicide operation against the French engineers at the Sheraton, and, finally, the kidnapping of Daniel Pearl. "The HUM and the HUJI had nothing to do with these things," said the mysterious caller. "The operation was planned by a 100% anti-Musharraf organization. We are that 100% anti-Musharraf organisation. We are 100% angry with the politics of Musharraf, who has become the Americans' lap dog. And here is the best proof, that only we can supply: The cadaver found at Gulzar e-Hijri is not Daniel Pearl's. The Americans are well aware of this, and that's why they have never made public the results of the DNA tests run on the skeleton."

Propaganda, obviously. Manoeuvre immediately exposed. But isn't it the same strategy? The same desire to confuse the issue? Another effort to divert suspicion from all the groups related in one way or another to the Pakistani government and the ISI?

I watch Khawaja.

All of a sudden he seems strange.

Too jovial, too self-satisfied.

And I wonder what game, ultimately, he is playing by planting these doubts in my mind.

Because, after all, shouldn't it be in the interest of the attorney for Sheikh Adil and Fahad Naseem, who both belong to Jaish e-Mohammed, to turn the spotlight, instead, on the Lashkar?

And how can he at once use the arrest of Fazal to demand a retrial for Omar and then, in the same breath, imagine the same Fazal is an agent who has been manipulated?

After all, perhaps he's the one who's trying to misinform me.

Or perhaps Khawaja thinks the best way of exonerating his client is to bury the crime in an immense plot, indemonstrable, indecipherable, that goes all the way up to the highest level of the State.

I think of his main argument: Why didn't Fazal, or the "special informer," go to the Americans to claim the reward rather than end up in prison? There could be a simple explanation: Fazal is really guilty, he really held Danny's neck so the Yemeni could begin his work, and he couldn't go see the Americans and thereby take the risk of giving himself up and ending up in the electric chair.

I think about Omar. I don't understand his attitude either. In my mind I go over all his declarations, during and after his trial, that I found yesterday with Abdul. Suddenly I find them very restrained, very sensible. And, apart from obligatory provocations for their own sake, in the end rather reasonable. Why doesn't he himself protest this scandal of the "detained but not indicted" more vehemently? Why, if Khawaja's last hypothesis is right, don't we hear him shouting that he's being made the fall guy for a crime committed by many and, perhaps, with the support of people in high places?

It's all becoming so complex....

So terribly contradictory, dizzyingly so....

An imbroglio. In the true sense of the term, a nebula where I have the feeling of watching the cloud of dust around the mystery of the Pearl affair become denser and denser....

I leave Khawaja, with his knowing smiles, his bearded men, his wild hypotheses, his questions, in a state of even greater confusion than when I arrived.

CHAPTER 4 THE DOUBLE LIFE OF OMAR

As has often been the case in this investigation, it's luck that sets me on the path to clarification.

I'm at my hotel.

I'm thinking about all Khawaja's disconcerting hypotheses.

Feeling lost, almost demoralised, I'm thinking of even going back to France and returning in a more official capacity that would allow me to go back to the authorities and ask them the questions I've been thinking about.

And then Abdul, who has taken beautifully to his new role as fixer, comes to my room without warning—meaning, in our old code, that he has some information so sensitive that we should avoid using even the phone line within the hotel.

"I don't have what you asked for," he begins mysteriously, with a triumphant look.

I had asked him to find a contact on the staff of Lashkar i-Janghvi which, at that time, wasn't yet on the Americans' blacklist of terrorist organizations.

"No, I don't have it. But I have something better. Someone who heard what we're looking for contacted me. He says everything that's being said about Omar Sheikh's arrest is bullshit, and that he knows the truth . . . ."

I know what's being said. I know the official version, which had been distributed immediately to the press agencies and the embassies. Having arrested the source of the e-mails they had traced, they wrapped things up the day the police raided Omar's aunt's house in Karachi and his grandfather's home in Lahore. They forced Ismaïl, the grandfather, to call Omar and plead with him to surrender. One of the inspectors grabbed the phone from the old man. "You're done for, Omar, give yourself up," he said. And the good Omar gave himself up to spare his family danger.

"So how is that bullshit? How can the e-mails they traced be bullshit?"

"That's exactly what we're going to find out!" Abdul replies excitedly. "You have a date with this guy today, at 6, in the old city, near Aurangzeb Park, where the junkies hang out. It will bring back memories. Don't worry, he's safe. He comes through my friend X, who's one of the best journalists in town and has my complete trust."

I'm a bit hesitant.

I can't help thinking that this kind of encounter, in one of the most squalid parts of the city, is precisely the kind of thing I should avoid.

And I recall the virtual catalogue of advice, a Bible for any journalist arriving in Karachi and which Pearl, unfortunately, ultimately didn't take into account: never take a hotel room facing the street; never flag down a taxi in the street; never, ever speak of Islam, or of Pakistan's nuclear program; and especially and above all, never go to street markets, cinemas, crowded areas, or public places in general without taking precautions, without telling someone you trust where you are going and what time you should be back—and Aurangzeb! A neighborhood known for drugs and crime!

Nonetheless, the proposition is very tempting.

Abdul explains that, in any case, the man would never come to the big hotels in town, where we usually arrange meetings. He says we have a phone date with the man in an hour, and then I can request that the meeting take place in our car, and that under no circumstances should we get out of the vehicle. Finally, I accept.

So here we are, a little before 6, at the intersection of Aurangzeb Park and Jinnah Road, Abdul behind the wheel and me in the back seat, watching for a man whose only clue as to what to look for is, in itself, rather reassuring in its naïveté: He will be waiting under the billboard for Pepsi-Cola, and will be wearing, under his jacket, "a very elegant, embroidered, multicolored vest."

Around us, groups of shaggy-haired young people with puffy features have taken over the sidewalk, the pale blue imitation ceramic-style steps that climb to the gates of the park, and farther, inside the park, the wooden benches and the pathways.

From afar, you would take them for beggars, waiting for rich people coming from the nearby Sabri restaurant and giving them free food. You would also take them for members of some strange, black-magic sect, or a legion of the supine, bivouacked in the middle of the city.

But they're just addicts.

They are the Karachi contingent of a reserve army of drugs and crime.

God knows I've seen sanctuaries like this before!

I remember the part of Bombay around the Stiffles Hotel, thirty years ago, where every junkie in the city—of the country, even—seemed to congregate: Young drifters off to nowhere, fanatic users, hooked on needles, with dead eyes, ready to kill mother and father and, above all, themselves for a fix of bad coke cut with talcum powder and medicines, worth, at the time, the price of a can of beer—and yet, as I once had the misfortune to discover, such force left in those apparently wasted bodies when they confront you!

But this.... This shady hellhole.... The scorched esplanade turned into a dumping ground for syringes.... These heaps of bodies, with faces at once patient and feverish, some of them huddled around a camping stove cooking a tin of *Nihari,* the beef marinated in thick, spicy sauce, the favorite dish in Karachi....These two men fighting over an old rope mat.... That person lying on a slightly better looking rug, seemingly dead or at least dead to the world.... These others, pressed against each other, nearly comatose, around the ruin of what might have been an ancient fountain, which is in the center of the esplanade.... These stunted trees, covered with black soot, that border the gates and provide these poor people an imaginary shelter.... Down to the dogs and cats (for it's the only place in Karachi where I've seen so many animals that no one will bother), the mongrels wandering between the rugs, bizarre, moaning, sort of floating along, looking for a piece of vegetable peel, a little bone—Karachis say they inhale so much of the smoke or the fumes that they end up drugged as well.... No, I've never seen this!

"Sorry!" says the man we neither saw nor heard arrive, as he opens the front door with an air of authority.

"Sorry!" he repeats as he sits next to Abdul, pointing out a pair of dirty, rag-clad youngsters, probably foreigners, who have followed him, and whom he dismisses, through the window, as one would flick away flies—I barely have time, before the car drives off, to catch the delicate features and the pleading expression of one, a young girl.

"This was the only solution. It's one of the rare areas where the police don't venture," he says.

He turns half-way around. What strikes me is not his vest, but the too-large shoulder pads of his jacket. And then the bony face, black hair with a low forehead, the Nietzschian moustache, with fine, tight wrinkles around the eyes. He smiles, with a roguish air, and adds in a gravely voice: "Except me, of course."

For the man—I shall call him "Tariq"—tells us he is a policeman. He explains he has information about Omar's interrogation by police officers Athar Rashid and Faisal Noor in Karachi. And if he sought us out, it is because some people in the Sindh police are not happy about the way things transpired.

"First question," he begins, after a brief reminder of the conditions of our meeting and the precautions I should take so that he will not be identified: "Do you know when the Sheikh was arrested?" I know what everyone knows. I know what the European and Pakistani press printed.

"The 12th. According to the press, he was arrested on the 12th of February, just a few days after. . . ."

He interrupts me with the teasing expression of someone who has set a trap into which you have just, obligingly, fallen.

"One sentence, two errors, Mr. Journalist! Omar was not arrested, he turned himself in. And he didn't turn himself in on the 12th but on the 5th, Tuesday, the 5th, in the evening."

The car turns down a road which could take us far from the park in the direction of Jinnah Road and the Jama Cloth

Market. He gestures to Abdul to make a right. Since he's gotten in the car, he hasn't stopped stealing furtive glances right and left, punctuated by slight, jerky movements of his neck.

"Next question," he continues. "Do you know who Brigadier Ijaz Ejaz Shah is?"

I don't know who Brigadier Ijaz Ejaz Shah is.

"What? I thought you came from Lahore...."

I glance at Abdul in the rearview mirror to express my surprise that the man knows this. Abdul looks incredulous, lifts an eyebrow as if to say, still another mystery of Karachi....

"You've come from Lahore, but you don't know who Ijaz is? Think again," Tariq insists.

I think about it and remember the tall silhouette of a thin, bald man I met at the Liberty Lions Club in Lahore. He was introduced to me as the Minister of the Interior of Punjab, the strong man of the region, and I seem to recall his name was Ijaz.

"Brigadier Ijaz," he continues in a resonant voice, like a teacher instructing the class dunce, without turning round to face me, "is not just the Minister of the Interior of Punjab. He is also a close friend of Musharraf. More importantly, he's an ISI man, a very high-ranking agent, ex-chief of the agency's Air Force, in charge until only recently of relations with the Harkat ul-Mujahideen and the Harkat ul-Jihad al-Islami. Now, attention!"

He turns around and looks at me with a frankly hostile expression. I can't say if he's doing this for effect, or if he is suddenly seized by a genuine rush of contempt for an ignorant Westerner.

"He is the one the Sheikh turned himself in to on the evening of the 5th. The Sheikh knows him, of course, because the HUM and the HUJI are the two groups Ijaz is associated with and so he decides to give himself up to this old acquaintance."

Now I vaguely remember, as though in a fog, the Brigadier's reaction when the diplomat accompanying me had introduced me to him, his visible recoil, his smile turned glacial at the mention of my project, a "novel" about Daniel Pearl.

"Meaning..." I say to him, taken aback and not sure I understand.

The car turns and starts up a narrow, steep street, a dangerous back alley leading back to the park. Past a butcher's stall that smells of meat gone bad. Next to it, a bunch of skinny dogs are fighting over a pile of stinking fish viscera. With the overhead light on, Tariq reaches into his pocket and hands me a wrinkled piece of paper without actually letting go of it. Then he takes it back quickly. But I have time to see it is a carbon copy of a note, in English, on police letterhead, confirming the surrender of Omar on the 5th, to Brigadier Ijaz.

"This means that seven days go by between the moment when the Sheikh turns himself in to this high-ranking ISI official and the time, on the 12th, when he is handed over, by a special flight from Lahore to Karachi, to us, to the police. During those seven days, he is kept in secret in an ISI safe house, solely in the hands of ISI agents. The police know nothing about it. The FBI and the American Embassy know nothing about it. No one, do you hear me, no one knows, during those seven days, that the presumed organizer of Daniel Pearl's kidnapping is there in Lahore, in the hands of the Pakistani secret services."

The car pulls close to the wall to let pass some young people walking right down the middle of the street, weaving, as though they were drunk. I'm not sure I understand him.

"Meaning...?"

"Meaning that things happened the way they always happen in this country. When a jihadist is arrested, he always has the name and the number of a brigadier he asks us to call and who always tells us, the cops: let him go."

"Except, this time—"

"You understand. In this case, the Sheikh didn't wait to be arrested. As soon as he saw that it was going badly, he decided to take things in his own hands and get in touch with his contact. The fact is, the Sheikh is one of the ISI's men. He has been for a long time. And all this is the story of an agent who plans an action, and sees things go wrong, and, when they go wrong, goes to report it: 'Chief, we've got a problem, what shall we do?'"

"And so, what do they do?"

"They spend seven days and seven nights, among people from the services, trying to come to an agreement. On what? On what to say and not to say to the police. On what is going to happen to him once he's turned himself in, and on the guarantees they can grant him. I won't tell them anything I know, he promises. I'll protect the ISI. I won't tell anyone about its role in the Pearl affair, or in the combat of jihadists in Kashmir. But you have to commit to protecting me from being extradited and, if I'm condemned, to getting me out of this situation as quickly as possible. For seven days they negotiate this. Seven days to put together a scenario. Seven days to find the best way for everyone to get out of the mess they've gotten themselves into."

I remember all the things I read about those days of fever and anxiety. I remember that, at the time, the authorities were still hoping to find Pearl alive and were racing against the clock, counting the hours and the minutes. Can't we imagine, I ask, that those seven days were used to give Omar the third degree? Weren't there people in the agencies who felt that the only thing that counted was to make him reveal, by any means necessary, where the journalist was being held? And moreover, isn't this what Omar told the court in Hyderabad in a 21 June declaration cited by the *News* that dovetails, as a matter of fact, with this story of disappearing for seven days but gives the opposite interpretation—he talks about a week of "harassment," of them "breathing down his neck," a week in which they had "fabricated evidence" against him?

Tariq shrugs his shoulders.

"On the contrary. Those seven days were seven days lost for the investigation. You're not a cop, but you can imagine. Seven days is the time it took for the people who killed him to hide the body, erase any clues, and disappear."

"And the accusations of harassment? The idea that the people he was dealing with brutalized him?"

"The risk, in situations like this, is always that the agent who has been burned panics and spills everything to the press. So, of course, the services conditioned him. They may even have threatened him. Musharraf talked to the father, who talked to the son, pleading with him to avoid any declarations harmful to Pakistani national interests. But look at his face when he came out of the safe house and was delivered to us. He was fine. He was smiling. He had the look of someone who had been given assurances. He didn't appear to be a man who had been raked over the coals for seven days. And, for that matter...."

He takes his time. Then, the sardonic smile of a brute. I hadn't noticed that half his front teeth were capped in silver, like the whores in Tashkent.

"...for that matter, we would have liked to have given him the third degree when we got him ourselves. We know how to do that sort of thing. But I'll give you another scoop—the order came down from the highest level not to do that. And one of their men was sent, unannounced, to keep an eye on our men during the entire interrogation. Result: the Sheikh said nothing. Nothing. And there was a moment, apparently, when he wanted to talk about what he did when he left the Indian prisons. But 'they' were immediately informed, and we got a phone call from someone in the President's cabinet telling us: 'Watch it! Stop everything! Keep him quiet and turn him over to the judge.'"

I sense that Tariq is telling the truth. And I add what he says to some bits of information I picked up in my research: A report on Pakistani channel PTV2 presented, in April, a thesis not far from his.... The 13 March *Newsweek* article describing an Omar arrogant before the police who interrogated him—"sure," he declared, that he would not be extradited and that he wouldn't pass more than "three or four years" in Pakistani prisons.... Another article citing his lawyers' protest of a procedural trick that prevented the reintroduction of the testimony of Hamid Ullah Memon, the superior police officer in charge of the arrest and responsible for the February deposition.... Still another reporting the judge's complaint that the police interrogation was incomplete, lacking in depth, and when a mocking Omar said, "What do they mean by saying the interrogation is incomplete? They stopped interrogating me more than a fortnight ago. I am prepared to talk to them, but they are afraid of my talking."

I start again.

"Let's back up for a second. What 'went wrong,' as you put it? Why, in your perception of things, was Omar forced to turn himself in and set all this in motion?"

Tariq hesitates once again and looks outside for a long while. Perhaps he's not really sure himself.

"There are two theories. The first is that the team bungled things. The story about the e-mails for example. The inexperience of Naseem who was picked up almost immediately and who, of course, ratted on the boss. Or, even dumber, the fact that they continued for several days to make calls on the journalist's mobile phone, which were traced. Everything was planned, except for the novices' errors...."

I think of the obscenity of this mobile phone, continuing, like nails or hair, to live its own life after the death of its owner.

I think about Abdul Majid, the cell phone salesman I found on Bank Road, in Islamabad, who had sold Omar two of the six phones he had used during the operation. He also told me a story about the kidnappers—that they had been thrilled like kids to be using a triband mobile phone with an American number, from which they could play at threatening the investigators, their families, their children.

I think also of another story, strange and unexplained: a plane ticket for Pakistan Airlines flight PK 757, London to Islamabad, file number EEEFQH, was purchased in the name of Daniel Pearl on 8 February, eight days after his death, by someone who would have had to present his passport and a valid visa.

"Or else, the second hypothesis," Tariq continues. "We're not actually certain Pearl's execution was planned. When Sheikh says that he learned of it when he called 'Siddiqui' from Lahore on 5 February to give him the order to 'send the patient to the doctor' but was told 'too late! Dad is dead, we did the scan and the X-rays,' I'm not excluding the possibility that he was telling the truth. So maybe things went off the track there. Perhaps Pearl was executed against the instructions of Omar and the people behind the operation."

Tariq turns to face me again, and takes my arm, violently, with a feigned intensity which, I guess, is supposed to convey the sorrow we share, the sympathy.

"The piece of the puzzle I lack is who decided to contravene the instructions. The actual team themselves, who went off the deep end? Or other sponsors, interfering with the orders of the original backers? It often happens that way. You think you're alone in an action, but in fact, there are two of you. And the second one shows his hand while your back is turned. Sorry. I really don't know."

"All right," I say, removing my arm from his grasp. "But one last question, the very last. Why seven days before giving Omar back to your colleagues? Did they really need all that time to put together a scenario?"

"There are two things," he says, still turned towards me, with his sardonic Tashkent smile. "You're right to ask, because there are two different things. First, it's not an easy case. Imagine, once more, the panic of these people when they discover that these guys have lost it and executed the hostage. The panic in the services! The frenzied attempt to cover things over, disconnect the circuits, erase the traces that could lead to the higher-ups, convince the Sheikh to take the responsibility and not to finger too many people, save what they can and invent a whole story for the Americans. And then. . . ."

I get the impression he's hesitating again. I try to catch Abdul's eye, to see if a bill won't fix things. But no. That's not it. There's the beginning of a fight, two guys, in the light of a doorway, with broken bottles. For a second, his cop reflex has resurfaced. Then he continues.

"Think about it.... Five and seven equals twelve—the day Musharraf is to arrive in Washington. Add another two and it's on the 14th that Omar's first interrogation began. The same day Musharraf was received by Bush, the end of his trip to the United States."

"So what?"

"I don't know. You tell me. Musharraf is a President who's playing a difficult role in terms of diplomacy. He discusses, he negotiates. His primary request when he met with Bush, the delivery of F-16s, frozen because of our conflict with India, is, by the way, the same request that appears in the kidnappers' communiqués. And yet, all through the negotiations, Musharraf says nothing. Above all, he doesn't want to worry the Americans. He even has the nerve to declare, in his press conference with Bush, that he is 'reasonably sure than Daniel Pearl is still alive' and that we're 'as near as possible to these culprits.' And when it's all over, when the negotiations are finished, when everyone realizes that the Americans won't give, when there's nothing left to negotiate, the truth explodes—Omar's name, his arrest, and the death of the American journalist. Don't you find that disconcerting?"

"Too much so, perhaps. It looks like a crude manipulation."

Tariq shrugs his shoulders, like someone who has said all he has to say and leaves you to figure things out yourself. We've come back to Aurangzeb. The gates of the park are closed. It looks to me like the small crowd on the sidewalks is not as dense as it was a while ago. Besides the addicts, there are now, wandering around some brand new cars, a group of young aspiring starlets, maybe leaving Radio Pakistan, which is nearby, 100 meters away. He turns one last time towards me and offers his hand amicably. His gaze is distracted now, absent.

"Be careful. This is a sensitive matter. I know them. I know how the Mohajirs think. And I know they wouldn't like the idea that someone new is meddling in this—especially a foreigner. God keep you."

I had forgotten this other factor in the Pakistani equation: the hostility that has existed since the birth of Pakistan between the native Punjabis and the ones they call here the Mohajirs—the millions of people who came from India in 1949, at the time of Partition. Could it be that this rivalry is a dimension of the Pearl affair? Is it conceivable, for example, that the Punjabi high command (contrary to what Tariq pretends to believe, 90% of the ISI's superior officers are Punjabis) has found an excellent means of destabilizing Musharraf (who is, as no one here forgets, the most eminent of Mohajirs and who, when the Pearl affair exploded, had just completed a radical purge whose aim, under the pretext of fighting the Islamists, was to rid the ISI of Punjabis)? And is this the real reason Tariq wanted to see us, and to talk to us?

But he's already out of the car. Now that I see him standing, he looks smaller than I thought. He leaves as he came, a little man with oversized shoulders who plunges into the night, leaving Abdul and me to some new theorizing.

Let's say that Omar is, as Tariq says, an ISI agent.

Let's say that's a possible explanation for his attitude during and after his trial.

Let's say that that's one of the reasons for this strangely docile attitude that makes Omar accept, basically, being the fall guy.

The real question then becomes who, exactly, in the services set him up, and with what end in mind.

Because it's either one or the other.

Either Musharraf has a hold on his country, he is informed, in real time, of the work of his services, and, in fact, Tariq is right: Musharraf knows, when he is in the United States, where Pearl has been detained; he knows, especially, that Pearl is already dead when he declares to the American press that he has every hope of seeing him liberated. On this point, why not? We can well imagine a forceful negotiator like the General-President—formerly of the ISI himself, let's not forget—keeping the card of a journalist's liberation up his sleeve, taking advantage of it to make things last, and showing it at what he judges the opportune moment. The second point, however, is not so simple, it is hard to see why a head of state nurturing a strategic alliance with the United States—F-16s notwithstanding—would add cynicism to a crime. It's hard to see why, knowing that Pearl is dead and the announcement of his execution is a matter of days or hours away, Musharraf would chose to offer one last lie that could only, in the end, add to his partner's anger.

Or, alternatively, Musharraf is in control of nothing. He is deceived by his own services. The man officially charged with keeping him abreast of developments in the affair (who, by the way, turns out to be none other than Brigadier Cheema, the man at the Ministry of the Interior who answered my questions regarding Omar) makes a point of providing him with erroneous information. This so-very-fragile head of state, this king without crown or territory, who has already escaped—no one in Pakistan can forget it—six assassination attempts and who had to cancel an August 2000 visit to Karachi because his own security said they could not protect him, knows, perhaps, where Pearl has been held. But he does not know of Pearl's possible murder, nor that the deed has actually been done. The very fact that he says he has good reason to believe that the American journalist will be liberated soon, the confidence with which he utters those words, the political risks he takes by saying them, all this, rather than prove his duplicity, tends to demonstrate his innocence. And the whole thing would amount to a gigantic maneuver on the part of the services, or, at least a faction of the services, seeking to ridicule, destabilize, and place in an awkward position a president whose Western alliances they contest and whose authority they seek to undermine by any means possible.

What better means to discredit Musharraf, in fact, than to let him say, "Pearl is alive" when they know that he no longer is?

What better way to mark the balance of power and to tell the world—starting with the Americans—that this man is a puppet and that the real power is in other hands, than to let him get tangled up in his own promises. Or, better still, to inflate them by feeding him, and the press, erroneus information—and, then, to pull the rug out from under him at the opportune time?

The services have their policy on Kashmir. They had a policy—perhaps they still do—on Afghanistan. In all probability, they have a policy for the Pearl affair, and we have witnessed a new stage in the power struggle between the State and the State-within-the-State that is the Pakistani services.

Ten days before the kidnapping, and not without courage, Musharraf made a long antiterrorist speech that half of Pakistan assumed was dictated by Colin Powell. Right after that, he had two thousand jihadists arrested, the majority from groups black-listed by the United States. He closed the training camps in Pakistani Kashmir. He started cleaning up the services them-selves by placing his old friend Ehsan ul-Haq, a man who is con-sidered a moderate, representative of the "secular and kemalist" wing of the organisation, at their head. And there it is. The kid-napping, then the execution of Daniel Pearl is tit for tat. Omar Sheikh, the young Londoner who became a warrior of Allah, must have been exploited by the branch of the ISI hostile to Musharraf. And there's every reason to believe the message got through because in the following weeks, after a vague and comic promise not to dabble in terrorism, the police released half of the assassins they had previously arrested.

Who rules Pakistan?

The President, or the services?

That is the question the Pearl affair raises.

That is the question raised by an agent named Omar.

CHAPTER 5 WHEN THE KILLER CONFESSES

There's one place in the world where no one has the slightest doubt that Omar is an ISI agent—India.

Of course, I know there are many things to consider.

I know that India can derive great advantage from the idea that the murder of a prominent American journalist was commissioned by their sworn enemy, Pakistan.

I also know my own biases: I love this country so much! I feel, particularly after being in Pakistan, so happy here! I haven't been here in thirty years, and it takes me only an hour on Connaught, ten minutes at the Gandhi Memorial and five at the Chandni Chowk Bird Hospital to be flooded with a stream of memories that have been languishing in my mind and which I suddenly rediscover, with incredible precision: emotion, sensuality, a nostalgia of mind and sense. The jacket I wore, the woman I loved, her tight little chignon. The lights of the temple where we slept without permission. The money-changer/magician, that first evening on Connaught, who, by folding the bills in half as he was counting them, had robbed me of half my meager fortune—funny, how the love for a place is a love that never dies!

Anyway, I wanted from the start to have the Indian point of view on the case.

I meet with journalists, intellectuals, retired and active military men, scientists, heads of "think-tanks"—those American-model idea shops flourishing in the India of the new millennium.

Using what little influence my Bangladeshi past seems to give me here, I schedule meetings at the federal Ministry of the Interior; then at the Research and Analysis Wing (RAW), India's equivalent of the ISI, with the few people assigned to follow not only the Pearl affair but also Omar.

Which is how I found myself in the heart of New Delhi in a mini-Pentagon—composed of a series of bunkerized buildings, with walls of sandbags and cement, a veritable fortress against the suicide bombings regularly threatened by Muslim fundamentalist—swarmed from morning until night by men and women in Western-style dress, who look more like the employees of any big bureaucracy than like spies.

"A book about Daniel Pearl?" asks Sudindrah Datta, deputy to the head of the RAW. He's around thirty, square-jawed and good-humored with the manner of a gym teacher, and is receiving me in his huge and bare office, which has no files, no furniture, just a table, a couch, a chair on which he has hung his windbreaker, and an old, wheezing air-conditioner. From next-door, the clacking of secretaries typing. "Yes, that's interesting. We know you are an old friend of our country. But first, tell me. It seems you've just been in Pakistan.... How are those lunatics?"

A long day, then, spent in a universe so bizarre I never thought I'd have to deal with it except in novels.

A day spent poring over dusty documents produced on old-fashioned typewriters, seeking the overlooked detail that changes everything, the decisive clue, the lie that exposes another lie, the mystery that opens, like Russian dolls, into another even thicker mystery, the forgotten name, the word which in a flash reveals the country behind the lies and the crime.

And at the end of the day, three exceptional documents and several pieces of information—some of which had never before come out of these archives.

Document no. 1. The most exceptional and perhaps most fascinating, even if it is not the most directly tied to my investigation—in cramped typing, single-spaced on an old typewriter, in the nothing-but-the-facts language common to all the police forces of the world, a copy of the transcript of the interrogation of Masood Azhar, the future boss of the Jaish-i Mohammed and already at that time—summer 1994, after his arrest in Kashmir—a most-wanted terrorist.

No direct link, then, with the Pearl case. Not a word, for example, about his disciple Omar Sheikh. But a precise description of the relationships between the different groups that comprise the Pakistani Islamic movement during those years. A description, from within, of the series of schisms that endlessly divide it. The trips to Albania, Kenya, Zambia, Great Britain, taken by this relentless propagandist for a jihad that must set fire to the planet before submitting it to the law of Islam. The extraordinary freedom with which he moves around London, which, we discover with horror, is already the real bridgehead of terrorism in Europe. How he thinks he's too fat—"I am a too fatty person"—to go through complete military training. How he makes up for it by managing newspapers—*Sadai Mujahid,* for example—that spread jihadist propaganda all over the Pakistan. His campaign in favor of Islamabad's withdrawal from the international forces in Somalia. His faith in a Pakistan that would, via fire and sword, deserve its name of "Country of the Pure." In short, an amazing intaglio portrait of this holy man—because Masood presents himself as a holy man, a religious person, a pious soul—who holds the Koran in one hand and a machine gun in the other. And then, reading on, as he recounts his difficulties in obtaining a visa for Bangladesh and India, comes the tale of the deception—how, with the help of the Pakistani government and in fact the ISI, he obtains a fraudulent Portugese passport in the name of Wali Adam Issa.

Omar is not cited by name. Still, I can't help thinking about the fact that Masood is his mentor. They were both freed together, as we recall, after the terrorist operation at the Kandahar airport. It has not been ruled out that Masood was among those who, with Omar, planned Pearl's kidnapping. And I can't help but consider that Omar's mentor, who is possibly one of the Pearl abduction planners, has strong enough ties to the Pakistani secret service to be given a fraudlent passport—one which, as the transcript clearly recounts, would fool even the most discerning Indian customs officials.

Document no. 2. The transcript of Omar's own interrogation, after the abductions of Rhys Partridge, Paul Rideout, Christopher Morston and Bela Nuss, the English and American tourists he kidnapped in New Delhi in 1994.

He's just back from Bosnia. He's just gone through weeks of military training in the Miran Shah camp. He's part of all those jihad troops on meager pay, born too late in a world that is too old, who have seen the wars in Bosnia and Afghanistan end before they could really participate, and who are desperately seeking another "great cause" to embrace. Palestine, whose sinful leaders, in the wake of Oslo, are making compromises with the Israeli Satan? Chechnya, where the Russian army is involved in its war of conquest, control and—some aren't afraid to say it—extermination? Maybe the Philippines, where the Abbu Sayyaf groups are marking out their territory? No. For him, as for many other Pakistanis of his generation, it will be Kashmir, the province Pakistan and India are fighting over, where Pakistani terrorist groups, supported by the secret service, have been engaged in terrorist guerrilla warfare for nearly forty years.

"There are things to do within India itself," he was told by a man he calls in the transcript Maulana Abdullah, a Jihadist chieftain, member of the Harkat ul-Mujahideen, whom he met in the Afghan camps. "There's combat on the ground in Kashmir. There's a military battle against the occupying forces. But there's also work to be done behind the Indian army, in Delhi. You've got dual nationality, Pakistani and English. You can even give up your Pakistani passport and apply in London for a visa for India, which you'll get in a heartbeat. You're exactly the kind of man we need. We're waiting for you." After which Omar finds himself, on 26 July 1994, at the Holiday Inn in New Delhi, the same city I knew so well—but twenty-five years before him, in the year of his birth, I realize. He finds himself in New Delhi with a clear mission: to kidnap foreigners, hold them, and make a deal to exchange their freedom for that of six leaders of the Harkat ul-Mujahideen, including Masood Azhar, languishing in Indian prisons.

So Omar recounts this story. He goes into detail on his series of kidnappings. You see him running around town like a rutting animal, hunting for victims. He describes a method, which is exactly the one he will put into use eight years later with Daniel Pearl: the strategy of making them trust you; setting up a house in a remote area of town, in Saharanpur; purchasing a camera; the chains; everything down to the snapshots he sends to the press and which I saw—gun against the temple, the day's newspaper as background. At least the script was well-rehearsed! Then, as his narrative continues, three elements emerge that indicate the entire operation would not have been feasible without the active support of the Pakistani embassy in Delhi.

The house. The fact that he buys the house. He gives the price, 130,000 rupees, and explains very clearly that he doesn't rent it, he buys it. Where did he get the money, the 130,000 rupees?

The weapons. The day Yusuf, his sidekick, finds him in a park, near Jama Masjid, with a plastic bag containing two handguns. The day, not long after, he brought an AK-47 and two grenades back to their hideout. Impossible, I'm told by my sources, and I think they're right, to bring an AK-47, grenades and handguns into India without diplomatic assistance.

And then, the most significant, this admission, on page fourteen of the transcript. He comes back to his military training stints in Afghanistan. He talks about the two times, in 1993 and 1994, he stayed in the Miran Shah and Khalid Bin Waleed camps. He explains in detail how he is trained to "handle pistols, revolvers, assault rifles, AK-47 machine guns, LPG and GPMG rocket launchers." He recounts his apprenticeship in those actual "techniques" of "organizing an ambush, handling grenades, mines, explosives. Living clandestinely, the art of shadowing someone, of moving around at night." And, in passing, he gives the names of his two instructors, two men to whom he owes everything because they taught him everything on these subjects: Subedar Saleem and Subedar Abdul Hafeez, who are, he specifies, former members of the SSG—otherwise known as the Special Services Group, the elite unit of the ISI!

Document no. 3. His diary. Not the police transcript anymore, but his personal diary, kept by Omar himself, at the beginning of his stay in Indian jails, in which he recounts in even more detail the series of kidnappings that have brought him to this point.

The Pakistanis, who know about this diary, regularly make it known that it can only be a fake, fabricated by the Indian police—who ever heard of a terrorist, in jail, starting a diary which is a chronicle of his life? Everything is possible, of course. I've seen enough dirty tricks in my life to know that everything is possible and that the Indians, just like the Algerians or the Israelis or any other secret service in the world, are capable of anything when it comes to disinformation. But in this case I don't believe it. First, you see everything in jails; anything is conceivable. Why not a killer keeping his own diary? Omar, furthermore, has never denied it. He read, as did everyone, excerpts published in the Indian press. He knows that the Pakistani papers also talked about "Omar's Diary" as an essential element of the case. And he never in the slightest denied its authenticity. And then I saw the text, finally. I went to the Records Room of the criminal court in New Delhi, in Patiala House, where I managed to get them to take the original fifty-page manuscript out of the archives, declassify it, and photocopy it for me. And, from the very first pages, I recognized the handwriting, only slightly more mature than that of his school homework. Which means that the theory of a fake diary can only stand up if it's leaning on another, and that supporting theory is itself not very convincing even though you regularly find Pakistani diehards propounding it: that Omar was an accomplice in its counterfeiting, because he has ties to India. Or, to be more exact, he was recruited by the Indians during his years in prison at Uttar Pradesh and then in Tihar Jail, and has since become their man. (Aren't there even sources—the *Pittsburgh Tribune-Review*, of course—that came up with the idea that Omar was a CIA agent, used in the CIA's hunt for bin Laden?)

The first thing that strikes you, in those fifty pages, is the writing itself. You actually have to say the *writings*. Good in the first pages, with round letters, nicely shaped and regular, with mistakes crossed out neatly. And then starting on page 13 or 14, the penmanship goes awry: it becomes smaller, less readable, slanted slightly towards the right when up until that point it had been vertical, with unfinished letters, *G*s that look like *Y*s, *D*s you mistake for *L*s, the writing of a fifteen-year-old. And even younger in the last pages which are a chronology of his life before India, then very brief biographical sketches of his parents and the people he is close to, and finally some samples of his writing and his signature—obviously provided at the demand of prison authorities—which have been stapled to the rest. In those last ten pages, yes, I'm struck by the clumsiness, the scribbled, fly-speck aspect of the handwriting. Here, too, as in his photos, Omar is someone who can change age in front of your eyes. Here, too, a peculiar capacity for splitting in two, for being sev-

WHEN THE KILLER CONFESSES

eral people in one. The faces.... The talent for changing his accent, almost his voice, according to circumstances.... And now, writing that is so unsure of its identity.... Despite my distrust of the so-called rules of the so-called science of handwriting analysis, how can I not in this instance let myself be tempted?

The second thing that amazes me is the language. The poverty of the language and the style. The childish nature of the narrative. And even, according to Lara Fielden and James Mitchell, English and American friends and fixers, to whom I showed this document, the numerous bizarre turns of phrase, not exactly improprieties but slightly off in a way unexpected from the pen of a former student of the Forest School and the London School of Economics. "Female partner" instead of "girlfriend"... "Member of the public" instead of "someone in the street" or "passerby"... "I clasped" instead of "I shook" his hand... "I espied" Siddiqui, instead of simply "I saw" or "I spotted".... And, in a passage about the "village" that he tells his victims he just inherited and which he invites them to come and visit, his weird way of saying that it is "on" instead of "in" his name.... A sign that the text is deliberately flawed? A message—and if so, what is it, to whom is it addressed, and what does it say? Or is it a sign of pomposity, of preciousness, the linguistic equivalent of the arrogance I noted in his youthful photos?

Interesting, too, the extraordinary amateurishness of the little gang of kidnappers he forms with Amine, Sultan, Osman, Farooq, Salahuddin, Nasir and Siddiqui. The feverish hunt for victims. The clumsiness in approaching them. The slipups. The driver of the van, whom he notices, too late, doesn't pray with him and is therefore not as reliable as he had assumed. The incredible story of Akhmir, the Israeli giant who immediately falls into the trap, whom he brings back one night, at two in the morning, to the house in Ganda Nala where they plan to hold him. "You're crazy!" shouts the boss when he sees, through a chink in the curtains, this oversized guy, too strong, too threatening. "You're going to get us all killed! Take him back to his hotel!" The contradictory orders. The permanently make-shift atmosphere. Excursions, hand-in-hand, talking about what a good time they're having. The telephone numbers that are always wrong. The agencies, newspapers, and embassies whose addresses they realize—right at the moment they're supposed to be sending them the message claiming responsiblity for a job— they don't have. He goes himself to the *Hindustan Times* to deliver one letter. Catastrophe! The managing editor is out, it's his deputy who takes the letter, opens it in front of him and starts to read it, barely giving him time to gallop down the stairs two at a time. The photos.... Hey, boss, what if we took photos of the hostages. Yeah, boss, you remember, like they did in Lebanon, with the newspaper in the background to show the date. OK, says the boss. We hadn't thought of it, but it is indeed a good idea, we'll buy a camera and take the photos. Fearsome killers. The heart of the contemporary terrorist machine. But also the Three Stooges.

And the boss himself, the only one without a name, whose mysterious shadow haunts the pages. Sometimes Omar calls him "Big Man." Other times "Shah Sahab," the name he'll give to Gilani eight years later in his e-mails to Pearl. In another police interrogation I also had access to, he also calls him "Shahjoi." In the paragraph Omar writes about him in the biographical sketches at the end of the text, he refers to him as "the chief of the mission" and calls him simply "Commander." And in the "Personality" section, he says that, although the Commander is "moody at times," he's "very good at controlling the people." He's the real boss of the group, in any case. The strategist. The man who decides the Israeli must be set free, that they need to concentrate on Americans, or, if there aren't any Americans, go for English or French. He's the man, too, who draws up the list of Kashmiri militants whose freedom will be demanded in exchange for the four hostages. The wily one who decides to add several unimportant names to the list of who they really want freed, to cover up their tracks. The treasurer. The one who decides whether or not to buy the house or the van, and who makes sure that the group, should things go wrong, has enough cash to beat a retreat. He's the man who, finally, has the contact with Islamabad and who keeps saying, about the money and everything else, "I'm calling Islamabad.... I've called Islamabad.... Islamabad agrees... the instructions from Islamabad are...." Omar points out, in fact, that it's in Islamabad, in July before his departure, that he meets this harsh, passionless character, the commander—who is using the name Zubair Shah and in the company of Maulana Abdullah— for the first time. Except Omar, still in his diary, says the man is rather "paternal" towards him.

So who is Shah Sahab, exactly? Why is he never named? And why is he the only one who feels the need to conceal his face when he goes to see the hostages? Omar says, "Shah Sahab veiled himself." The former hostage Rhys Partridge will remember the arrival of a character everybody called the Commander, with a kitsch watch on his wrist and "a tea towel on his head." For the Indians, the reason is obvious: the tone, the way he's constantly asserting his link to Islamabad, all this indicates a high-level agent—very probably General Zahir ul-Islam Abbasi who was, that year, the Pakistani military attaché in India, and who, when he returned in 1996, had a hand in an attempted coup d'etat, was court-martialled and convicted, then freed in 2001, after which he became one of the star orators of the Harkat ul-Mujahideen, Harkat ul-jihad al-Islami, Lashkar e-Toiba and so on. For me, the situation isn't that simple and two details in the diary give me pause. The fact that on at least one occasion—the day of the aborted kidnapping of the Israeli giant—we see the "Big Man" spend the night in Ganda Nala, with Sultan, Nasim and Farooq: Would the military attaché have done that? Would he have shared the discomfort of this shack? And more particularly the fact that twice—the day he visited the hostages and also the day they composed the letters to the press—Omar says he had to translate Shah Sahab's words into English: Would a diplomat have needed that? Wouldn't he have written the letters himself? On the whole, though, I think you have to go along with the Indians on the idea that Shah Sahab is an agent. And were I to doubt it, there's a little note, right at the end of the diary, in the "previous association" section of the biographical notes, that supports this: "SSG," says the note. Shah Sahab's "previous associations" are the Harkat ul-jihad al-Islami, and the Hizb e-Islami, but also, like Subedar Saleem and Subedar Abdul Hafeez, Omar's instructors from the Miran Shah camp, the SSG—the Special Services Group, the elite unit of the ISI.

The Indians also tell me that it was the station chief of the ISI who, under the cover of the Pakistani embassy in London, paid Omar's lawyer when he was arrested.

They give me the list showing how many times the various embassy attachés—and particularly the military attachés—came to visit him in prison.

"How's that?" I ask. "His friend Peter Gee told me it was the British consul who was taking care of Omar, and of Gee as well."

"There you are," Datta replies. "Omar was British, as you say. A subject of Her Majesty. Treated in the same way as the musician smuggling marijuana. Except that it really was the Pakistanis who came to visit him the most often, and here's proof, here's the visitors' register."

They also inform me that, six years later, in the spring of 2000, when the time came for him to return to Pakistan after his liberation in Kandahar, it was an ISI colonel who was waiting for him at the border to drive him to a safe-house where they debriefed him.

"Here's a man," Datta continues, "who owes his freedom to an exceptionally serious plane hijacking. Every newspaper in the region and even the world was full of photos of him, of Masood Azhar, and of the poor passenger who was horribly decapitated a few hours before their liberation. And, along the same lines, Masood Azhar, as soon as he was home, held meeting after meeting, founded his Jaish e-Mohammed, showed off at the Karachi press club, and traipsed around every town in Pakistan, surrounded by a veritable private army of turbaned men. And Omar Sheikh, instead of staying in Afghanistan, or fleeing to Yemen, Iraq or North Korea, instead of hiding, goes back to his house on Mohni Road in Lahore, gets married, has a child and gives press conferences, too. How do you explain that? How do you explain this insolent impunity without assuming an active complicity, from the beginning, with the Pakistani governments, the visible and the invisible one?"

I see a note—but this one I'm not allowed to take with me—which apparently is based on the contents of an FBI report: 0300 94587772.... Omar's cell phone number... the tracing of all his calls between July and October 2001 on that line. And among the numbers called, the number of General Mehmood Ahmed, who, until right after September 11, was the general director of the ISI.

Talking to Mohan Menon, communications director of the RAW, I'm treated to an analysis of the series of messages claiming responsibility for the kidnapping of Pearl that were sent to the press. What is strange, Menon tells me, is not the sudden appearance of this "Movement for the Restoration of Pakistani Sovereignty," which was said in the United States to be unknown to Pakistani authorities. It wasn't unknown at all! It had already claimed responsibility in October for the peculiar kidnapping of Joshua Weinstein, a.k.a. Martin Johnson, the Californian they accused, like Daniel Pearl, of being a CIA agent—and whom we saw in the photos with two hooded men on either side of him pointing an AK-47 at his head, and he, too, is holding a Pakistani paper showing the date. No. What's interesting is how the messages are written. You have three of them. The last awful one, sent on 1 February from an Internet address (antiamerican-imperialism@hotmail.com) unknown to police: "We have killed Mr. Danny now Mr. Bush can find his body in the graveyards of Karachi we have thrown him there"—because of which the police spent two crazy nights, punctuated with crackpot confessions and phone calls from pranksters, searching the two-hundred-plus cemeteries in the city. There's the message from the day before, 30 January, when Pearl is already dead or about to die, which allows twenty-four hours and not one more for the kidnapper's demands to be met—"U cannot fool us and find us," it says, in a bizarre, incomprehensible English riddled with mistakes. You will never find us because "we are inside seas, oceans, hills, graveyards, everywhere; we give u one more day; if America will not meet our demands, we will kill Daniel; then, this cycle will continue and no American journalist could enter Pakistan; Allah is with us and will protect us." And then there's the very first message, the day after the abduction, which is written in perfect English with impeccable spelling and addressed like the others—but through another e-mail address (kidnapperguy@hotmail.com)—to the international press: Daniel Pearl is being held in inhumane conditions, was its gist. But these conditions are merely the reflection of the fate inflicted on the Pakistanis being held in Cuba by the American army. Improve the lot of our people, give in to our demands, and Pearl's fate will automatically be humanized. The message went on to outline the demands (which we would see again, white letters on black background like a macabre signature, at the very end of the 3 minutes and 36 seconds of the video of the decapitation): the right for Pakistanis arrested after September 11 to have a lawyer; the return of the Afghan and Muslim prisoners held by the American army on the Cuban base in Guantanamo, to be tried in Karachi; the liberation of Abdoul Sala Zaeef, former Taliban ambassador in Islamabad; and finally the resumed delivery of the F-16 jet fighters blocked in 1998 as reprisal for Pakistani nuclear tests, which had become ever since one of the constant demands of the country's military. Since when, Menon asks, do terrorists demand ambassadors and airplanes? Who are these jihadists who talk like a press release from the Joint Chiefs of Staff? Where are the screams of hate for the infidels and the Zionist conspiracy that jihadist communiqués are normally riddled with?

And then this final piece of information. Or, to be more exact, this story: I am in the office of A. K. Doval who is now the head of the Domestic Intelligence Bureau but who was, nine years ago, at the time of the Indian Airlines plane hijacking, a member of the delegation which brought Masood Azhar, Mushtaq Zargar and Omar Sheikh to Kandahar for the exchange. "Here's the hijacked plane," he tells me, pencil in hand. "Ours, coming from Delhi, landed here, at the other end. But theirs is exactly here, at the end of this runway in the deserted Kandahar airport. Here to the right you have the Taliban, who, when they realized we had brought commandos with us, disguised as nurses and social workers, were ready to move in, lined up two armoured vehicles, rocket launchers and a handful of sharpshooters all along the runway, aimed not at the hijackers but at us. On the other side of the runway, on the left, you have this little building where Erik de Mul is with the other UN people, seriously handicapped by the fact that they don't speak Urdu. Then here, just next to that, you have an officers' mess where we've set up with walkie-talkies to finish, in the place of the UN, the negotiations with the hijackers, who in any case only want to talk to us. It's cold. The tension is extreme. Nobody dares make a move. We're all expecting that, at any minute, either the hijackers or the Taliban will lose it. At one point, one of my sharpshooters gets a guy in a turban in his sights who's jumped out and is standing in the doorway of the plane, shouting, holding a hostage and a box-cutter—'Do I shoot?' asks my guy. And then here, a little farther, you have a last building where there are three high-ranking officers of the ISI who also have walkie-talkies. And that's when three incredible things happen."

"1. When the hijackers forget to turn off their receivers, we hear the voices of the ISI guys, telling them what to do, what to answer, how to handle the situation.

"2. When we finally reach an agreement and we bring Sheikh, Azhar and Zargar to the plane to proceed with the exchange, it's not the hijackers, it's the ISI guys who, as it were, on their own account, come to check their identities.

"3. And when the trade is finally made and the ISI officers take charge of the prisoners—here, you see these three little rectangles, those are their vehicles, which the Taliban lent them—I see the one who seems to be their leader kiss Omar Sheikh, call him by his first name and say, 'So, back to Kandahar. I'm so happy to see you.'" Doval is looking at me, his eyes twinkling behind his round, intellectual's glasses: "Could you dream of any better proof of the collusion between Omar and the secret service?"

That's the Indian point of view.

I give it, I repeat, for what it is: the point of view of an enemy state who, involved in a total war with a hereditary adversary, can't be negligent on any front.

I don't exclude, may I stress, the possibility of having been manipulated by Doval and Datta on a particular point or perhaps a document, as I could have been by any Pakistani I spoke to. That's the game, I'm not unaware of it.

But, really, all this is too convergent not to make sense, finally.
Omar Sheikh, from Delhi's perspective, is an agent.

He has been for a long time: from his London School days, more or less.

He's one of those brilliant, competent young people that the Pakistani secret service spots when they're in college and tries to win over.

And, parenthetically, that's probably even the explanation of the mystery I bumped up against in Sarajevo and in London—it's the key to the trip to Bosnia, the strange trip that left no traces, which has puzzled me so much and for which I have dilligently but unsuccessfully tried to reconstruct an itinerary.

"Too ill to accompany them to Bosnia," writes Omar on page 36 of his Indian diary.... Too ill, yes, to follow the mission of the Convoy of Mercy to the end, after it leaves from England to bring supplies to Jablanica.... Asad Khan's version, in other words. Omar, in this document, confirms the version of the Convoy's organizer! And the idea that occurs to me is the following: What if the whole Bosnian affair—trip, humanitarian aid, emotion felt from seeing the film *Destruction of a Nation*, anger, the fact that nobody can say whether the guy went all the way to Mostar or stopped in Split, but everybody keeps saying, that he experienced the great turning point of his life with the martyrdom of Sarajevo—what if all of it were a fabrication, window-dressing after the fact, a way of inventing a plausible biography for someone who, for a long time, maybe since London and his admission to the London School of Economics, had been working for the ISI?

I don't claim that Omar *never* went to Bosnia.

I don't exclude the possibility that Saquib Qureshi, his friend from student days, was *also right* when he told me Omar could have made a second trip to the Balkans, without the Convoy of Mercy.

And I would get confirmation of that second trip long after my stay in India, reading an interview Omar gave in jail on 6 February 2003 to *Takbeer*, an Urdu Islamist weekly, in which he describes, as if they were scenes he'd *witnessed*, "Serb attacks" against Muslim villages, "women and children reduced to cinders," a "child's burned hand on a pile of ashes," "babies' legs in a heap," "piles of corpses."

I simply say that there is a Bosnian legend in Omar Sheikh's biography that serves to glorify—adding anger, thought, compassion—a much less honorable exploit of a very young man caught up in the destiny of a cop and a secret agent.

I say that this Bosnian affair is like his relationship to "Being Muslim" and like the way he tells Peter Gee, after the fact and in the face of contrary evidence, that he was a persecuted Muslim, victimized, the prey of little English boys' mundane racism—all packaging, a red herring, retroactive justification.

Bosnia is not, as I had first thought, a hole, an enigmatic blank spot, a section of his life that had fallen into oblivion and that everybody, starting with this investigator, had lost track of. Instead, it is a lie, a deliberate invention, a construction—as often with this kind of character, the production of a piece of biography that serves as a decoy and a false trail.

CHAPTER 6 IN THE DEMON'S LAIR

Omar, ISI agent.

The child from Deyne Court Gardens, the good student, Saquib's friend, the gifted individual with the brilliant future ahead of him, the pride of his family become a slave of the state, a dog of war for the Pakistani powers-that-be, a killer— Islamabad is where I would find the final confirmation of this spectacular turnaround.

We are in October 2002.

It's my third stay in the Pakistani capital.

I am busy trying, for the third time, to find the trace of this man that everybody here seems to want to forget.

Because the Indians are right, finally!

How could a felon, convicted of kidnapping and freed by another kidnapping, move around so freely on these vast avenues, crammed with military?

How does this man, who is supposed to have gone underground—because of what he is about to do as much as because of what he has done—move around so easily, without taking any precautions? How does he break all the rules—how to avoid being followed, taking safe routes, changing addresses—that are obligatory for shadowy characters, terrorists included?

It would be understandable in Karachi, where we all know that nobody has had anything or anyone under control for a long time.

It's all right in Lahore, where he lives in a beautiful house, gives a party in January to celebrate the birth of his baby, receives local dignitaries, is received by them, goes to the same clubs they do, moves in the same high society circles and is counted among local personalities—he's from Lahore, after all. You could say to those who have doubts that he's at home in Lahore, in his and his family's fiefdom.

But Islamabad!

The Potemkin village of those in power!

The center of gravity, the nerve-center of the state and its agencies!

How to explain that he is like a fish in water in Islamabad?

How can a supposedly hunted man matter-of-factly order a book on the Kandahar airplane hijacking from the "Mr. Books" bookstore, which everyone knows is just a stone's throw from ISI headquarters, on Khayaban i-Suharawardy Road?

Here's a man who has already spent five years in jail in India for a series of crimes of the same kind as the one he is preparing to commit. Here's a jihadist suspected of complicity in the attack on the Jammu-Kashmir assembly in Srinagar with a truck full of explosives, then in the 13 December grenade attack on the New Delhi Parliament, and then, again, in the 22 January operation—right before Pearl's kidnapping—against the American Cultural Centre in Calcutta. Here's a repeat offender whose extradition—we know this now—Washington had demanded just a few weeks earlier, in November, in connection with the 1994 kidnapping (one of the victims, Bela Nuss, fortuitously, was American), sending the ambassador Wendy Chamberlain to

Islamabad in person on January 9, fourteen days before the abduction, to insist he be arrested. Here's a man who is not only one of the most dangerous, but also one of the most wanted on the planet. Who can believe that this man is able, without very solid support, that is to say without ties to the country's secret service, to move around the way he does, with total impunity?

I'm thinking about how arrogant he looks in the photos at the end of his trial.

I'm thinking again about his answer to the FBI agents who asked him in February if he had links to the ISI: "I will not discuss this subject. I don't want my family to be killed." Whether he feels any remorse: "My only remorse is the child. I have a child who is two months old. So the idea that Pearl was about to become a father, too, that makes me feel a bit of remorse." Another answer he gave, which I was told about in Washington, that was accompanied by a huge burst of laughter: "Did you say extradition? You really think I can be extradited? Come on, gentlemen, you're dreaming! Three, four years maximum, here in Pakistan! And then I'm out." Almost the same words as in the 13 March *Newsweek* article.

I'm reflecting on the article by Kamran Kahn, in the *News*, which had so much impact at the time, that evoked his ties to General Mohammad Aziz Khan, Chairman of the Joint Chiefs of Staff Committee of the Armed Forces as of 8 October 2001. Was it true that he had gone with Musharraf and Aziz to the headquarters of the Lashkar e-Toiba, in Muridke, near Lahore, before Musharraf's visit to India in July? Is it true that he knew Aftab Ansari, the mafia man, and that their relationship had the blessing of the ISI?

I'm thinking about what is known of the personality of Mohammed Adeel, one of the three plotters of cell number two, the one that took care of writing and sending the e-mails: policeman in Karachi; former member of a counter-terrorist unit; former intelligence officer; directly tied, therefore, to the ISI.

I'm thinking about the remark Musharraf made to the U.S. ambassador who had just expressed to him the USA's wish to see Omar extradited: "I would prefer to hang him myself than to have to extradite him." Resentment? Anger? Hatred overcoming him, making him capable, with his own hands, etc.? No doubt. But it's hard not to hear as well in his exclamation the willingness to do anything, absolutely anything, to avoid a public trial and the possible exposure of the murky connections between Omar and the ISI.

I'm thinking about the story of the taxi driver who claims he drove Omar to the Hotel Akbar, and the account I got from him: he was stopped at a checkpoint in much the same way I was the evening I first arrived. Armed soldiers—this is in the middle of Musharraf's phase of pro-American anti-terrorist zeal—hustle the driver out of his taxi, push him up against a wall with his arms outstretched, and search him. But when it is Omar's turn to show his papers and be searched, a word seems to suffice, maybe a document he stuck under their noses—and the embarrassed soldiers let him go on: "No problem, welcome, you can go."

I'm thinking of Saquib again, the friend from London. It was a little story that at the time hadn't really struck me. But now, in the light of what I know.... This story takes place in April 1996. Saquib has finished school. He has a job at a big bank—I think the HSBC—and he's been sent on business to Pakistan. And there he is one night at dinner, in Islamabad, at the home of a vice-admiral whose name he forgets, seated next to a brigadier who is known to belong to the ISI, who says to him: "You went to the London School? Bravo! Perhaps, then, you know Omar. Maybe you were in the same class." Not Omar Sheikh. Just Omar.... As if there were only one, the one everybody knew in Islamabad, and who was, in any case, close to the brigadier....

And then finally I think, one last time, about his first meeting with Pearl, at the Hotel Akbar in Rawalpindi, 11 January, twelve days before the abduction. Well.... What is this Hotel Akbar, exactly? What does it look like? Why in fact did he choose it? And why is it that no one, as far as I know, has asked these questions? How come no one has had the idea to take a closer look and to spend an hour, or why not a night, in the room where contact was made?

I go to the Hotel Akbar.

I leave Islamabad and its wealthy districts.

I take the Aga Khan Road with its beautiful opulent houses and its look, common to most of the avenues in this perfectly artificial city, of having come straight out of a de Chirico painting.

I pass the Super Market, which is lively and animated and where, among photo shops, perfume boutiques, an "Old Books Sell and Buy," and a Konica camera shop, the "Mr. Books" bookstore is located.

I get to Murree Road, the main avenue of Rawalpindi, which is clear and open at first, and then, as soon as you get into town, choked with traffic. The cars move at a snail's pace. Clusters of kids are hanging from the ladders that climb to the roofs of multicolored buses. The group taxis bursting with people still manage to suck in more passengers. A horse cart.

Women in headscarves, not burqas, headscarves, uncovered smiling faces under the headscarves—I note that Rawalpindi is the only place that I see women's faces. The vast fabric shops. The jewellery district. The chemists district, where I suspect they also do the major drug deals. The signs for Habib Bank and for Honda and Suzuki shops. The beggars. The hovels. The side streets where you can sense the disease of the decaying neighborhoods. Just in front of the English Language Institute, the sign that identifies the Jammu and Kashmir Liberation Front. And then at the end of Muree Road, on the right, at the entrance to the old city, where the houses take on shades of ochre and the colonial style of all the old Indian cities, is the Liaquat Bagh, very green, with its flamboyantly colored flowers, and its spacious esplanade where they've been holding mass meetings since independence. And facing the Liaquat, set back, stuck between a boys' school and the Khawaja's Classic Hotel Executive—the windows, adorned with dark green balconies, of the Hotel Akbar.

At the door—it's a bizarre (and quite cruel) custom in midrange Pakistani hotels—a dwarf is greeting guests, his antics intended to cheer up weary travelers.

"Do you have any rooms?"

For once the dwarf doesn't laugh. He looks at me suspiciously without answering, apparently very surprised to see a foreigner, and makes gestures to indicate that I should ask at the reception desk, behind him, to the right.

"As I was saying, do you have any rooms?"

More suspicion from the desk clerk who takes a step back behind his counter, as if my simply coming in were an act of aggression. He's a man of about 40, dressed Western-style, clean-shaven with a slightly swollen face and hair that sticks up. Is he Aamir Raza Qureshi, the receptionist who was on duty on 11 January? Was he the one who first greeted Omar and checked him in, then later greeted Pearl? For now, I consider it useless—and unwise—to try to find out.

"Someone in France told me about your hotel. Because of the view on Liaquat Bagh."

The man takes my passport. And still without opening his mouth, acting as if he really wasn't looking for customers, he makes a gesture for me to go and sit over in the lobby, where there are pillows and low glass tables set on colored earthenware elephant feet.

At one of the tables, a strange child, all wrinkled, his forehead blotched with brown spots, wearing rags, stops drawing to stare at me.

At another, a group of five bearded men, in grubby white clothing, wearing turbans, suspicious.

All the tables, in fact, are occupied by bearded characters with not very engaging attitudes, who stop their conversations abruptly and look at me, not even trying to conceal their hostility.

Behind us, a small featureless room, very dark, that serves as the restaurant, and where I know that Omar, when Pearl arrived, was finishing dinner: the place is full, Chinese and Pakistani food, about forty people.

There are brown, fake-wool rugs everywhere, matching the curtains and the tapestries that go up to the ceiling—and everywhere the smell of haphazard housekeeping, of encrusted dirt and cigarette smoke that makes the air almost impossible to breathe.

The clerk has gone into the little office next to the reception desk, he's hanging on the telephone, flanked by a male housekeeper and a waiter from the restaurant who have just joined him, and seem equally intrigued, elbowing each other, sniggering.

Some of the time he's watching me, with a weird, murky look that could be threatening. Some of the time he's leafing through my passport. But mainly he seems very attentive to what he's being told over the telephone. After two minutes, unwillingly, almost angrily, he comes toward me.

"What floor?" Reluctantly he explains that the price is not the same—six hundred rupees for the first and second floors, twice that for the upper floors where the rooms have just been redone. I ask for the fourth floor, of course. And here I am, if not in Omar's room (it was number 411, but I'm told it's occupied), at least on the same corridor, facing it.

The difference is that my room looks out onto the Liaquat and from the window I can see, and hear, the kids coming out of school and further away, in the park, the neighborhood kids playing cricket with improvised bats, balls made from rags, and goals made from hastily stacked bricks.

The difference is that room 411, judging by the way the corridor is situated, must look out on the other side, onto a courtyard or a blank wall—it must be quieter, more peaceful, but also, and this was probably the idea, more isolated, and, in case of trouble, with no contact to the outside, and little chance of being heard.

Apart from that, it must have the same wooden bed, no pillows, with a blanket in the closet.

The same smell of cheap soap powder on the sheets.

The same dingy gray carpeting, and even dustier than on the ground floor. The same black formica on the walls, up to a man's height, and, facing the window, an engraving which depicts, like the one at the lawyer Khawaja's, Srinagar's snowy mountains. And, beneath the engraving, a minibar sits on top of a small television, which—incongruous luxury!—seems to get the regional cable channels.

The same laminated wood table where room-service put the club sandwiches, sodas, iced coffee, and, when night had fallen, when the conversation had become lively and an atmosphere of trust was beginning to prevail, more sandwiches and more iced coffee.

Pearl is there on the bed with his notebook open on his lap.

Asif, the fixer, who set up the meeting, is sitting on the floor, his back against the door.

Omar is sitting in the only chair, with Pearl 's and Asif's tape recorders on the table in front of him.

He's feeling awkward, at the beginning. Evasive. He can't bring himself to look at Danny directly and punctuates his answers with big embarrassed gestures. His missing beard, perhaps.... This new chin, smooth and clean-shaven, which he's no longer used to.... The thin, somewhat weak mouth which looked so strange to him that morning in the mirror, and which he's afraid will arouse suspicion—how absurd! The idea was to give himself a reassuring look, and now he's wondering if it isn't his shaved face that will betray him! No. Danny is trusting. He has a way of listening, of asking multiple questions, of letting the answer come, of extracting everything it means to reveal, then of coming back to a detail, and from this detail, starting up the questioning again. He has this very characteristic way of holding his breath when the other person is talking, or else of nodding his head in encouragement, accompanying the speaker almost as if he were an orchestra conductor—Ah, Danny and music! Danny and his violin! Those photos I saw in Los Angeles, of him with his violin, are coming back to me!—until he succeeds in putting Omar at ease and getting him to open up. And that's why, very quickly, they decide to relax and turn off their mobile phones and embark on a four-hour frank and open conversation about the Jaish e-Mohammed, the Lashkar I-Janghvi, the Harkat ul-Mujahideen, the Lashkar e-Toiba, the Gilani sect, the whole galaxy of Islamist organisations proliferating all over Pakistan; the relationships between them fascinate Danny.

It takes a long time for me to fall asleep that night.

I'm here to play the game and to experience this hotel from the inside, the full experience, in the hope of seeing a sign, I don't know what kind of sign but a sign, something which has yet to be revealed to the investigators or the press—but I confess to great difficulty in passing a normal night.

A swarm of questions are buzzing around in my head. Pearl's thoughts? His reactions? Was Pearl greeted the way I was, with the same visible suspicion? Or, on the contrary, were the people at the reception and in the lobby accomplices, briefed by Omar and so on his side? Was Pearl suspicious? Did he wonder, too, what was this strange place he'd happened upon? Did Omar have to provide explanations, justifications? How, in general, did their first meeting go? Did they talk about London and Los Angeles? About their babies? Their wives? Was the room service waiter the same little bearded guy in a djellaba, with one leg shorter than the other, making him walk hesitantly? Did it take him two hours to get up to Pearl's room, as well?

I am obsessed and tormented by the same doubts, which, with the night, take on awesome dimensions: Who were those men downstairs? Why was the desk clerk, when the hotel is visibly empty, so reluctant to give me a room? Why, in an empty hotel, do I hear the sound of footsteps, of stairs being climbed softly, those creaks of an old spring mattress in the room next door, these whispered conversations outside my door? Are they conversations, in fact? Or labored breathing? Moans of pain? Or the sound of furniture being moved? Why do I feel as if I am not alone? As if I'm being spied on even in my room? What if this Hotel Akbar, in other words, was not exactly a normal hotel?

The next day, as I'm paying my bill, I get the first part of an answer to my questions.

In front of me are some of the same men from yesterday, also waiting to pay—except that they present a card and repeat an identical phrase as they do so, a phrase which I don't understand but which seems to give them the right to a substantial discount.

Further away, in groups of five or six around the low tables, are other men, less prosperous, who don't seem to have rooms but are there nonetheless, regulars, silent, getting warm and drinking large cups of tea with milk, very hot, without saucers, with endless refills.

And finally in the restaurant, which has been rearranged during the night with the tables set up as if it were a classroom, thirty other men, who also look poor, with beards, are listening to a man of military bearing give a lecture.

The truth, I'm starting to realize, is that I have fallen into—or more importantly Daniel Pearl fell into—an unusual hotel, a refuge for visiting Kashmiri militants and fighters when they're in Rawalpindi.

The truth—I learn in the hours that follow when I find my local source—is that Kashmiri fighters get rooms at a discount (those rooms on the third and fourth floors, in fact) and free tea in the morning.

The truth—from the same source—is that, besides these fighters and fierce peasants who come here seeking a bit of warmth, other much more important men are regulars here, men who have in common a close tie to the country's special services: prominent advocates of the Kashmiri cause, like the journalist from Jammu, Ved Bhasim, or the pro-Pakistani Indian politician Bzaz; Abdul Ghani Lone, another notorious Kashmiri, who housed the guests to his son Sajjad's wedding here; all the big jihadist leaders, who, until the recent wave of restrictions, would organize their press conferences here, with the blessing of the ISI.

In short, the place Omar chose for his first meeting with Pearl is a place where the Pakistani secret services are at home.

The hotel he chose for their first encounter was not in fact an ordinary hotel, but rather one controlled, almost managed, by the ISI.

There are three hotels of this kind in Pakistan. Surely there are others. But I spotted at least three: the Sangam in Mazzafarabad; the Margalla, in Islamabad, two kilometers past the French embassy on the Serena road; and the Hotel Akbar, which I discovered belongs, officially, to a Kashmiri named Chaudhary Akbar but which is one of the ISI's locations in Rawalpindi.

Everything converges.

From the organization of the crime to the biography of its authors, from Omar's past to that of certain of his henchmen, from India to Pakistan, from Lahore to Islamabad, from backstage at the plane hijacking in Kandahar to backstage at the Hotel Akbar, everything points to the direct and close involvement of the Pakistani secret service.

No more psychology, at this point.

Yes, Mariane was right, at this level you can no longer see how analyzing the psychology, the moods, of Omar could have any effect on the obvious reality.

Daniel Pearl was kidnapped and then murdered by Islamist groups who were manipulated by a single fringe group of the secret service—the most radical, the most violent, the most anti-American of the factions fighting for control of the services; but how can it be denied that this faction behaved, from the beginning to the end of the affair, as if it were perfectly at home in Musharraf's Pakistan?

This crime was not petty, a murder for nothing, an uncontrolled act of fundamentalist fanatics—it's a crime of state, intended and authorized, whether we like it or not, by the state of Pakistan. As Aldo Moro, to quote him again, said in his tragic letter to his wife Noretta, in which he announced to the likes of Cossiga, Zaccagnini and Zizola that his blood would fall on them, it's a "state massacre." The paradox, of course, is that it implicates a country which is a friend to the United States and the West, an ally in the fight to the death against the "Axis of Evil," in other words, a full-fledged member of the antiterrorist coalition.

That's the provisional conclusion of this book, in October 2002.

At this stage of the investigation, that's my first and terrifying conclusion.

PART FOUR
AL-QAIDA

CHAPTER 1 RETURN TO THE HOUSE
OF THE CRIME

But that's not all.

I was far from finished being surprised.

And I had yet to discover the most extraordinary, and edifying, aspect of the story.

It is now November 2002.

I am, again, back in Pakistan.

This time I'm here officially, with a visa, a stamp, I go through the whole business: visit to the ambassador in Paris, meeting in Islamabad with the Minister of the Interior, to whom I have to show at least part of my hand—"I am writing a novel about the death of Daniel Pearl... yes, yes, don't worry, a novel... we're like that, in France, we produce works of imagination based on reality...."

The idea is in fact to see as many officials as possible.

As soon as I arrived, I asked to see everybody who had any knowledge of the case, from Musharraf to the fourteenth sergeant of the Lahore police force.

Your version, Sir?

What are your reasons for thinking that Omar might be an Indian agent?

Can you show me the transcripts of his interrogations? The Indians did—are you going to do less than the Indians?

Why don't you extradite him to the United States? Did they demand him as forcibly as they say they did? Which of you is the more reticent to extradite him?

So, I'm waiting for appointments. And while I wait quietly, I decide, again with Abdul, to revisit some of the obscure areas of my earlier investigations, particularly the very beginning, the point of departure—I decide, without really knowing why, to visit again the farm where the body of Daniel Pearl was found. I decide, in fact, to seek out a character whom the Pakistani press had talked about a great deal at first, but who seems to have been completely forgotten since: the owner of the land, the house, and the entire complex where the drama took place—the millionaire Saud Memon.

Who is Saud Memon?

Why do the terrorists end up there, at his house?

To what degree is he involved in the logistics of the crime?

And how come no one, either in Pakistan or anywhere else, seems to be interested in getting his testimony?

First surprise: Saud Memon is not to be found.

Access to Gulzar e-Hijri having been denied to me this time, I ask Abdul to take a casual look around—the place, he tells me, is in exactly the same state as when I was there in May. Neither Memon nor any other member of his family has reappeared since. The big house on the edge of the farm is empty, abandoned—shutters closed, big, rusty padlock on the iron gate, and the front garden overgrown.

Then, I obtain from the Sindh police headquarters the interrogation transcripts of Memon's brother-in-law, who teaches at the neighboring *madrasa*, and of his brothers—there are three—all arrested by the Rangers at the end of May, in their house in Nazimabad. None of them seems to have the vaguest idea where Saud could be now; despite the harsh methods I know are customary in these circumstances, nothing further has been extracted from them than "no, we know nothing, we haven't seen Saud since last May, maybe he's in Dubai, or Ryad, or Sanaa, or maybe even London, he has so many friends in the world, you know, so many friends...." I have in front of me the statements made by all and sundry, as well as the text of the Supreme Court appeal lodged by Najama Mehmood, wife of one of the brothers, protesting the "illegal detention" of her husband—and I could be wrong, but I find in every single one of them a tone of sincerity in their way of protesting that the man has disappeared.

I go to Peshawar, a city of three and half million inhabitants connected to the famous tribal zones that are like a sieve between Pakistan and Afghanistan and which, for all practical purposes, elude the control of the central powers. I was told that Memon was hiding not far from there, in a *madrasa* in the province of North Waziristan. A professor from the *madrasa* next door to his home told Abdul: "This Pearl affair was an ordeal for him. Imagine! It all took place on the Memon clan's land, and therefore you could even say under his roof, so he's devastated. And because he's devastated, he wanted to get some distance, to forget, to be forgotten...." But no one in Peshawar has the slightest idea of where he is. Nowhere did I find any evidence of his passage. Not a trace of the billionaire stricken with remorse and commending his soul to God, which is the idea that is being promoted. (Meanwhile, it's true that bin Laden himself seems to have succeeded in entering the city, in the second week of December 2001, with a guard of fifty men without, apparently, attracting the attention of the authorities.)

So here's a man about whom you can say, at the very least, that his name is known in Karachi. Here's a personage whose influence is great—the Memon clan, everyone assures me, rules a part of the Punjabi business world—and everyone knows of their comings and goings and what they're up to. Here's an entrepreneur who personally manages—as does Omar Sheikh's father—a clothing export company that is entirely aboveboard and that has a warehouse in another building at Gulzar e-Hijri, very close to the farmhouse where the murder took place. That man has disappeared. He has vanished into thin air with wives and children. He's faded into the scenery like one of the minor thugs: like Mussadiq and Abdul Samat, the two unidentified members of the detention cell; like Hyder, a.k.a. Mansur Hasnain, who made the last two telephone calls on the afternoon of the 23rd, and whose family, we recall, told the police that he had just been "infiltrated into the Jammu Kashmir"; like Arif, a.k.a. Hashim Qader, supposedly off to the Afghan front, leaving the household in Bahawalpur in mourning, bereaved....

Another surprise.

I'm in the office of one of the deputies of the Minister of the Interior of Sindh.

He is a tall man, vain, all uniform and moustache, who looks at me suspiciously and seems very concerned about the honor of his police force.

"Tell me, Mr. Chief of Police, about the famous antiterrorist operation conducted by your men last September 11, at the end of which you arrested ten Yemenis, including Ramzi bin al-Shibh. Tell me how the Rangers came to be outside the Defence building that morning. Tell me about the raid and the surrender of the terrorists. Tell me how all that was organized—did the Americans help you? Was it their agents who had tracked down Ramzi and his gang? Their satellite systems for intercepting and wiretapping? The CIA? FBI?

And him, vexed:

"Why always the Americans? Do you think we're not capable of conducting our own antiterrorist operations? As it happens, this affair had nothing to do with the CIA. It was Pakistani intelligence sources that did the preliminary groundwork. Here, listen . . . ."

And he tells me how everything started two days earlier in the Badurabad district when they broke up a fake-ID ring involved in the exfiltration of al-Qaida members. How, from there, they followed the trail of a smuggler who dealt not only in fake documents, but also in the export of illegal workers to Ryad—children from Dacca to be used as jockeys for the camel races of Dubai. He specialized, last but not least, in getting al-Qaida fighters out of the country to Yemen, and other countries of the Middle East. That man, the Minister's deputy told me, was the real target of the antiterrorist raid on the 11th—he's the one, even more than Ramzi bin al-Shibh or the flashy Khalid Sheikh Mohammed, that we wanted to capture; his name is "Mr. M.," and Mr. M. is none other than... Saud Memon.

I realize that this version of events does not coincide with my thesis.

It exonerates, if I can put it that way, Yosri Fouda, the Al-Jazeera journalist, by making his interview—or at least the timing of its airing—no longer the catalyst for the Rangers' decision to conduct the raid.

It allows one to imagine, instead of the comedy I had envisioned, an investigation, a real one, with suspicion, witnesses, prolonged shadowing of the suspects, multiple phases, and at the end of the road, the final raid on the al-Qaida hideout.

But for the moment, that's not the crux of the matter.

The crux is that Memon, in all likelihood, is far from being an honest and naïve merchant whose good faith has been taken advantage of by a gang of terrorists squatting on one of his properties.

The important thing is that we have here a man with two faces, much more complex and mysterious than his peers in the Karachi Chamber of Commerce suspect. On one hand, the innocent importer-exporter of textiles, serving as cover—and on the other, a darker and more troubling character, which leads one to believe that it is not by chance nor unbeknownst to him that a gang of jihadists took up residence on his property to murder Daniel Pearl.

Need I add Abdul's discovery when he returned to the Gulzar e-Hijri farm? The property, like a number of its neighboring properties, had been bought fifteen years earlier, taking advantage of legislation that allows tax breaks for "industrial and commercial profits reinvested into agriculture." Except that not the slightest sign of an agricultural project was ever seen there. Agricultural activity on the property, according to witnesses, never went beyond the bamboo and acacias that grew wild. And Memon seems to have become very quickly involved in other, infinitely less legitimate, missions. Starting with this one, in fact, long before Pearl: serving kidnappers and hosting prisoners in need of a prison. *Specialité de la maison.* Premises for rent, furnished and equipped, for needy jihadists. Memon as a dealer in abduction. Amateurs need not apply. A millionaire at the heart of the Islamist murder industry in Karachi.

And the third and last surprise: the al-Rashid Trust, of which Memon is one of the administrators, and which is tied to the property, although I don't know from what angle.

In theory, it's quite clear.

Al-Rashid is a Pakistani organization that has taken on the task of helping Muslims in need all over the world.

There's the All-Party Hurriyat Conference, the United Jihad Council, the Markaz al-Dawah al-Irshad with headquarters in Lahore. There are a number of more or less well-known and powerful charities. And then there is al-Rashid, the most important of these NGOs that collect from all over the country the famous "*zakat*" or "Islamic tax," which is then redistributed to great and noble causes of Muslim human-rights: Kosovo, where the organization apparently gave away the equivalent of $35,000 in 2002; Kashmir, its burning obligation; Chechnya, where, indignant over the systematic embezzlement of funds provided by the UN, al-Rashid used its own networks to bring in $750,000 worth of food and medical supplies over two years; Afghanistan, where for the annual cost of $4 million, it prides itself on running a network of bakeries all over the country, capable of providing bread daily to 50,000 men, women and children. And that's not including the sewing machines for war widows, the computer training centers for Kandahar youth, the ultramodern clinics set up in Ghazni, Kandahar and Kabul, or, in Pakistan itself, the free distribution of sheep for the Aïd holiday. Is not charity the first duty of the pilgrim on the path to God?

The problem is that when you dig a little—as I did by going to the headquarters of the charity in Rawalpindi, and examining its books, and questioning one of its "volunteers"—you discover some very troubling details.

The date the Trust was set up, for example: 1996. Which is when the Taliban come to power.

The context of its activities. The money, in Chechnya, is given to Sheikh Omer Bin Ismail Dawood, who is one of the fundamentalist chieftains opposed to the authority of Maskadov. In Kashmir, it goes to terrorist organizations and the most fanatical and criminal combatants. And, as for the bread distribution in Afghanistan, the only thing that isn't mentioned in the Trust's annual report is the fact that the withdrawal of the World Food Program and the subsequent takeover of its 155 bakeries in 2000 and 2001 was linked to the prohibition against women working. At the time, it was the height of the confrontation between Western NGOs and the Taliban authorities, and the NGO's policy was to say "ease up on the status of women, let them work, and we'll maintain aid." The fact that the Trust took over the bakeries from the WFP was a political gesture that supported the position, the ideology, of the Taliban.

Its premises. The al-Rashid Trust, like all the big NGOs, has headquarters, offices, warehouses, and just simple addresses where donors are invited to send their money. But something else that goes unmentioned—yet is supported by a 22 November ad in the newspaper *Zarb-e-Momin*, for example, detailing where to send donations for "Afghan victims of U.S. terrorism"—is that in a lot of medium-sized cities, such as Mansehra, Mingora, and Chenabnagar, or even in the really big cities such as Lahore, Rawalpindi or Jalalabad in Afghanistan, the Trust shares its offices (and therefore probably its staff, its fund raising structure, and even its bank accounts) with a party, the Jaish e-Mohammed, whose humanitarian mission is not so obvious. What the report is careful to avoid saying is that, like a number of Islamic NGOs whose do-gooder mission is often only a cover (although it's rare to have blatant proof, as it in the newspaper ad), the al-Rashid Trust has links with a terrorist organization, which itself is linked to al-Qaida. These links are not merely ideological but structural, forged in organizational and financial logic. The Trust claims that these links were severed the day after September 11. The "volunteer" I speak to even gives me the account numbers and the names on the Jaish accounts at the Allied Bank in the Binori district of Karachi. Except there is the aforementioned issue of the *Zarb-e-Momin* with their joint advertisement—send your donations... cut along the dotted line... Jaish and al-Rashid, common cause and same struggle.

Its newspapers. Al-Rashid has newspapers, real ones. A daily in Urdu, *Islam*. And a weekly, the *Zarb-e-Momin*, which is also published in Urdu, every Friday in two versions, paper and internet, and whose circulation, in Pakistan and Afghanistan combined, adds up to 150,000 copies for the paper edition alone. (Another version comes out in English with the title *Dharb-el-Momin*.) It so happens that *Zarb-e-Momin*, until 2000, was the central organ of the Taliban leaders. Since their fall, it has become one of the outlets—along with *Al-Hilal*, which is more linked to the Harkat ul-Mujahideen, and the monthly *Majallah al-*

Daawa—for all the hacks who are to some degree nostalgic for the black order the newspaper advocated. And it's in *Zarb-e-Momin*, finally—and not, for instance, in the bimonthly *Jaish e-Mohammad*, supposedly the official paper of the party—that a man like Masood Azhar, boss of the Jaish, Omar's mentor, and high dignitary in the assassins' sect, has continually published his prison writings for the last eight years. What does this have to do with humanitarian aid? Is it the role of an NGO to publish, every Friday, appeals to murder Jews, Hindus, Christians, Westerners?

Its finances. They are opaque, naturally. They are opaque neither more nor less than those of most NGOs, Islamist or not, and it is therefore very difficult to calculate how much of its resources come from individuals or states, from Pakistan or some country in the Middle East, from a big private donor in South Africa or Indonesia. But several things are certain. Here's one: it is the al-Rashid Trust, on the strength of its international contacts and also, I imagine, its competence in these fields, that manages the foreign holdings of a certain number of terrorist organizations, such as the Jaish or the Lashkar e-Toiba. Here's another: until November 2001, that is to say until the fall of the Taliban, the Trust systematically shared bank accounts in the Afghan branches of the Pakistani Habib Bank with another NGO, the Wafa Khairia, which has the distinction of having been founded by Osama bin Laden himself, as a sign of gratitude for the hospitality offered to him by Mullah Omar and his relatives. A charitable organization functioning as a banker for criminals? People who swear that all they care about is caring for the dispossessed, who are themselves associated with one of the al-Qaida organizations? Curiouser and curiouser....

And then, even more curious, and confusing to boot, this singular mix: in 2000–2001 al-Rashid organizes military training sessions in Afghanistan; its founder Rashid Ahmed holds active positions in the leadership of three terrorist groups, the Harkat ul-Mujahideen, the Edara ul-Rashid, and of course the Jaish, all involved in terrorist actions in both Kashmir, and, increasingly, in Pakistan itself; and it's Rashid Ahmed who appoints Masood Azhar "emir" of the Taliban in Kashmir and thereby launches his career; it's Rashid Ahmed yet again who, at the beginning of 2000, promises in the Trust's newspaper, a 2 million rupee reward to whomever can furnish proof that he has managed to "send to hell" an infidel guilty of killing a martyr. And I mention, only as a reminder, the revelations of the *Washington Times* on 6 November 2001, stating that the Trust had been for years in the middle of a gigantic arms-smuggling operation benefitting the Taliban: light or medium-weight arms arriving as contraband in the Karachi port, concealed under the tarpaulins on trucks meant to be carrying flour and food aid, and then speeding to Quetta and Kandahar, where they were distributed to the international militias of Allah's army—humanitarian aid as the fuel for paramilitary activities.

For me, it is obvious: Al-Rashid is a cog in the al-Qaida machine.

Far from being helped, and financed, by al-Qaida, al-Rashid instead finances the terrorist organization itself through its collection network.

And that is the fact that we must accept: Daniel Pearl was tortured and murdered in a house belonging to a fake charity organization that serves as a mask for Osama bin Laden.

CHAPTER 2 THE MOSQUE OF THE TALIBAN

The "seminary" of Binori Town.

The grand *madrasa*, the heart of Sunni and, in particular, Deobandi, spirituality, where some of the Taliban dignitaries were educated and where, we remember, Omar spent one of his last nights before the kidnapping.

For a long time now, I've wanted to go inside.

I requested permission through the embassy—rejected.

From the police—rejected as well. The *madrasa*, they told me, is surrounded by the minority Shiite neighborhood of Karachi, which is engaged in open war against the Sunnis. So there are security problems, the risk of deadly assault. Wasn't it right there in the heart of the city, at the corner of Jamshed and Jinnah Roads, that Maulana Habibullah Mukhtar, the rector of the mosque, was shot point blank with four companions by a motorcycle squad of Shiite extremists a few years ago?

I tried to simply walk in, like a tourist coming to admire the place and passing by the adjoining grand mosque—turned back.

Finally, I talked to Abdul about it—don't even think about it! Very restricted place! As far as I know, no Western journalist has ever gone inside! You have to be Pakistani, know a teacher, work for an Urdu paper with jihadist tendencies, or, even better, go through the bureau of donations—otherwise, it's forbidden.

289

In short, I had finally given up. Every time I passed by, I was reduced to speculating about the mysterious world hidden behind the high walls, the barred doors, and the rust-colored iron grilles, and about Omar's reasons for going inside there twice before the crime. That is, until the morning of 24 November, the day of the great Shiite demonstration commemorating the death of the fourth caliph Ali, when, paradoxically, the riot inspired by this occasion nearly every year in this part of town gave me the opportunity I had been waiting for.

The wave of the faithful surges along Jamshed Road. The merchants have all lowered their security gates. Cordons of policemen, rifles at their sides, are keeping a watchful eye all along the avenue. There are tires burning on the sidewalks. The most fanatic of the participants are lacerating their faces and torsos, as is often the case at Shiite mass demonstrations. The others, long-haired dervishes with wild, bloodshot eyes, are shouting murderous epithets at their Sunni neighbors, then suddenly, to a man, they stop and begin chanting incoherent litanies full of, I am told, blood, vengeance, and martyrdom. My car is blocked. The mob, realizing that I am a foreigner, begins to violently rock the vehicle. One man, the victim of his own frenzied slogans, foaming at the mouth, his face bathed in sweat, brandishes a rock at the windshield. And so I get out. On the pretext of the mounting violence, I slip away from my driver, Abdul, and the official minder the ministry insisted on assigning me in light of the mood of the day. I thread my way through the crowd to the cross street, Gokal Street. In the crush, waving my expired diplomatic passport, I ask for passage through the cordon of terribly nervous policemen who are trying to block the way between the demonstrators and a hundred or so Sunnis who have just emerged from the *madrasa*, fists raised defiantly, shouting their own anti-Shiite slogans. The police let me pass and, without even knowing where I'm headed, I end up right at a door on the south side of the *madrasa*.

"What do you want?" asks the orderly, a consumptive-looking little man with a bit of a goiter, huge eyes in his moon face looking me up and down with distrust.

Behind him, in the interior courtyard, I see a group of armed men, mullahs, to judge by their turbans. Better armed, actually, than the policemen—strange for a *madrasa*....

"I am a French diplomat," I say, holding out my passport and one of the calling cards I had printed, quite illegally, at the time of my Afghan mission. "Bernard-Henri Lévy," it reads, "Special Representative of the French President."

"I am a diplomat, and I would like to see the Mufti Nizamuddin Shamzai, the rector of the seminary."

The man examines the card. Leafs through the passport. Looks at me. Goes back to the passport. Behind me, a loud speaker squawks: "Don't take the law into your own hands, stay in the mosque." The chief of the patrol of mullahs advances towards me, Kalashnikov in hand, ready to intervene. I'm expecting them to throw me out at any moment—"Diplomat or not, infidels are not allowed here.... You can just go back and rub elbows with those bastard Shiite demonstrators...." But, is it the passport? The calling card? The fact that I don't introduce myself as a journalist? The riot? Whatever it is, the little orderly motions for me to follow him into the interior courtyard, which is vaster than I had imagined, and a group of the faithful gawk at me. From there into a waiting room, empty except for some rope matting, and a moped in one corner.

"Have a seat," says the little orderly, "I'll be back."

And off he goes, my passport in hand, shuffling along with a sort of Chaplinesque gait, while the apprentice *ulémas* peer through the window to look at me. Most of them are very young, with scraggly adolescent beards, thrilled to see a foreigner, crowding and elbowing each other, bursting out laughing, with their black and red *keffiehs* on their shoulders. They look like Yemenis.

The man comes back after about five minutes. Grave. Self-conscious. "Very honor-due-to-our-foreign-guest."

"Mufti Nizamuddin Shamzai cannot receive you. Nor Doctor Abdul Razzak Sikandar. But one of the doctor's assistants is here. He will see you."

As extraordinary as it seems, my strategy has worked. And we're off again, one following the other, he with his penguin waddle and me opening my eyes wide, inside the Forbidden City of Karachi.

We take a left turn and find ourselves—inside the *madrasa*—behind a string of little stores: an Eskimo ice cream booth, "Master Cakes" bakery, and at the end, the "Café Jamia," which opens onto Jamshed. There, a sort of canteen, ill-lit and windowless, where several dozen poor devils, apparently students, are squeezed in together around big plates of rice; the little orderly presents me to an older man, a bearded colossus, who is seated with them.

We go back the way we came, down a poorly paved alley that opens out on the left onto a row of rooms, apparently class-rooms—a ground floor, then a first story painted hot pink with a wooden latticework that allows a glimpse of a sort of fog inside. What is the source of this fog? I don't know. But it gives the scene a ghostly quality. Young people, who obviously come from all over the Arab-Muslim world, are busy studying there: Yemenis, again, but also Asians and Afghans, Pakistanis of course, Uzbeks, darker-skinned Sudanese, and, at the back of one of the rooms, all alone, his eyes lowered, a very pale man with long grey hair who seems to be European.

I make a mental note that I'm moving away from the actual mosque, which is on the left and slightly raised, its dome sepa-rating the two wings.

Then there's a courtyard on the right, planted with scraggly trees, with a fountain, a dry, mildewy basin, finely carved columns that are half destroyed, signs in Arabic, a loudspeaker, some mopeds parked against a wall, a few 4x4s (probably "company" cars reserved for *madrasa* dignitaries), and another room, in a recess, where I can see no one except, I think, another Westerner.

At the end of the alley, another larger, cloisterlike room with inscriptions carved around the frieze of the walls, undoubtedly verses of the Koran, where I briefly catch a glimpse of a giant, vividly colored portrait, stylised and naïve, of a mujahid, hung on the wall facing the door and surrounded by a greenish light the source of which I again cannot see, and bearing a curious resemblance to bin Laden.

And then, right across from me, the office area (admissions, registration, donations, and administration for this city within the city which is the Binori Town *madrasa*) and housing for students and professors. Some of these are dilapidated blocks, like the unfinished constructions, with the structural steel beams exposed, that I have often seen in the Maghreb and the Middle East. And some of them are small houses of two or three stories, more cheerful, with an interior courtyard and, upstairs, rows of rooms that open out on to balconies.

With the exception of the bin Laden cloister, what is striking is the rustic quality of the place—rooms lacking shadows or mystery, naked ceilings, laundry drying on the railings of the balconies.

It's a series of lanes and courtyards that all look alike, giving the impression of a maze, a real labyrinth, where I would be hard pressed to find the path myself if I had to escape.

And then, of course, there's the crowd of faithful, sitting on the grass, walking in single file or hand in hand, cooling off outside their rooms on the balconies. Some really look like students, meditative, concentrating and, contrary to those I ran into a while ago, paying no attention to me whatsoever. Others look like ruffian soldiers, dressed in fatigues, with long hair, a harsh eye, and the ruddy, tanned complexion of Kashmiri montagnards. I can count a few, at least five, who are armed and don't hide it—another bizarre element of this strange "seminary" where it seems natural to walk around carrying a Kalashnikov. They say there are 3,500 boarders in Binori Town. My rough guess is that there are many more. And another thing is striking: the silence. Or rather, not exactly silence; people talk, but softly, in muffled voices, and the result is a slight, dull, continuous background noise, as though their voices were incapable of individual identity.

"I don't see any children," I say, both to say something and to slow the pace so that I can see more. "Aren't *madrasas* supposed to be for children?"

The colossus looks back at me, wary. And, maintaining his pace while giving a nod of recognition to a squad of *ulémas* he mutters, in good English, "Ask the Doctor. I'm not authorized to answer you."

"What do they teach here, then? Can you at least tell me what kind of teaching goes on in this *madrasa*?"

"The Koran," he says, this time without turning around, "Just like everywhere, we teach the Koran."

"All right. But what else besides the Koran?"

He stops. He seems both offended and appalled by the question, so he stops to reply to me.

"I don't understand your question."

"Not everything is in the Koran, as far as I know."

"No. There are the Hadith, the sayings of the Prophet."

"And then?"

"What do you mean, 'and then'? What more do you want besides the Koran and the Hadith?"

He seems irritated this time. His face, his beard, are shaking with anger. He's probably trying to understand why the hell anyone let a fellow who's capable of asking you if there are other books besides the Koran into such a place. I take advantage of the pause to sneak a look inside two more rooms whose doors are ajar. In one, as if in answer to the question I just asked, a circle of imams—real imams, except that they're young and clean-shaven. These are junior imams. In the other room, ten men—adults this time—sitting at wooden school desks, wearing long, white robes, black jackets, and, on their heads, white or red-and-white *ghutras* held in place by the traditional double band of the Bedouins and the Saudis. And, like their guns, which clash with the image one has of a place of fundamentalist worship, I'm pretty sure I see computers on the desks.

"What do you know about the Koran?" he goads me suspiciously, as though testing me.

"I know, more or less, what French people know about it."

This time it's too much. He shrugs his shoulders; obviously the absurdity of the Koran in French is beyond him.

"You are," he says simply, "at Jame'a Uloom ul-Islameya Binori Town—the Islamic University of Binori Town."

And, as though this response makes any further discussion unnecessary, he continues on the path towards a last courtyard, this one deserted and quite silent, with just a muffled, faraway sound, like a groan, or a scraping, or maybe a slow jig. A very old, hoary imam, his bony head like that of a sad-eyed dog, deep wrinkles beneath the cheekbones of his chapped face, waits there and takes me in hand. We go up a rather steep staircase, where he must grip a railing recessed into the wall, down a gallery crammed with closed boxes, and finally, into a small room much like the others, where Doctor Abdul Razzak Sikandar's assistant awaits, sitting on the ground, steeped in piety.

Fiftyish. Black beard, like the colossus. Full *djellaba* of immaculate white, like the Saudis, earlier. On his head, a skullcap. A low, melodious voice and quiet, grey eyes. A great deal of presence. Twenty or so books, bound in blood red, line a shelf on the wall behind him. In front of him, on a wooden stand inlaid with mother-of-pearl, the Koran, and right next to it, my card.

"You are French?" he begins, without looking at me.

I nod modestly.

"France is generous with us. We receive donations from all over the world, but also from France. You have many good Muslims."

Long silence. I don't dare ask him what kind of donations he is talking about.

"And your religion?"

No matter what, they always pull this one on me, but I never seem to get used to it. I can never repress a sense of revulsion, a nausea, but more than ever, the thing here is not to show it.

"Atheist. In France, there are many of us of the atheist religion."

He makes a face.

"You know that non-Muslims are forbidden to enter the madrasa."

"Yes, but atheists...."

"It's true. The rule applies to Jews and Crusaders."

And then, in a lower tone, as if he were talking to himself, eyes still fixed on the stand (the Koran? my card?): "But mind you, don't go saying the Pakistanis don't like the Christians. It's not true. Not only have we nothing against the Christians in principle, but we believe that Jesus Christ is not dead, that he was taken bodily into heaven by Allah, peace be upon Him, and that he will soon return to accompany the army of Allah."

He shrugs his shoulders and then, as though it were a butterfly, or something vaguely disgusting, cautiously takes my card with the tips of his fingers. I sense a note of distrust in his tone—maybe the name Lévy makes him stop and think, but perhaps I'm mistaken....

"And you are the representative of the French government?"

I nod yes.

"Well, tell your president that we, the Pakistanis, appreciate the French position. Give him our apologies, as well. Tell him the Pakistani people are sorry for the recent attacks that caused the death of Frenchmen who were here to help our country."

In plain language he is admitting guilt. I cannot help thinking that when you excuse yourself, you accuse yourself. It is hard to say more clearly that the Islamists in general—and perhaps those of Binori Town in particular—are behind the recent wave of anti-Western attacks, especially the one at the Sheraton. All the more so, since he adds, as though reading my thoughts:

"Tell your president it was a mistake.... A very unfortunate mistake.... The people who did that honestly believed that those were Americans."

"Should I understand this to mean, honorable mullah, that you know who is behind the suicide bombing at the Sheraton?"

He doesn't hesitate a second.

"Wicked people. People we strenuously condemn. Islam is a religion of peace."

"And the organizers of the attack, the people who have done so much harm to my country, would they be rejected if they came here?"

"Ah, no! We reject no one. All men are our brothers."

"And bin Laden? A little while ago, in passing, I saw a portrait of bin Laden. Has he come here? Would you welcome him if he did?"

He frowns. And for the first time, he looks in my direction—but it's a blank stare that seems to look beyond me.

"Osama is just a Muslim. No one needs to know whether or not he has come here. Do not ask this question, you are not entitled to."

"All the same, in Islamabad people told me that the grand mufti of your madrasa, Nizamuddin Shamzai, attended the marriage of one of bin Laden's sons last year with the mufti Jamil. Is that possible?"

"Do not ask this question," he repeats, raising his voice. "You are not entitled."

I know that during the American bombing of Afghanistan, this holy man, Nizamuddin Shamzai, personally supervised the recruiting of volunteers—starting with his own two sons—who crossed the frontier to fight beside the Taliban.

I know that in August, before September 11, when the Americans were putting pressure on Pakistan to send the foreign fighters of al-Qaida back to their own countries, in order to prevent this "betrayal," he personally threatened the Minister of the Interior with the rage of Allah and his followers.

And I know of the innumerable calls for jihad emanating from Binori, where this man the Mullah Omar considered his guru—Nizamussin Shamzai, again—cursed the Americans, the Indians, the Jews, and Westerners in general. Abdul translated one of his fatwas for me. It was from 1999, printed in *Jasrat*, the Urdu daily of Harkat, and in it, he said it was permissible to "kill and plunder the Americans, and to enslave their women."

But Doctor Abdul Razzak Sikandar's assistant stares at me now, and a flicker of hostility that wasn't there before prompts me to compromise.

"If I'm asking you this question, it's only in relation to what you told me: Islam is a religion of peace."

"That's true," he replies, a little more softly.

"Which means that, according to you, Osama is a man of peace?"

"Osama, I repeat, is a good Muslim. He is our brother in Islam. He fears no one but Allah. He may have made mistakes. But when he distinguishes between dar al-islam (the home of peace), which unites all the Muslims of the world, and dar al-harb (the home of war), which encompasses all the rest, he is right; that is our position."

"All right. But the result, in concrete terms, is what? Man of peace or man of war?"

He's irritated again. Again the inquisitive look, a restrained anger in in the voice. Behind the doctor lurks the jihadist.

"War against the infidels is not war, it is a duty. Since the American attack in Saudi Arabia, and then in Afghanistan, it is the duty of the Muslims of the world to support the jihad against America and the Jews."

"Why the Jews?"

Stunned, this time. Like the mullah earlier on, he seems dumbfounded by the question. He takes up my card again. He puts it down. He places his hand on the Koran, as though, unsettled, it is only through contact with the book that he will find the strength to respond.

"Because they are the true terrorists. And because they lead their crusade on the soil of Palestine and Afghanistan. Zionist agents have infiltrated even here, in Pakistan. Why do you think the government accepts their orders? It should place its confidence in God. But it accepts orders from the Jews."

Am I going to bring up my questions now? Do I dare? I have a feeling I've almost said too much, that the interview is drawing to a close. So I plunge in.

"Is that why they killed the American journalist Daniel Pearl?

Because he was a Jew? Do you have an opinion about this affair, which has attracted a lot of attention in my country?"

Just mentioning the name Pearl sets off a very strange reaction. First he curls up, pulling his head down between his shoulders, clenching his fists and drawing in his elbows as though he were about to face an agressor and wanted to reduce the target area. Then he straightens up, unfolding his big body, nearly rising, and extends his arms in my direction—the gesture of a preacher or of someone preparing to strike. It's funny, I think, seeing him suddenly so tall, towering over me—the Pakistani activists seem enormous, full of themselves, self-satisfied, nothing like the raw-boned desperate killers I'd seen in Afghanistan.

"We have no opinion!" he finally utters in an oddly solemn voice. "We do not think anything about the death of this journalist! Islam is a religion of peace. The Pakistanis are a people of peace."

And with that, he signals to the old imam, who has been standing in a corner of the room during the entire interview without my noticing him. It's time to take me back.

On the way back I see a large trap door, half hidden by a bush, which I suppose leads to an underground passage.

I catch a glimpse of a room my guide identifies with pride as the *madrasa*'s library: two sets of metal shelves going halfway up the wall, both half-empty.

I pass by an elaborately tiled prayer room, where two large portraits preside, no doubt of Allama Yusuf Binori and Maulana Mufti Mohammed, founders of the seminary.

In another room, I see a portrait of Juma Namangani, the former Red Army soldier who became the head of the "Islamic

Movement of Uzbekistan," then commander-in-chief of the Arab battalion of al-Qaida before he was killed in the American bombing of Kunduz in November 2001.

Portraits in a *madrasa*?

In a place where the representation of a human face should be considered profanation?

But that's not the least of the surprises this strange visit had in store for me.

As earlier, with regard to the portrait of bin Laden, I'm dying to ask how these images could be considered compatible with the prohibition of representation.

But I prefer to remain silent.

I have only one pressing need, to get out of this place and go back to the Shiite riots in the street, the wailing flood of bloody and hysterical faithful whose threats seem almost reassuring when you are emerging from the house of the Devil.

Later that day, I ask the same questions to other people, elsewhere in the city. For example, the station chief of a Western intelligence agency, who fills me in on some of the missing pieces.

It was here in Binori Town, early in 2000, that Masood Azhar and the Mufti Nizamuddin Shamzai, the mosque's reigning holy man whom I was unable to meet, announced the foundation of the Jaish e-Mohammed. Here, in the presence of—and with the blessing of—the country's most respected *ulémas*, the organization that would furnish the elite battalions of al-Qaida was baptised.

A month later, in March, a quarrel broke out between Azhar and Fazlur Rahman Khalil, the man who had, while Azhar was in an Indian prison, risen in the hierarchy of Harkat ul-Mujahideen and usurped control of the organisation. As Jaish is a splinter group of the Harkat, to whom should the offices, the fleet of 4x4s, the arms and the safe-houses belong? The deep conflict inflamed the Islamist movement of Karachi. Once again, it was at Binori Town, under the authority of the same Nizamuddin Shamzai, that the appointed scholars gathered to arbitrate the question and to arrive at a *harkam*. They decided the Harkat should retain everything and pay financial compensation to the Jaish. Binori as a tribunal! Binori as the arbitration court for the internal conflicts of the al-Qaida conglomerate!

In October, when the Americans launched their political and military offensive, word circulated around Karachi of a possible inclusion of the Jaish on the American's list of terrorist groups. Once again, Nizamuddin Shamzai rose to the defense of the organization—from his base at Binori, he organized a new group, the Tehrik al-Furqan, of which he immediately assumed leadership, to replace the threatened group, taking over its financial assets, its bank accounts, its files and its activities. Binori—the linchpin of politico-financial trafficking... the spiritual head of one of the world's largest seminaries transformed into a front for an association of assassins.

After the fall of Kabul in November, bin Laden's defeated troops fled Afghanistan, and the survivors of Pakistani paramilitary groups tried to escape the crossfire of the Northern Alliance and the American bombers. Some of them (members of Harkat ul-Mujahideen and Harkat ul-Jihad al-Islam) retreated to Kashmir. Others (like the Lashkar e-Toïba), headed for hideouts in the tribal zones of the North, at Gilgit and Baltistan. But the most radical, Lashkar i-Janghvi, Jaish, and a Harkat subgroup, the Harkat ul-Mujahideen al-Almi-Universal, found refuge in Karachi, and, in particular at Binori. Are they still there? Did I pass an hour in the sanctuary of bin Laden's lost soldiers? Is that what the portraits I saw meant?

The famous audiocassette of 12 November 2002—in which bin Laden spoke of the terrorist attacks in Djerba, Yemen, Kuwait, Bali, and Moscow, and called for new actions not only against U.S. President Bush, but also his European, Canadian, and Australian allies—originated at Binori, and was sent from there through Bangladesh to the Qatar television station of Al Jazeera. A recording studio in a mosque? Binori transformed into a logistics base for al-Qaida propaganda? Yes! This is the hypothesis of the American, British, and Indian intelligence services. They don't know what Bangladesh has to do with it, or to what degree ISI is involved in the operation. But they have no doubt whatsoever that the cassette was put together here, in the depths of the terrorist Vatican.

Finally, Osama bin Laden himself is said to have stayed at Binori on several occasions. The most-wanted terrorist on earth, global Public Enemy Number One, the man worth $25 million or more, this shadowy character who may or may not be alive, or who may survive only as a legend, is said to have stayed here in the center of Karachi right under the nose of the Pakistani police during 2002. A serious wound necessitated special medical treatment (and may explain his silence of the past several months). Binori as a hospital. Binori the sanctuary, inviolable by any authority, where Pakistani military doctors are said to have come with impunity to care for him. Other *madrasas* are said to have given him sanctuary as well. I heard the name Akora Khattak cited several times. A military hospital in Peshawar or Rawalpindi, where he went for treatment of kidney problems in the fall of 2001, just before September 11, has also come up (in

Jane's Intelligence Digest of 20 September 2001, for example, and on CBS News on 28 January 2002). But the most reliable sources, the most well-informed observers, speak of Binori as the inner sanctum of all sanctuaries. (B. Raman *South Asia Analysis Group*: "Were are all the terrorist gone," 29 July 2002 and "Al Qaeda, will it or will it not," 30 August 2002).

Abdul, when I meet him again at the Sheraton bar, the only place in town a Muslim can get a beer or a sandwich during Ramadan, mocks me: "So, the house of the Devil was empty?"

And me, irritated and slightly pompous: "Normal, old friend; the Devil doesn't make appointments; he's at home everywhere, except in his own house; the Demon's laugh, as we all know, is like Minerva's owl—it screeches once you've left, but at the same time...."

Yes, at the same time, perhaps I saw nothing in Binori Town.

Perhaps, I still don't know what Omar came to do or to look for on the 18, 19, and 21 of January in Binori Town.

But I do know a little bit more about the mosque.

I know that this place of prayer and meditation where he spent one of his last nights is a headquarters for al-Qaida in the heart of Karachi.

I know, I feel, that what exists there is a kind of central reactor or machine room of the Organization—right in the middle of Pakistan, not far from the American consulate, a Taliban or post-Taliban enclave, to which the worst of Afghanistan, bin Laden–ists included, have withdrawn.

What if, in reality, the trail of Omar Sheikh passed through Afghanistan?

Is it time, in order to move forward, to return to Afghanistan?

CHAPTER 3 JIHAD MONEY

Stopover, Dubai.

I'm on my way to Afghanistan, but I stop in Dubai.

In the back of my mind, I'm hoping to pick up a trace of Saud Memon.

And, since I'm here, I hope to glean a little information on al-Qaida's finances, networks, trafficking, and how it functions.

We are still at the end of 2002.

It's the beginning of the debate on whether or not to go to war with Iraq.

I'm among those who, at the time, doubt the existence of the famous links between Saddam Hussein's regime and bin Laden's organization, America's justification for the war.

I'm among those who are—regardless of the regime's obviously criminal character—more cognizant of the rivalry between Hussein and bin Laden, and their competition for a supreme emirate, than the possibility of their alliance.

I haven't changed my mind either since my book *Reflexions sur la Guerre, le Mal, et la Fin de l'Histoire,* finished shortly after September 11, in which I described al-Qaida as an NGO of crime, a cold stateless monster, an organization of a radical new type, which didn't need the support of any major power to prosper, any Leviathan, let alone Iraq.

So I am in Dubai and determined to move on both fronts—that of the book and that of the general debate—in a city I know a little from the coincidence of previous investigations....

The first time was during the war in Bosnia—because some of arms dealers who dared violate the embargo on arms destined for Izetbegovic's army were here. I went to Ankara, but also to Dubai, in 1993–1994, to investigate how one could circumvent the embargo.

Then, in 1998, returning from my stay with Commander Massoud in the Panshir—the chief of his secret services, General Fahim, had explained to me that all the support for the Taliban, all the violations of the UN resolutions that went in their favor, and all their logistics, are connected to the United Arab Emirates. And I had begun to consider two aviation companies, twenty kilometers away, Air Cess and Flying Dolphin, which were at the center of the affair and were based in Sharjah, the neighboring emirate. One furnished spare parts for Mullah Omar's remaining fighter planes, and the other supplied arms and sometimes, in conjunction with the Afghan national airline Ariana, "foreign volunteers."

And finally, my last visit to Dubai was in 2000, when I was reporting on forgotten wars, particularly on those in Africa. I was finishing my story on Angola, trying to trace missile and canon shipments to Unita, when, to my considerable surprise, I came across the same Air Cess and its nefarious boss, ex-KGB agent Victor Anatolievitch Bout. Cess's planes, used throughout the African wars—notably in the Angolan zones controlled by Jonas Savimbi—were key to the ongoing infernal exchange of arms for diamonds.

I am here, then, in one of the world capitals of dirty money, a nexus for the uncontrollable trafficking of some of the planet's most sinister contraband. But also, and these facts are not unrelated, it is the most open city in the Arab-Muslim world—the wildest and, in a certain way, the most free. Of course I know the limits of this freedom: I know the case of the French woman Touria Tiouli who was thrown in jail because she had the audacity, after being raped in October 2002, to complain publicly. Yet, at the same time I must admit that I never return here without a certain pleasure at finding again the madness and the artifices of Dubai—its lunar landscape, its flavor of a middle eastern Hong Kong or an Arab Las Vegas, its kitsch, its skyscrapers on the beach, its silly submarine restaurants, its steel and glass buildings, its islands shaped like palm trees, and its ice-blue Mexican sky.

I reactivate the old networks from my earlier investigations.

I make contact again with a staff member of the Civil Aviation Ministry, who once told me how some old Iliouchines, long banned from the transport of cargo or passengers, would land at night on the fringes of the airport to load mysterious cargoes unbeknownst to customs or the police.

I find my friend Sultan B., a manager at an Arab bank, who is second-to-none for guidance through the financial maze of offshore accounts, combined with *hawala*—the system of compensation and transfer based on word of honor, which is as old as commerce itself, and, by definition, leaves no trace, no matter how large the transaction.

And, if I find nothing on Memon, if in spite of everything I was told in Karachi about the master of the house of torment, he remains more than ever the invisible man of this affair, I still observe some things about the other aspect, al-Qaida and its finances—and the least of these, which will bring me quite unexpectedly back to the main subject of this book.

First observation. The freezing of suspect accounts, under pressure by the Americans following September 11, is seen in Dubai as a big joke. Too slow. Too forewarned. Too many problems of identification, if only because of the Arabic names, their English transcriptions, and homonyms. It's the classic story of the Americans sending notice to an English bank that says to freeze the account of Mr. Miller, or Miler, or Mailer, resident of London, we're not quite sure. What to do? Given that there are thousands of Mr. Mailers in London, and even more Mr. Millers, how do you find the right one? It's exactly the question which was raised here, in Dubai, when the FBI sent their lists of Mr. Mohammed or Mr. Mohammad, or Ahmed, or Maulana. Add to that the problem of pseudonyms. Add to that the Muslim charitable organizations, which deftly mix money from criminal activities with that of humanitarian aid. And then add the embarrassment of Western banks themselves which, before September 11, having no major reason to be suspicious, blithely and without knowing, took part in these dealings: Didn't Mohammed Atta, right up to the end, keep an open account here, in the emirate, at CitiBank? What about the pilot of the second plane, Marwan al-Shehhi, opening his main account at the HSBC branch here in July 1999, and using it right up to the very eve of the attack? And what about the fact that he and the others managed to open dozens of accounts in major American banks, 14 of them alone at Sun Trust Bank, often with false papers? So the record is disastrous. The terrorist organizations had more than enough time to re-deploy their funds and protect themselves. "Guess," says Sultan handing me a report from a local think-tank, "how much money was left in the Harkat ul-Mujahideen account the day it was seized: 4,742 rupees, or $70! Or the account of Jaish e-Mohammed, immediately re-baptized al-Furqan, which therefore nobody thought to freeze: 900 rupees, $12! And in those of al-Rashid Trust—guardian, don't forget, of the assets of the Taliban as well as Lashkar e-Toiba: 2.7 million rupees, or $40,000—relative to the wealth of the Trust, another joke. Guess how much they seized from Ayman Al-Zawahiri, the Egyptian who, as you know, was one of al-Qaida's financiers: $252! The al-Qaida fortune, its war chest, reduced to $252, we must be dreaming!"

Second observation. Al-Qaida resources. Everyone acts as though al-Qaida and bin Laden were one and the same. Everyone, in the West as much as the average Arab on the street, seems to hang on to the idea of a terrorist organization financed out of the pockets of the Saudi billionaire and his family, propaganda to which he is not indifferent—the cliché of the family scion immolating his colossal fortune on the altar of Arab revenge is a powerful part of his legend. What better way to enhance his popularity than this idyllic image—drawn in part from the red millionaires of our past, romantic financiers of world revolution like Hammer and Feltrinelli—the cursed and rebel son, the ascetic heir who decides to bequeath his inheritance to the damned of the earth and to Allah? Unfortunately, it's false. Al-Qaida, I come to understand in Dubai, is no longer the virtuous self-sufficient, family-type enterprise it once was. It's a Mafia. A trust. It's a gigantic network of extortion extending worldwide, from which bin Laden himself, far from depleting his capital, continues to profit. It extends from the common racket of taxes on gambling, such as those the Macao mafia levies, to percentages taken on the Afghan drug trade, to the sophisticated, almost undetectable mechanisms of financial fraud based not on theft, but on the duplication of credit cards. These young financiers, not unlike Omar Sheikh, have become masters in the art of selling to the West the rope with which to hang itself—which is to say in this case, to turn the West's own arms, and often, its own vices, against itself. "You know the technique?" asks Sultan. "It consists of selling a stock that you don't have but that a bank will lend you for a commission, and that you buy back later at the market price when the time comes to return it to the bank. Suppose it's worth 100, but you have reason to believe it'll go down to 50. Suppose you know that an attack on the World Trade Center is going to happen, which will drive the market down. So you rent the stock and immediately sell it at the market price, which is still 100. When the attack comes and the stock takes a dive as expected, you buy back at 50 what you sold for 100 and pocket the difference. This is a technique American and English banks perfected, and here in Dubai we caught on quickly. We know a bank here that made this kind of transaction between the 8th and 10th of September on certain Dow Jones blue-chip stocks for accounts linked to bin Laden—I know the name of a bank that, by shorting 8000 shares of United Airlines on the 7th of September, then 1,200 shares of American Airlines on the morning of the 10th, allowed the attack to finance itself." What bank is it? Sultan won't tell me. But the next day he gives me the translation of an interview with bin Laden published on 28 September, in *Ummat,* one of Karachi's Urdu dailies: "Al-Qaida is full of young, modern, and educated people who are aware of the cracks inside the Western financial system, and know how to exploit them. These faults and weaknesses are like a sliding noose strangling the system." That says it all.

Third observation. Or rather a statement. That of Brahim Momenzadeh, a liberal Saudi attorney who receives me in his futuristic office facing the sea, on the top floor of a glass and black marble building, and who was described to me as an international specialist in sophisticated occult financial systems. "Islamism is a business," he explains to me with a big smile. "I don't say that because it's my job, or because I see proof of it here in my office ten times a day, but because it's a fact. People hide behind Islamism. They use it like a screen saying: 'Allah Akbar! Allah Akbar!' But we know that here. We see the deals and the movements behind the curtain. In one way or another, it all passes through our hands. We do the paper work. We write the contracts. And I can tell you that most of them couldn't care less about Allah. They enter Islamism because it's nothing other than a source of power and wealth, especially in Pakistan. It's true of the big ones, the chiefs who make fortunes with their benevolent associations which are just fronts. But take the young ones in the *madrasas*. They see the high rollers in their SUVs having five wives and sending their children to good schools, much better than the *madrasas*. They have your Pearl's killer, Omar Sheikh, right in front of their eyes. When he gets out of the Indian prisons and returns to Lahore, what do the neighbors see? He's very well-dressed. He has a Land Cruiser. He gets married and the city's big shots come to his wedding. They notice that Islamism is very good to him, that it is the sign of his success, a means of promotion. They know it's a good way to get protection from government agencies and the powerful. Believe me—very few people in Pakistan become Islamists out of conviction or fanaticism! They're just looking for a family, a Mafia, capable of protecting them from hard times. And Islamism is the best solution. It's as simple as that." Is it really as simple as that? Can we skip over ideology and fanaticism so easily? I don't know. That is, in any case, the point of view of a Dubai businessman. That is the other face of the madness of these times, as perceived in the Arab financial capital. The young lions of radical Islam? The Golden Boys of jihad.

Fourth observation. Kamikaze money. In Sri Lanka I had met a repentant former member of the Liberation Tigers of Tamil Eelam, or LTTE, a movement grounded in the ideology of the suicide-attack. She told me about the intellectual mechanisms at work in this kind of enterprise. I also met in Ramallah a Palestinian father with ties to Hezbollah—therefore, and I hasten to make clear, not representative of the general mentality of Palestinian fathers—who told me how happy and proud he was to know that one of his sons was going to sacrifice himself for the anti-Jewish jihad: "It's an honor," he explained, "but also a chance for all of us—doesn't it say in the Koran that a family who gives a martyr to Allah is automatically provided sixty places in heaven?" Here in Dubai, I gather more precise and detailed information. Here, thanks to Sultan and to others, I have the impression of entering of the financial underside of the self-sacrificial world.

The al-Qaida militant has a price. Between 2,500 and 5,000 rupees (5,000 and 8,000 if he's foreign, meaning, in fact, Arab). The grenade launcher has his: 150 rupees per grenade (bonus if the results are good). An attack on an Indian army officer in Kashmir has its own: between 10,000 and 30,000 rupees (bonuses varying with the rank of the target). And the kamikaze, too, has his price, decided ahead of time in an actual negotiation between himself, the organization, and his family, which assures the family of almost decent living standards: 5,000 and sometimes 10,000 rupees—but per year, and for life, and, when the contract is negotiated well, indexed for inflation and based on strong currencies.

There's the case I read somewhere of an Afghan refugee, a father living in the greater suburbs of Dubai, who received after the death of two of his children in Tora Bora in November 2001, the necessary funds to open a butcher shop. There's the case of a Yemeni drowning in debt who found himself one day, after the departure of his son for unknown parts, delivered from his predicament as if by magic wand, and able to return to Sanaa. There are agencies, not quite banks but more than simple money exchangers, where suicide-attack candidates come to fill out applications almost as naturally as for a loan. There are foundations—the Shuhda e-Islam Foundation, for example, created in 1995 by the Pakistani Jamaat e-Islami—whose *raison d'etre* is to assume responsibility for the killers' families. And then, most horrible of all, the *madrasas* where the future kamikazes are raised, or one should say trained, with the full consent of their families.

Martyrdom as a social program to assist needy families?

Suicide-attack as both social ladder and life insurance?

And then the last observation—and the most important because I'm going to pick up again the thread of my investigation, from a most unexpected angle. By searching the apartments, the hiding places and the cars abandoned by the hijackers of September 11, Sultan explains, the FBI had traced some of the money transfers that served as the financial basis of the operation as early as 18 September: roughly speaking, and corroborated by evidence, $500,000 to possibly $600,000—a considerable sum compared to the $20,000 or $30,000 that the first attack on the World Trade Center cost eight years earlier. More precisely, the investigators focused on one of these transfers, possibly the first, since it dates from August 2000, coming from a major bank in the Emirates and going to the first account opened in the United States by Mohammed Atta after his Hamburg period: $100,000 expedited by a mysterious character who had arrived two months earlier from Qatar with a Saudi passport and who called himself Mustafa Muhammad Ahmad. Even more precisely, the investigators following the $100,000, reconstituting its trail, made four discoveries:

1. In the month following its opening, Mohammed Atta's American bank account is the starting point for a series of smaller transfers—$10,000 dollars, sometimes less—to a dozen other accounts, most at the Sun Trust Bank in Florida, in the names of his accomplices.

2. Once credited to these accounts, the money was withdrawn in cash amounts of $100, $200, and $300 from ATMs. Abdulaziz Alomari for example, Mohammed Atta's companion on the American Airlines flight, was videotaped on the night of the 10th, a few hours before the operation withdrawing money from an ATM at a bank in Portland, Maine.

3. The next day, September 11, Atta, along with Marwan al-Shehhi and Waleed al-Shehri, two hijackers who were on the first plane from Boston, send back to Mustafa Ahmad, the originator of the initial transfer, $4,000, $5,400, and $5,200 respectively, a total of $14,600 dollars, corresponding to unused mission expenses scrupulously returned like all good bureaucrats to an organization's treasury.

4. Mustafa Ahmad, who hasn't budged from Dubai, receives these leftovers, transfers them to an account in a bank in Pakistan, and flies the same day, September 11, still using his Saudi passport, to Karachi, where he proceeds on the 13th to make six cash withdrawals emptying the account, before disappearing completely.

5. Mustafa Ahmad's real name isn't Mustafa Ahmad, but Shaykh Saiid, also known as Saeed Scheik, or Omar Saeed Sheikh—my Omar, in other words, the author of Daniel Pearl's kidnapping, and the villain of this story....

No need to say what effect this had on me. At first I don't believe it. I think: the polite and plump little Englishman, student of the London School of Economics with a passion for chess and arm wrestling, flower-lover at the Aitchinson School, good fellow at the Forest School, the moderate Muslim never objecting to Anglican payers at chapel, Omar, involved in September 11—it's impossible! It's absurd! Too much, too crazy, too perfect, to be true! The "Panther" and the "Force" were hard-pressed to imagine how their old partner could be mixed up with Daniel Pearl's assassination. Saquib Qureshi and the others couldn't believe their eyes and ears when they saw him on television in the role of executioner, their good friend, their brother. What would they say now if they heard this? What will they say when they read, if they read it, that a good friend—who opposed with them the fundamentalist takeover attempt of their school's "Bosnia Week" and whose single exterior sign of being Muslim was to arrive at a bar for an arm wrestling match bearing a carton of milk—was, not just at the controls, but at the cash-box of the greatest act of terrorism of all time?

I had to be certain.

I turned toward the Emirate authorities: "What does Sheikh Abdullah bin Zaid al-Nahayan, the Minister of Information of the United Arab Emirates, have to say? What do the banking and finance authorities of the country have to say?"

I went back to New Delhi to question those who had already given me the interrogation transcripts and the prison diaries from 1994, to pose the question: "Can you see Omar in this role? Does he have what it takes? Above all, do you have any evidence that would confirm or deny the theory that Ahmad and Omar are one and the same?"

And finally I went to the States, to consult the archives of several major media sources (CNN, NBC, *The Washington Post, The Wall Street Journal, The New York Times, Time Magazine, The Los Angeles Times, Newsday*) and see the officials I thought closest to the case—Ann Korky at the Department of State, Bruce Schwartz at the Department of Justice, others.

From this new investigation, especially from my conversations in Washington, I gather subtle impressions that don't lead to any hard and fast conclusions—but they are troubling enough that I put them out, not in any particular order, but as they came.

1.September 11, it must be quickly pointed out, had other paymasters than "Mustafa Ahmad" (alias, or not, Omar Sheikh). There were other transfers, in addition to the mysterious $100,000 sent to Mohammed Atta in August 2000. There was Mamoun Darkazanli for example, a Syrian businessman who operates out of German banks, whose contribution to the operation—two transfers at least, on the 8th and 9th of September—was probably greater.

2. As to the identity of Mustafa Ahmad, there are other theories circulating besides the wild one about Omar. In the 3 October 2001 *Newsday* John Riley and Tom Brune figure Mustafa Ahmad is the alias of a certain Shaykh Saiid, one of bin Laden's financial lieutenants (not in itself contradictory to the Omar hypothesis), but who they say was arrested at the time of the 1998 bombing of the American embassy in Tanzania, then quickly released by the Dar Es-Salaam police (and here the Omar theory no longer works, because in 1998 Omar was still in jail in India). The Associated Press in a 18 December dispatch says Mustafa Ahmad is in fact Sheikh Saiid, or Sa'd al-Sharif, or even Mustafa Ahmad al-Hisawi, or Al-Hawsawi, and he's a thirty-three-year-old Saudi brother-in-law and finance minister of bin Laden, who has been at his side since the Sudan years (and who is also known to have opened an account in Dubai for one Fayez Rashid Ahmed, alias Hassan al-Qadi Bannihammad, who was in the second plane, United Airlines 175).

3. The problem is all the more complex because there is another transfer of $100,000 that no one denies is linked to Omar but that nothing indicates is linked to September 11. We are at the beginning of August 2001, one year after the transfer to Mohammed Atta. In all probability the financing for the attack is already in place. Daniel Pearl's future killer writes to mafioso Aftab Ansari that he would like to see him give $100,000 dollars to a "noble cause." Omar writes to Ansari again on the 19th to inform him (according to *The Times of India,* 14 February 2002) that "the money has been sent." To whom? For what purpose? Nobody knows. Nothing, again, indicates this transfer was connected to the attack on New York's Twin Towers. But, if the two are confused, if one thinks of the 2001 transfer when we're actually talking about the one in 2000 and transposes what is known of the former onto the later, if one doesn't see there are two transfers of $100,000, one could postulate: "Omar's $100,000? Yes, we know! The August 2001 transfer, of which nothing allows us to think there is a connection to al-Qaida," and further conclude that Ahmad is Ahmad (first transfer) and Omar is Omar (second transfer) and that Ahmad is not Omar (clever demonstration—but is it the truth?). Again the trap of homonyms. But it doesn't stop with names. Because there also exist heteronymous transfers, financial quid pro quos, dollars which, like the Millers and their aliases, pass for other dollars. Masked money. Money as mask. In the world of shuffled identities it is money, of course, which provides the ultimate mask.

4. Meanwhile, the Omar hypothesis, according to which Ahmad is Omar, is one I discover has indeed circulated, was in print soon after the attack, and reprinted numerous times.

Except that Omar at the time was not yet Omar, and his name meant nothing to anyone. So that in the CNN report shown on 6 October, the day of the attack on the Kashmir regional assembly, it is clearly stated that "Omar Saeed" and "Mustafa Mohammad Ahmad" are one and the same, and that this person would still be in prison were it not for the December 1999 Indian Airlines hijacking which freed him. Then two days later, also on CNN, the journalist Maria Ressa, reporting on another subject, describes Mustafa Ahmad as a young Pakistani twenty-eight years old, formerly of the London School of Economics, who was freed from prison in India in late1999 as the result of an airline hijacking resembling those of September 11. Then an article appearing under the byline Praveen Swami in *The Hindu* of New Delhi, reports on a communiqué from German intelligence attributing the $100,000 transfer to Ahmad Omar Sayed Sheikh, close associate of Masood Azhar, commander of Jaish e-Mohammed. This information will be repeated here and there until Danny's murder. For example, up until 10 February, *Time Magazine* and *The Associated Press* take seriously the idea that Daniel Pearl's killer was involved in financing September 11. Amazing hypothesis. Seen from Europe it seems incredible. But neither the State Department nor the Justice Department, nor the major media of Washington or New York seem to find it unreasonable or absurd.

5. Better still, in two major American newspapers I find confirmation of the sensational information that the Indians had given me, implicating the chief of Pakistani secret services, General Ahmad Mahmood, in the financing of the attack. The information, according to *The Times of India* of 7 October and

The Daily Excelesior of the 10th, was that "at the instigation of General Ahmad Mahmood" the enigmatic "Ahmad Umar Sheikh" had "transferred electronically to hijacker Mohammed Atta" the famous $100,000. And the very same day, 10 October 2001, the *Wall Street Journal* writes: "The American authorities confirm the fact that $100,000 was transferred to Mohammed Atta by Ahmad Umar Sheikh at the request of General Ahmad Mahmood." The 18 May *Washington Post* goes further: "The morning of September 11, Goss and Graham (respective chairmen of the House and Senate intelligence committees) had breakfast with a certain Pakistani general, Mahmoud Ahmad, who a short time later was dismissed as head of Pakistani secret services; he had directed an organization that maintained ties with Osama bin Laden and the Taliban." And then, even more incredible, I find in the 9 October *Dawn,* one of those small news items that pass through the censor's net without being denied or obfuscated: "The general director of the ISI, Géneral Mahmoud Ahmad, was replaced after FBI investigators established a credible link between him and Omar Sheikh, one of three militants exchanged in the Indian Airlines hijacking in 1999." And further: "Informed sources say that American intelligence agencies have proof that it was indeed on instructions from General Mahmoud that Sheikh transferred $100,000 to the account of Mohammed Atta." The hypothesis, in other words, is no longer that Omar is the financier of September 11, but that Omar is operating on orders from the ISI. The hypothesis is no longer just that an Omar is linked to al-Qaida and a most spectacular terrorist operation, but that there is an Omar whose role is even greater than that—to facilitate a collusion between al-Qaida and the ISI, working together toward the destruction of the Twin Towers. For Indian agencies, the connection is not in doubt. In New Delhi I saw the results of decoding the telephone chip of Pearl's killer, showing, during the summer of 2000, at the time of the money transfer, repeated calls to General Mahmoud Ahmad. The FBI, of course, is more diplomatic, but I've spoken with people in Washington who confirm unofficially that the cell phone number decoded by RAW—0300 94587772—is Omar's, and that the list of calls made from it are the same as were shown to me in India. So, if Omar is proved to be the originator of the transfers it would be difficult to deny that it was done with the knowledge of the head of ISI.

6. We're left then with two distinct questions. And, in fact, three, which plunges us more than ever into the whirlpool of hypotheses and truths. There's the question of the link between Omar and the other Ahmad, of the ISI—established by the Indian Secret Service as almost certain, and not really astonishing to me: Hadn't I already established Omar as a man of the Pakistani services, and therefore Ahmad's agent? Then there's the question of the link, or more exactly, of the identity of Omar and the first Ahmad, originator of the September 2000 transfer—probable although not certain, but if confirmed, shedding a new light on the personality of Omar, agent of both the Pakistani ISI and Al Qaida. And lastly, the question we can no longer dodge, of the responsibility of the Pakistani secret service, or of one of the ISI's factions, in the attack on America and the destruction of the World Trade Center. Assuming that the answer to the first question is yes, and supposing as well

that the answer to the second question is yes—how can we not think that the September 11 attack was desired and financed, at least in part, by secret agents of an officially "friendly" country, a member of the antiterrorist coalition, which offered logistical support and its intelligence services to the United States? These three questions, of course, are at the heart of my conversations in Washington. To the first, as I said, the American reply is yes: the proof from the cell phone, verified contact between Omar and the head of ISI—it's clear. To the second, it's more ambiguous: I'm told that two documents exist which may identify Ahmad; the indictment of Zakarias Moussaoui, of which I know nothing, and a video tape from a surveillance camera showing Mustafa Ahmad entering the Bank of Dubai at 1:15 on September 11, to recoup the funds transferred by Atta during the preceding days from a Western Union—no one has seen the video, but I think it confirms what the press still says as to the identity of Ahmad and Omar. And to the third question, finally, concerning the ultimate responsibility of Pakistan in the September 11 attack, it remains part of the great unspoken in the America of George Bush and Donald Rumsfeld: If you accept that Ahmad and Omar are the same, and that Ahmad/Omar is the originator of the wire transfer, and you recognize the co-responsibility of the ISI in the attack, doesn't that call for a re-examination of the standing foreign policy which already positioned Iraq as the enemy and Pakistan as an ally? What remains essential for me is that I have a third reason to think (after Saud Memon, after Binori Town) that the murder of Daniel Pearl could have been, also, sponsored by al-Qaida.

Omar's staggering complexity.

The stunning obscurity of a person of double or triple depth.

Each time, we touch bottom....

...But at the bottom of each new depth, there is always a new trap door opening beneath our feet.

On the walls of the cave, behind the ultimate screen, always another screen that pulls us away, farther, into another spiral of this vertigo of Evil.

Unless, of course, this is the investigator's own vertigo, investigating vertigo. Unless he too is sucked into the hole, swallowed in this matrix, carried off on this nightmare ride—the intoxication of a mystery that ends by thinning out to nothing.

CHAPTER 4 AT THE HEART OF DARKNESS

I had all kinds of reasons to come to Kandahar, in southern Afghanistan.

I know this is where the Indian Airlines plane landed in 1999 when it was hijacked by Pakistani jihadists from Harkat ul-Mujahideen and its 155 passengers were exchanged for the release from prison of Omar, Masood Azhar, and Mushtaq Zargar.

I know that, once set free, Omar did not return immediately to Pakistan like his two comrades. Either he had some personal business here, or he wanted to pay tribute to the Taliban, whose mediation had facilitated negotiations with the hijackers and, consequently, his release, he stayed a few months in the country of the "students of religion."

I know (since I read it in Delhi in his "prison diary") that as early as 1993–1994, at the end of his stay in Bosnia, and while the mortal struggle between Massoud and his fundamentalist enemies was in preparation, Omar had already done two tours in training camps: one of them was near Miran Shah in the tribal zones of Pakistan; the other at Khalid bin Waleed inside Afghanistan.

And I'm mulling all this over when, as discreetly as possible, without informing the embassy—which would give my visit and the steps I plan to take a uselessly official connotation—and, without passing through Kabul, late in 2002, I land at the airport in Kandahar, the capital of the Taliban.

Of course, I have only one idea, an *idée fixe*. Omar. Omar more than ever. To confirm—or disprove—the ties between Omar Sheikh and Osama bin Laden. To find, or not, proof which, if it does exist, can exist only here, in the city that was once the capital of al-Qaida. To find out if I was dreaming in Dubai. To find out if I've let myself be taken in by a game of infinite theories, or if what I am really dealing with is one of those individuals with multiple faces—like Oswald, or like so many of the great spies of Cold War mythology—who invariably turn out to be different from who they seem and, when we think we have located them at the center of a great riddle, show up as part of another, even greater riddle, which clarifies the first... or makes it dissolve.

I spend the first day looking for lodgings that accept foreigners.

The next day, not really knowing where to begin, I roam around near the airport, now under American control, where I finally find someone who worked here ten years ago, at the time of the hijacking, and who confirms the overall picture outlined for me by A. K. Doval, the man from the Indian secret services.

Just in case, I pass by the hideous Hollywood-style villa, half candy-pink, half pistachio-green, that Mullah Omar had specially built and furnished on the outskirts of the city. Stucco and radar; kitschy turrets; rococo bedrooms and anti-aircraft installations; gigantic murals in the most pretentious styles, that mix visions of a future Afghanistan with freeways and dams, with bucolic scenes of life in paradise.

I wander around the Aïd mosque, the ruined offices of the Ministry for the Repression of Vice and the Promotion of Virtue, the flourishing music stores, the little arena where the Taliban held wrestling matches and where, occasionally, the Taliban's supreme chief would come in person and, like a modern-day Nero, provided he was having a good day, would bring his personal body guards to fight in a match. (Legend has it he would even occasionally come on foot. Since no one knew his face, he could be there incognito.)

But I'm having great difficulty finding any trace of the other Omar, my Omar, the one who really matters to me.

I go to see another religious official whose name and address were given to me in London, and he tells me about yet another Omar Sheikh, also Pakistani, but it is a different man with the same name.

I go to one of the *madrasas* where I've heard the Pakistani "brothers," who had come for the jihad, were welcomed—but no one there remembers him either.

I look up Mohammed Mehran, an intellectual I met on my Afghan mission a year ago, and one of the leading experts on Arab and Pakistani training camps—Omar's world when, as a young student barely out of the London School of Economics, he was here for a few months in 1993–1994. But although Mohammed is an inexhaustible source on the structure of the camps and the kind of training received there, spending hours answering my questions about how they function, he can scarcely shed any light on the particular case of Omar Sheikh.

Everywhere I go, I feel he has been—and yet I find no trace of him.

With every step, I sense his presence—but it is as insubstantial as shadows.

I know that here, in this maze of narrow streets, lies hidden another key to his mystery and to the nature of his ties with al-Qaida, but nothing tells me how, if I were to come upon it, I would recognize it.

In a word, the investigation is at a standstill.

For the second time, as in Bosnia, I've run into a complete lack of clues or witnesses.

For three days, it goes on like this.

I spend the time reading, reflecting, walking through the bazaars, daydreaming, listening to the call of the *muezzin*, which seems (or is it my impression?) more aggressive than during my other stays here. I reread *Les Amants de Kandahar* late one afternoon, seated at a table on the terrace of a café on "Mujahideen Square," waiting, losing patience, waiting some more. And then, since I have to wait, I spend the time trying to imagine Omar's life, not here, but at Miran Shah, then Kahlid bin Waleed, during the time of his first visit, when he completed his first two training sessions—and as long as I'm daydreaming, I linger one last time over what remains the most disconcerting part of the puzzle: the transformation of a young Englishman into a fanatic of holy war and crime.

There are no direct witnesses, of course. No one to tell me, "I knew Omar at Miran Shah and Khalid bin Waleed, and this is what he was like." Instead, Mohammed's stories, and bits of secrets confided to Peter Gee, to Rhys Partridge and to his other kidnap victims, whose police depositions Indian services gave to me and I recall. And then, my own knowledge of him. Because isn't that what it means to know someone? To be able to imagine how he would behave, even in situations of which we know close to nothing.... And by drawing on all this, I have the feeling I'm beginning to know Omar....

The layout of the camps of Khalid bin Waleed and Miran Shah: The camps are all alike, Mohammed Mehran told me. Built along the same lines. At the bottom of a very green valley, surrounded by snowy, deserted mountains. Hangars of poor-quality sheet metal that sparkle in the sunlight. Tents. A mosque. An immense parade ground where everyone gathers for prayers and for exercises. The exact image, in other words, of the naïve painting on the wall of my room in the Hotel Akbar. But Khalid bin Waleed, the second camp Omar attended, and the one Mohammed knew the best, having visited there just before the Americans razed the place, had one unusual feature. It had another, smaller parade ground, where the combatants' families came regularly to share their joys and sorrows, to be united in an ecstasy of shared sacrifice and death, and, sometimes, to inter-marry, widows and survivors, thus constituting a sort of a holy fellowship of relatives of heroes. They came also as if to the the-atre, with their children, to see the "holy warriors" act out, as though on a stage, their glory, their sacrifice, and their death. War and theatre. Crime and crime drama. A bucolic and austere setting. Luxuriant and lugubrious. Actors and martyrs. Allah Akbar. Omar is there.

Daily life in the camps: The days.... The nights.... I try to imagine Omar's nights at Khalid bin Waleed. Details.... Always details.... Because, as usual, everything is said and done in the details: Where does he sleep, for example? In a bed? On a mat?

On the ground? In the snow or on the stones? Alone? With the others? Response: on mats on the ground, under a tree, when it rains, without a pillow of course, without sheets or blankets, in stocking feet when it's cold, huddled against one another like sardines, to get warm. Terror and brotherhood. Terror-brotherhood. Heat, rank and exquisite, and, at last, the bliss of a sense of belonging. In the style of my dear Sartre: the experience of the hangar and collectivity, the sweaty stench of humans, their fetid breath, the nausea—in a word, the "autodidactic" destiny of a social misfit named Omar who, far from suffering from the fleas and bedbugs, the cold, the promiscuity of bodies, the mingled breath, the decaying human matter, finds the most profound and intense pleasure in them. If, as Peter Gee told me, Omar's problem really was that of the impossibility of his belonging, if his secret dream was really to escape his painful and guilty solitude, at Khalid bin Waleed, his desires were fulfilled. The hell, thus the heaven, of Khalid bin Waleed.

The days at Khalid bin Waleed: What did they eat? What did they drink? It seems like a frivolous question, but it isn't for Omar. Omar with his fragile health. With the body and the physiology of a prosperous European. Omar, whom I now know couldn't make it to Bosnia because the trip was too exhausting and, ultimately, made him ill. And Omar who, arriving directly from London at the camp at Miran Shah, had had the same problem. Dishes of poorly cooked rice. Old meat that has spoiled, eaten with the fingers off huge, communal plates. Rancid oil, cooked a hundred times over. Bad, stagnant water. Milk that has gone sour. Meager amounts of fruit. Filthy kitchens. Filth everywhere, all the time. Miran Shah turns out to be like Bosnia, only worse. Food poisoning that, this time, knocks him flat. Fever. Delirium. Dry, swollen tongue. The body—bathed in sweat— letting go at both ends. Left in bed, if one can call it a bed, while the others go out to drill. Off to the jihad and glory, Omar falls ill after twenty-one days (the end of the first leg of jihadist training) and must immediately leave for Lahore (either the home of his uncle, Rauf Ahmed Sheikh, a judge on the High Court of Lahore, or that of his grandfather, I don't know which—back to home base, Omar the weakling, the pitiful).

What does Omar do when he gets sick? At Solin, in Croatia, it was simple. He stayed in bed. Waited. And the Convoy of Mercy picked him up on its way back and took him home to London. But here? From what I know of Miran Shah, doctors and nurses are nonexistent, as are medicine and medical care. And what I know of that army, the army of jihadists, the holy warriors, the soldiers of God, is that it's the only army in the world where no one cares about the health, the physical state, or even the age of the soldiers. There is no age limit for recruitment, for example. No draft board to declare you exempt. Little kids and old men of eighty. And the little kids, by the way, can be ten years or ten months or ten days old—there are mothers who take their newborn to the camp! There are actually nurseries in the camps, for the babies dedicated to the jihad! In short, no hospital at Miran Shah nor, for that matter, at Khalid bin Waleed. The closest hospital is at Muzzafarabad, two hundred kilometers away, where those who are wounded in combat receive treatment. Sink or swim is the only choice. Omar, at Miran Shah, nearly sinks, and goes back to Lahore.

The schedule at Miran Shah and Khalid bin Waleed: The rhythm of the nights and the days.... The first thing that must strike Omar, I am sure, is the way time drags on slowly, without breaks or events. Five prayers don't make a rhythm; three meals aren't enough to organize a day around. The first thing that bothers and changes him is this slackness, time that's almost immobile, bloodless, like time during insomnia, when nothing happens except the succession of days and of nights, of dawns and of dusks. Time reduced to this? The time of these epic and beautiful moments—the sunrises, the sunsets—whose meaning, as it would be for all city dwellers, had been lost on him in London? Yet not even that, for, in the camps, one never sees the sun rise. And one never sees it set. Or, if one does, it is without looking at it—it is forbidden to notice, a European and Christian concern, a wonder of aesthetes and idolators, silence! The first commandment of jihadist time: act as though nothing were happening. The first shock of Omar the jihadist: the time that doesn't pass, time emptied of events, of thought, the pure passage of time. Omar no longer reads. He no longer reflects. Caught in the mechanism of the days, in the repetition of collective movements and that of survival, he scarcely has time to think. No longer an autodidact, but an illiterate. Drunk, no longer on the group, but on the void. The illiterate destiny of Omar. To become impoversihed in spirit. Amnesia. Brain washing?

The schedule, once more: The concrete filling of the hours. The same as in almost all camps. It's a protocol, almost a ritual, it doesn't change from one camp to the next. First prayer before dawn. Then, recitation from the Koran, in Arabic. Then a lecture by an emir, or an *uléma* who is passing through, on a point of doctrine, a saying of the prophet, a group of *suras*, a page of the *Kitalbul Jihad*, the "Book of the Jihad" by Abdullah bin Murbarik, the Koranic scholar responsible for a collection of the sayings of the Prophet regarding the holy war. Then and only then—it's eight o'clock—is breakfast served. After that—it's nine o'clock—military training. Prayers at noon. Lunch. Rest. Afternoon prayers. Training. New indoctrination session: the wars of Mohammed; the lives of his companions; his holy Face; the contours of his Face; why there is only One; the horror of video games, drugs, the films of Stallone and others that were so influential in arousing violence in Omar and that he sees, now, condemned, relegated to oblivion. Domestic work. Chores. Prayers at twilight. New recitation from the Koran. New lecture on the "jihad" (combat on the path of God) and on the "qital" (the art of killing, according to the path of Allah), on the holy values of Islam (fraternity and *oumma*, the community of believers) as well as the materialism of modern life and the moral decadence of the West (the incapacity, in Europe, of sons to love fathers, of fathers to love sons, of brothers to love brothers, as brothers love in the land of Islam—as in the camps). Last prayers. Sleep.

I add them up. Five prayers. Four or five time slots devoted to religious indoctrination and the Koran. As opposed to two, perhaps three sessions of actual military training (in sum: learning how to handle a Kalashnikov, an RPG-7, grenades, a rifle, a rocket launcher, and, the specialty at Khalid bin Waleed, remotely detonated landmines). Is this what they call a "training camp"? Is this how the dreaded camps of al-Qaida function? Is the religious more important than the military at Khalid bin Waleed? Does the minaret have control over the rifle? The *uléma* over the emir? And, in "holy warriors," does "holy" count more than "warriors"? Well, yes. That's right. That's what the West doesn't realize when we think of these camps, and yet, that is the reality. That these camps are about life as well as combat, that jihadism is a way of living and of being as well as a penchant for war—it's one of the things I have come to understand in the twenty years I have been interested in Afghanistan, and something that my conversations with Mohammed Mehran confirm. That the important thing is less the actual jihad than to believe in the jihad, and that the jihad is as much, if not more, of a religious obligation as it is a military obligation, that the liberation of Kashmir and Palestine are merely a point of departure, almost a pretext—this is also the first thing Omar realizes as soon as he arrives. It's his chance, actually. It's the card he's going to play. That's the only explanation for the odd title of "instructor" he boasted of to the Bengali and Pakistani inmates at Tihar Jail, a title I have long wondered about—how could it have been conferred upon such a weakling, such a city boy? Omar never would have been an "instructor" at the camp of Khalid bin Waleed if the actual military component had been more important than the religious.

A word about the readings from the Koran in Arabic. No one at Khalid bin Waleed speaks Arabic? It's true. The language of paradise is not Arabic but Urdu, or Punjabi, or Kashmiri, the vernacular languages of the illiterates that the camps produce in droves. Of course there are camps—those of the Lashkar e-Toïba—where the fighters have spent some time in Pakistani public schools, know the rudiments of math and reading and have a basic command of English and Arabic. This is not the case of those under the aegis of the Deobandi organizations (at that time, the Harkat; today, the Jaish e-Mohammed), that draw on the grand *madrasas* of Peshawar and Karachi (Akora Khattak, Binori Town)—and so this is not the case at Khalid bin Waleed. No matter. For the fundamentalists, the point has never been to speak but to listen, not to understand, but merely to be present—I can picture dozens of men of all ages assembled before the hangars on the parade ground, just before dawn; I can see them listening in ecstasy, repeating, reciting a text of which they do not understand a word. Omar? Of course, he speaks Arabic. In any case, he studies it. In the house in Delhi, when Shah Sahab was tired of having him underfoot, didn't he tell him to "go to your room and study your Arabic"? And in the report of the interrogation, under the heading "languages spoken by the accused," didn't he declare, "English, Urdu, Punjabi, French, and Arabic"? So he knows enough Arabic to follow the readings from the Koran. I would even be willing to bet it's the sole intellectual activity he has retained. And I suppose that also contributes to his influence over the others, his comrades and companions. I suppose that also explains his "command" over these peasants who speak only Urdu and Kashmiri.

What does "instructor" mean, then? How does the hierarchy work in a camp like Khalid bin Waleed? In general, what kind of hierarchy exists in the army of the jihad? What command structure? And ranks? What ranks? What, exactly, is Omar's status? Answer: emir. The only rank in the holy army is emir. Wherever there is a group, there is an emir. All powers belong to the emir, without recourse to discussion and without question (except questions the emir himself chooses to ask the assembly of scholars, the *jirga*, who meet at his request). So there are as many emirs as there are groups in the jihad. The only problem: what defines a group? How many men, starting from when, compose a group? A hundred? Ten? Two? In theory, in both Pakistan and Afghanistan, a group is simply more than one person—at two "holy warriors," you are already a group. In practice, there appears to be an average—according to Mohammed Mehran, who studied the camp of Ma'askar at Mansehra in depth, there are around eight professors and instructors for fifty or so "holy warriors." And what of Khalid bin Waleed? What kind of emir was Omar at Khalid bin Waleed? What level, what degree? When it is said that Omar was an "instructor" at Khalid bin Waleed, it means emir. But little or big emir? Reigning over a hundred, ten, or two fighters? Over the camp, or over his roommate? I don't know.

Omar religious? Pious Omar? Omar praying? For those who know him, that would be one hell of a surprise. For those who remember him at the Forest School and the London School, for Frank Pittal, who remembers their great conversations about Jews and Arabs, for Asad Khan who, on the trip to Bosnia, was surprised that Omar didn't come to pray with him more often, even for his friends from New Delhi, or for Rhys Partridge who saw with what aplomb he used the Koranic statute of "traveler" as a dispensation from prayer, for all those who, in a word, know what a modest place the idea of God has always occupied in Omar's life (although Peter Gee said, "He believes in the immortality of the soul 'like an egg is an egg'"), the idea is borderline credible, and it's hard to imagine him steeped in piety, waiting for the Last

Judgment. Am I worthy of God? Or unworthy? Nights going over and over in his mind his good and bad deeds? Not his style.... And yet, at Khalid bin Waleed, there is no choice. An iron-clad religious discipline. Punishment, even corporal punishment, for those who fail to say their prayers, especially collectively, at the appointed hour. So Omar behaves like everyone else. He conforms. He is submissive. Either religious crisis, or, for the first time in his life, the feeling of belonging, and the obedience that goes with it. Or else, mere cynicism, and the belief that this is the way to gain power at Khalid bin Waleed.

Memory. The past. What does Omar do with his memory? How does he live, in the midst of all these coarse beings, with his past as a Westerner? The knowledge and the science he has had access to, are they an asset or a sin? Should he get rid of them, and if so, how? Cultivate them in secret, and why? Does someone in the company of the soldiers of God still have the right to his memory, or must he, like the Khmers Rouge of Cambodia and the Tamil Tigers of Sri Lanka, kill the "old man" in himself, to be cured of the malady of the past? Yes of course, the pattern of the Tigers and the Khmers Rouge. Yes of course, the past is a sin, memory is shame. Yes, in theory the jihadist, once trained, is assumed to be pure, newborn, immaculate, and as for the rest, it's forbidden to remember—forgive me my past, Allah! Forgive me for what has past but is not entirely in the past. I suspect, however, that Omar is an exception and that, like a few jihadists of high rank, he plays both sides of the question: hate and love for the West; hide one's science and use it; deny it, but put it to service in fighting; support the common line that this knowledge is the source of all evil, but turn it around against the dogs who invented it; and, cleverer still—proof of the survival, in new clothing, of the Omar I know and of his cynicism—the temptation to create a leverage of distinction and influence, even amongst his brothers the jihadists. At least, this is the way I see him.

It's the same thing, I think, for the kamikaze tendencies of jihadism. Of course, not all jihadists are kamikazes. The Koran forbids suicide. This is clear when you read it closely, and when you read, in particular, the *suras* explaining that the distinctive feature of hell is that the soul of the damned to relive and repeat *ad infinitum* the scene of its last moments. And I think the "holy warrior," even in his most impossible missions, is bound to try to fight until the last against destiny, to do everything he can to come out alive and escape death—I know that martyrdom is only valid if it is at once passionately desired and desperately averted; and that to find grace in God's eyes, it is particularly important not to claim to be the author of a decision that is God's alone; I know the paradox of the kamikaze who, in Islam, and in defiance of all custom, is literally constrained to disguise a suicide as a natural and violent death. Notwithstanding, the death wish of these men is evident. That they aspire to death, that they pray day after day, begging Allah to call them to his side, is obvious. What did I do wrong? prays the surviving jihadist. What crime did I commit, my God, for you to put off your welcome? The misery of old jihadists. The ageless, soulless face of the forty-year-old jihadist who realizes that, despite his prayers, death has forgotten him. And Omar? His place in this drama? How can one imagine the young and lively Omar in this game of one-upmanship, of victimization and expiation? Well, cynicism, yes. Double-, even triple-talk. Nihilistic phraseology, without a doubt. Perhaps, also, a display of braggadocio from one who, as in his arm-wrestling days, intends to be the best, one of the lucky ones, the chosen, who will have the supreme privilege, to bear the mark of honor and the right to cross over the "line of control," the border between Pakistan and Kashmir, and become a combatant. In an article on the war in Kashmir, I read that there are five to six hundred thousand trained jihadists in Pakistan, among whom only a few thousand are engaged in active combat! But as for the rest, no, a solid will to survive.

The comrades of Omar? There are none.

Omar's sexuality? Like that of everyone in the world of the camps. Like Mohammed Atta, who had such an aversion to women that he stipulated in his will that they should be forbidden to approach his tomb and, what's more, when preparing his body for that tomb, from washing his genitals without wearing gloves. Latent homosexuality. Or, if not, perhaps no sexuality at all, pleasure is a sin, the purpose of relations with a woman is to procreate. Omar, at this time, if I take into account what I heard in London, has probably never slept with a woman. Omar, at this time, has never taken seriously a desire, an idea, a plan, that came from a woman. And since we can assume that nothing changed at the camps, or in Lahore at his uncle's, or later, in prison, we must conclude that when he meets his wife Sadia, he is a twenty-nine year old virgin. Is this a key to the psychology of Omar? A partial explanation of his mystery? Asexuality, and the will to purity that goes with it, as possible sources of the moral standards of the religion of fundamentalist crime? Frustration and morbid desire for the absolute as the double parameters of a new Mariotte's law—whereby the volume of a gas is inversely proportional to its pressure—applied to politics in extreme conditions? One has nothing to do with the other. But I remember, I cannot help but remember, a great French philosopher, Louis Althusser, still a virgin at thirty and who.... No. Out of bounds, precisely. Because truly blasphemous. And too flattering to Omar.

Pictures of Omar during those days? Photos? The camps of Lashkar e-Toïba are the only ones that forbid photos. So I looked. I asked. Somewhere, there must be some photos. I did not find them.

Omar's family? The beloved father, the adored mother, both remaining in London, of whom he told Abdul Rauf, the first man to invite him to enlist, at Split, "I shall do nothing against their will... they decide everything... they are the ones to convince to allow me to become a holy warrior." No more contact with the family. The jihadist believes he has the right to name 72 of the chosen—the same as the number of virgins waiting for him in paradise—to follow in his ascension. Perhaps Omar believes this. Perhaps he thinks, if he goes to paradise, he has a responsibility to give Saeed, Qauissia, and Awais a leg up.

Do jihadists change their names? Yes, of course they do. *Noms de guerre.* Disappear from circulation, become invisible, undetectable, camouflage and erase oneself. But for religious reasons as well. Like the companions of Mohammed. One changes names as one converts. A new name, like a rebirth. Part of the initiation into the jihad. Omar changes names then, like the others, out of religious duty. And I know all of Omar's names, seventeen of his aliases. But I don't know one, so important, decisive: His secret name.

The making of a jihadist.
Geneology of a holy warrior.
The school of religious war and the academy of crime.

That's where I am. I am in the midst of reconstructions and speculations about the most obscure area of Omar's life. And I'm having my umpteenth discussion with Mohammed. Do you think Omar knew how to shoot? The place of homosexuality in the camps? Is it possible that he never fought at all? Letters—weren't there combatants who, if they wanted to, received mail from their families, from their friends? In other words, I'm trying to fill in the details, to sharpen my portrait of him, but I'm fully aware that it doesn't in the least help further my central preoccupation, which is, his ties to al-Qaida. I'm in the midst of biographical rumination, morbid daydreams, unanswered questions, futile and pathetic speculations—when, one morning, I realize where I should have started: Gul Aga Sherzaï, the colorful and terrifying governor of Kandahar. Wouldn't the simplest thing be to return to see Gul Aga Sherzaï, this old acquaintance dating from the time of my *Rapport Afghan*, and, incidentally, the boss of this city? Isn't he still, today, the best lead and, in any case, the only one left?

I leave for the Palace.

And I pray that no one had the unfortunate idea of waving under his nose the less than flattering pages I had devoted to him in the book.

CHAPTER 5 BIN LADEN'S FAVORED SON

Apparently no one did.

Because the Governor remembers our meeting only vaguely.

He does remember, it seems, our wild automobile rodeo through the streets of his good town: "Show me, Mr. Governor, that you're as popular as you say among your people!" And he, stung to the quick, mobilizes his personal guard, his ceremonial motorcycle escort, his all-new armored BMW motorcade, its windows riddled with bullets, sirens blaring, and takes Gilles Hertzog and me for a tour of Kandahar. At each stop Sherzaï's helmeted infantry charged into the frightened crowd, whip or revolver in hand, to convince a swarm of terrified children to come have their heads patted.

Mixing up everything, he confuses this demonstration of popularity, this sinister and muscular walkabout, with the probably identical event he had to organize three months later for his "friend" Ahmid Karzai the day of the attack that almost left Afghanistan without a president and Kandahar without a governor. He takes off his general's operetta cap and, laughing very hard, almost shouting while his aide-de-camp laughs and snaps stupidly to attention, Sherzaï shows me his swollen, bruised ear: "Look at this! Does Gul Aga have a lucky charm? Could a bullet get any closer? You remember, what nerves of steel!"

But of the scathing portrait I made of him upon my return to France—his listless face, his soul-dead eyes, his nasal voice, his physique like the character out of *Tintin*, General Alcazar, stuffed in his too-new uniform with its too-red decorations and his too-black moustache, hat too high, epaulettes too starched, of his low forehead pretending determination that was only the expression of obstinance, of his terrible and absurd rages, of his taste for pistachios which he gobbled incessantly, mechanically, during our meeting, of his cupidity—he knows, it seems, thankfully, nothing.

"I've come to see you, Mr. Governor, because I'm interested in a man who was here at the end of the '80s."

"Oh the '80s... that's a long time ago, the '80s," he says, taking a handful of pistachios an aide has shelled, and stuffing them all in his mouth.

"Yes, but it's important... he's an enemy of Afghanistan. Remember our conversation last year when you said the Pakistanis were enemies of your country. Well, this man is Pakistani...."

"Yes, I remember," he grumbles, suspicious, then angry; but it's only a piece of pistachio stuck between two teeth—he glares at his aide-de-camp.

"I'm convinced, Mr. Governor, that this man who is today in prison in Pakistan underwent military training here in Afghanistan; and I'm certain he still has connections and support in the region."

He looks happy now. He's managed to extricate the piece of pistachio and so he's happy, and he smiles at me. And I choose to interpret this as an invitation to proceed.

"The name of the camp is Khalid bin Waleed."

BIN LADEN'S FAVORED SON

"I remember," he repeats, "I remember...."

But he is slumped over his table now, eyes half closed. His voice is husky, a little thick. I'm afraid he's going to sleep. Even the pistachios, he takes sluggishly, a few at a time.

"It's important, Mr. Governor. Very important. The French government attaches the greatest importance to the—"

A miracle! The words *French government* have the effect, one wonders why, of waking him up. He starts, twists his hat on his head, and stares attentively at me as if seeing me for the first time.

"The money," he says. "I hope you have the money!"

What money? What's he talking about? I won't find out. Because without waiting for an answer or even my question, he straightens up, barks an order to his aide-de-camp who again snaps to attention, takes me by the arm, and drags me to the giant stairway of the Palace where the motorcycle squadron waits, ready to go. But there, he changes his mind, barks a new order at his panicked escort, stumbles, turns red in the face, takes my arm again, and quick-steps back to his office where he stops in the middle of the room with a stupid look on his face as if he no longer knew why he had come. We are joined by a small, thin man with bright black eyes set in a face with the profile of an insect, who seems to be the only one who dares look the general straight in the eye.

"Amine is one of the heads of our police," he says, pulling himself together and affecting an absurdly sonorous voice as if he were awarding a decoration. "Ask your questions. All your questions. Amine is here. He will answer you."

And he goes to his chair, slumps down again, and grabs another handful of pistachios that his panting aide-de-camp has resumed shelling.

Amine asked me to give him two days.

He didn't promise anything. He said: "All that is long in the past; the Afghanistan of today is a new Afghanistan; we might have a chance, though—the Taliban was very organized, they recorded everything."

On the morning of the second day, one of the governor's cars preceded by a full-dress motorcycle escort, stops in front of my *pension* and takes me to the other side of town in a grand display of sirens, flashing lights, the jack-booted cycle escort kicking cars in their way, to a complex of buildings surrounding a courtyard. I don't know if it's an annex of the Palace or a Kandahar police station.

Amine is there with two colleagues in a dining room where a copious breakfast has been prepared.

"I think we've got it," he says. "Saeed Sheikh Omar. Born in London in 1973. Double nationality until 1994. Abandons his Pakistani nationality in January 1994. Is this him?"

He slides an old black-and-white photo, actually a photocopy of a photo, across the table to me, and immediately, despite his youth and his black turban, resembling those of the Ministry of Repression of Vice and the Promotion of Virtue, I recognize my man.

"Well then yes," he resumes. "In that case, we have a few things. Drink up your tea. And come."

Amine, his colleagues and I get into a new Toyota, which was a good-bye present, he tells me, from an American Special Forces officer. And we're off again, as always, with the jack-booted escort, toward Wazir Akbar Khan, the residential quarter of the city, near the Pakistan consulate. It's an isolated three-story house, modest and obviously empty, but guarded by armed soldiers as if it was the tomb of a *marabou.*

Inside, arranged on shelves like museum pieces: a flight manual with a newsprint cover; several Korans; Pakistani passports; video-cassettes; stacks of mimeographed pamphlets in Arabic and Urdu; photos of combatants, maybe Chechens; a map of American bases in Saudi Arabia and the Gulf; medicines; some cooking utensils. We are, I understand, in one of the al-Qaida houses discovered in November 2001, when nobody knew whether these houses were mines of information or decoys—if it's the latter, then the real secrets, the archival essentials, the names of bin Laden's operatives in the United States, had already been moved to Jalalabad by al-Qaida. And earlier, in January 2000 after Omar had been exchanged for the 155 passengers on the Indian Airlines flight, it was also one of the places foreign fighters were housed, and therefore it's possible Omar stayed here.

Amine, in other words, confirms for me his three stays in Afghanistan.

The first was in 1994. Probably in March. Maybe April. Omar spent, a few months before, a period at Miran Shah in the Pakistani tribal zones in a camp called—I had been missing the name—Salam Fassi Camp (this camp, contrary to what Mohammed Mehran told me, still exists since it seems, in January 2002, to have been a transit stop for Abu Zubaydah, bin Laden's deputy, as he fled Tora Bora on his way to Faisalabad). But his first real stay in Afghanistan is here, at camp Khalid bin Waleed, in Zhavar, which American bombardments, first in 1997, then in 2001, in this case, completely destroyed.

Instructor, really? Yes, really.

In a position to take his turn to run an *istakbalia*, a training session? Yes, quite probably.

Particularly because—and this is something I suspected and which Amine confirms—Khalid bin Waleed had the distinction of being oriented to the "intellectual" training of the combatants. The handling of Kalashnikovs, of course. The techniques of hand-to-hand combat, as well. The art of throat-slitting and remotely detonated explosions, yes. But also the art of camouflage and disguise. Of disinformation and information. Of intelligence and counter-intelligence. And, even more specifically, a section on the infiltration of militants, and eventually kamikazes, into "infidel" zones: life in the West, how to eat and dress, how to travel, how to outsmart police surveillance, remain a good Muslim, pray without raising suspicions—all questions to which Omar, given his biography, was supposed to provide more precise and reliable answers than anybody.

Anyway, he's there, in good health this time. For forty days he trains thirty or so young Pakistani recruits in the art of jihad. The student of statistics, the chess player, who said in London that he played the way Julius Caesar led his battles, has declared war without recourse on his former world. It's here, that he meets the man who will weigh heavily on the following episodes of his life—his mentor, his dark angel, the man who will send him to India to organize kidnappings of tourists, the man whom the irony of fate will send to prison soon after, and for whose liberation Omar takes his first hostages: Masood Azhar, who, on an inspection tour in the region's camps, with the flair of a gang boss that all jihad dignitaries have, spots Omar right away, the exceptional young recruit with a promising future.

In January 2000, after the hijacking and his exit from prison—Omar's second stay.

Omar is a celebrity. He was important enough that one of the Pakistani Islamist groups, with support from the secret services, put together a major, costly, internationally perilous, and spectacular media event to liberate him. The hijackers, as everybody in Kandahar knows, started with a much longer list of demands—they wanted the release of several dozen of their "imprisoned comrades." They announced they wouldn't budge for less than "two hundred million dollars." However, as the week progresses, they gradually renounce all their demands but one—the release of Omar, Masood Azhar, and Mushtaq Zargar. What privilege! What glory! And for the unknown jihadist, what proof of importance!

As soon as he arrives he is received by Mullah Omar himself, who naturally puts him in contact with the other foreigners stationed in the city, and through them, with bin Laden. With bin Laden they talk about Kashmir. The Pakistani tells the Saudi of the heroic struggle of the Kashmiri people against Indian occupation and asks for his help. The former student of the London School of Economics also explains how he sees the Koranic prohibition of "*riba*," literally, "increase"—in other words, the prohibtion of the work of money, and of the new mechanisms of financial capitalism. "It's not so simple," he expounds. "There are other readings just as orthodox, from *Surat* 2, verse 275... one can be a good Muslim and turn the methods of the infidels against themselves...." The Saudi observes him. He is obviously impressed with this rare combination of faith and culture, of fanaticism and competence. And he certainly sees what he can get from a fervent jihadist and a matchless financier, expert in electronics and the internet as well as a connoisseur of the West and its workings.

He is wary, I imagine. Amine doesn't say this, but I imagine he must be. Yes, a man like bin Laden wouldn't, without a minimum of caution, receive a young man who had just spent six years in Indian prisons, and could have well been turned into an enemy agent. So they study his case, test him discreetly. Does he know Arabic but hides it? Does he know Indian? Persian? Does he make suspicious phone calls? Does he overdo it—classic error—in his official hatred of America and England? Are they in the presence of another Ali Mohammed, the young Egyptian who in the '90s infiltrated Arab terrorist groups for the CIA? But the tests must have been conclusive because the Englishman seems to have been adopted.

According to some, Omar joins Majlis al-shura, the political council of al-Qaida. Others say he is put in charge of relations with the major allies outside Afghanistan—the Iranian Hezbollah, the National Islamic Front of Sudan. What Amine knows, and which the Indian services confirmed to me, is that Omar finds himself entrusted with extremely precise tasks for putting in place the logistical groundwork for the organization.

For example, he designs, puts on line and secures the al-Qaida websites.

He contributes to the creation of a communications system that will allow an obscure sect, closed in on itself, backward, to open up to the world, to capture the voices of friends and enemies, to circulate its fatwahs as well as its coded messages.

And finally, eighteen months before September 11th, at the time the organization begins to plan the operations that will give it its global dimension, he is among those set to work on its finances and secure the means to match its ambitions. With others he negotiates to buy land where the training camps of Khalden, Derunta, Khost, Siddiqui and Jihad Wal are based. He helps perfect a sophisticated system to reinforce al-Qaida's control over the Afghan opium trade. He ensures ties with Saudi NGOs, like the Islamic Relief Agency, whose Dublin office, since the 1998 attacks on the American embassies in Tanzania and Sudan, is one of bin Laden's largest suppliers of funds. Later, I will even hear that, in this Kandahar house, a computer is installed, possibly for Omar, that will function as a mini-stock exchange providing continuous on-line connection to the markets of the world: London, Tokyo, New York, Frankfurt—already "selling short," already perfecting the speculative techniques that in six months will be used to play the effects of September 11? Anyway, all the young trader *savoir-faire* of Omar in the service of an organization preparing total war against the American capitalist system!

"We are in the winter of 2000," concludes Amine, "maybe spring. Bin Laden, as you know, lost Mamdouh Mahmoud Salim, his finance minister, who was killed in 1998. At that point it seems that Omar Sheikh takes his place. Or rather, we wonder if this recruitment wasn't decided earlier still—if the organization hadn't already spotted him during his years in prison in Delhi, and therefore whether getting him back wasn't the reason for the hijacking. What? Harkat? You say it was public knowledge that Harkat was behind the hijacking? Yes. But it's compatible. The Harkat is part of al-Qaida .... The ISI? You're wondering if the ISI wasn't also involved in the operation? That I don't know. That's a little delicate. You understand that I prefer not to comment...."

Amine won't say more. But I can see, as I listen to him, new perspectives opening up—I can see the pieces falling into place, confirming, and going well beyond, what I learned in Dubai: Omar liberated by al-Qaida and the ISI; Omar an agent, very early on, of al-Qaida *and* the ISI; Omar as link between *both* organizations.

And then finally 2001. September 2001. Omar has returned to Pakistan. For six months he's been living the high life in Lahore, all the while making great and noble speeches on the misery he rediscovers there, the beggars going through the garbage who break his heart, the selfishness of his peers, their flinty souls. He enjoys his growing prestige conferred by his experiences in Bosnia and Kashmir, his years of prison in India, and now, his Afghan season. He sees his old friends. He makes little visits to his old Aitchinson College professors who also see him as a celebrity, almost a hero: "Oh yes, that scar, the arm slightly withered... so it's true those Indian bastards shot him savagely the day they freed the hostages.... Poor Omar! The brave Sheikh...." Far from concealing his connections to the Taliban and al-Qaida, he boasts of it, glories in it. Overtaken by his old tendency toward mythomania, he invents extravagant fables. To some he tells how, during the battle of Taloqan he almost, and with his own bare hands, strangled the renegade Masood, traitor to Islam—shame on him. He tells others that he witnessed the famous scene (which in fact happened twenty years earlier) in which Mullah Omar, in the heart of another battle, rips out his own wounded eye. And I know this mythomania is one of the reasons for the growing chill between Omar and Masood Azhar: Omar, undoubtedly, thinks the time has come to emancipate himself from his mentor and to forge his own legend; Masood has had enough of hearing the yarns his disciple feeds to the young leaders of Jaish, his imaginary exploits and Indian tortures: "They made me drink my urine... eat my own shit... enough to put you off food for the rest of your life...."

Then comes the attack on the World Trade Center. The announcement of reprisals against Afghanistan. Omar is fired up again. He says: "These are my brothers, the greatest power in the world threatens attack on my brothers—my place is at their side, I'm going." He continues, "Each man, the Koran teaches, comes into the world to accomplish a mission. Some missions are humble, others are great, mine is to serve in the great army of Allah." So here he is, in the first week of October, back in the house for foreigners in Kandahar, where preparing for holy war.

He is seen at Mullah Omar's headquarters.

He is again received by bin Laden, who, it seems, puts him in charge of new financial duties (notably, contact with a counterfeit money workshop in Muzzafarabad, in "occupied Kashmir" that Omar knows better than anyone, and where he still has solid ties). He brings books purchased from "Mr. Books" that are, I think, perhaps gifts for the al-Qaida leader or his principle aides (an anthology in four volumes, edited in Beirut, *The Strategies of Arab Conquests*; a book by Rifaat Sayed Ahmed on the war in Palestine, published in Cairo; and economics texts).

He is in contact with Tajmin Jawad, bureau chief of information for Mullah Omar, who in the beginning of November is named liaison officer to bin Laden, and is also linked to the ISI.

He sees Mulla Akhtar Usmani, commander in chief of the Taliban armed forces in the region, who puts him in charge of an accelerated training program for a group of newly arrived young recruits from Pakistan.

He sees Qari Saifullah Akhtar, the leader of Harkat al-Jahad el-Islami, one of Mullah Omar's close advisors, who will soon join him in escaping the country, but who looks askance at this strange, cultivated man so different from the saber-rattlers who make up most of his troops.

He drives a Toyota. He has his personal guard. He lives surrounded by mobile phones, computers, and other gadgets.

He has become, concludes Amine, one of the most high-profile characters of the small clan of foreigners in Kandahar, and he knows it. So much so that, in October, when the Americans unleash their offensive, he is there at the front with a few thousand combatants from the whole region, but especially from Pakistan. It doesn't appear that he actually participated in the battles, but he's there. He shares the fate of his "Afghan brothers." And he might be among those who negotiate, in certain surrounded areas, and notably in the face the battalion led by the future president of Afghanistan, Hamid Karzai, the surrender of Taliban forces.

Omar, as Robert Sam Anson (*Vanity Fair*) and Jon Stock (*The Times* of London) say, is now called by bin Laden "my favorite son" or "my special son."

The future kidnapper of Daniel Pearl has become, in a very short time, an active apostle of the clash of civilizations, al-Qaida style.

I don't know how he gets out of Afghanistan.

The fact that he reappears in early December in Lahore, ready for the kidnapping of Daniel Pearl, proves that his exit was relatively easy and that he didn't belong to the roughneck rank and file who had to go through Uzbekistan, Tajikistan, and in some cases Chechnya, pursued by American Special Forces and having to hide in Waziristan and Buner, the Pakistani tribal zones, before returning.

The fact that the adventure is resolved so quickly and so well, the fact that he obviously escapes this Afghan Rigadoon, this rout, this deluge of fire, and the flight that was the fate of most of the combatants caught like he was, in the rat-trap of Kandahar, the complicities implied by all that system of connivance that had to be put into action so that he could find himself from one day to the next, as if by enchantment, in his garden in Lahore—it all proves what we already knew, which is, his very particular status: inside this LVF, this collaborationist's militia, that is the Pakistani battalion in the Taliban army and, now, in the State of Pakistan itself and its intelligence services.

What we didn't know about, however, was his place in al-Qaida.

What I couldn't figure out, even after Dubai and the discovery of his possible role in the financing of September 11, was his position in bin Laden's entourage.

I don't need to go back and see Gul Aga, I know enough.

Daniel Pearl's killer is not just linked to al-Qaida. He is not one of the innumerable Muslims around the world in vague allegiance to it. He is the "favored son" of its Chief. He is a man with responsibilities in the organization's command cell. He is a crucial character in the "arm wrestling match" that the new barbarians have started against the democracies of the world. And this is how the Pearl affair takes on its full dimension.

CHAPTER 6 BAD OMENS
FOR THE INVESTIGATOR

After Dubaï and Kandahar, back again to Karachi.

The coolness of the air, salty and bracing as at the beginning of a storm, that reminds me, as always, of the presence of the sea.

The breathing of the city, under my windows, children crying, car horns, plaintive cries mixed with sounds of joy, right near the Village Garden—strange, the way I am drawn back to this place as though it were a magnet.

Tomorrow is Christmas.

It will be 328 days since Daniel Pearl was murdered.

And for the first time since the beginning of the investigation, I feel the atmosphere getting heavy.

The other morning, Grasset, my French publisher, told me the Pakistani embassy in Paris had requested a copy of my first book, *Indes Rouges*, which came out at the beginning of the '70s.

"So, what did you tell them?"

"Nothing, we were waiting for the green light from you."

"Well, no, no, of course not. Drag things out. Tell them the book is out of print. Tell the distributor to pretend they're out of stock in case they try to order it directly. I think it's better if they don't have this book in their hands while I'm still in Pakistan."

I sense them wondering, at the other end of the line, if I'm not getting paranoid. But I know this country is crazy and lives under the watch of the secret services, which really *are* paranoid.

Being a Jew is already less than an asset.

Being interested in Daniel Pearl doesn't earn you any friends here, either.

But worse still would be if these people knew that I am the author of a book you can't read for five minutes without realizing it is scarcely sympathetic to Pakistani policy; even if it was written in my long-ago youth, it would complicate things considerably.

That said, the information is there.

And the call from the embassy is no accident.

In Karachi and in Islamabad, there are naturally people who inevitably ask questions and find the answers.

Ikram Seghal, Danny's friend, proprietor of one of the largest private security companies in the country, welcomed me the other day and told me his mother is Bengali and he is happy to shake the hand of a Frenchman who, in his youth, knew this magnificent country....

Another person, the evening before, at a dinner in the home of a judge, suddenly leaning toward me as we were getting up from the table, to whisper, "I'm glad to meet you, I've been told you fought for Bangladesh when you were young...."

He is—like Seghal—a good man.

He's an industrialist from Lahore, pro-Western, liberal.

But in this country, how can one possibly know who is who?

How can you be certain people aren't double or triple-dealing?

The friendliest faces suddenly become suspect.... The journalist who inspires your confidence and who, you discover through conversation, is married to the daughter of a general.... Another guest at another dinner, who, comes on as a rational man, holding forth to explain to the assembled company that the second wife of Mohammed Ali Jinnah, founder of Pakistan, was a non-Muslim— "So our friends mustn't bother us too much with their Islamist zeal, hmm?" Still another guest, insistent and kind, who took the trouble to ask me if I had thought of encrypting my computer, of not leaving compromising notes in my wastebasket. "For example," he said, in the tone of a new friend initiating you to the mysteries of a dangerous country, "you must never write 'the services' on your personal papers, never. Write 'the bad guys' or 'Islamabad,' or 'the creeps'—anything you like, but never 'the services'...." The next day, Abdul tells me that this free spirit that I had listened to in all confidence holds a high position in the services!

You'd have to be an agent yourself to find your way in this labyrinth.

You'd have to be a specialist in semiotics or hermeneutics, in this country where everything is done in signs.

For now, the truth is that I have just received a clear message: my Bangladesh file, something I thought was buried in the depths of the ISI's memory, has resurfaced.

The day before, at my hotel—which no one should know since I change it nearly every night—there was another weird call.

"Hello, Mr. Lévy? I'm downstairs in the lobby. I'm a journalist from *Zarb e-Momin*, the English version. I'd like to see you— I'll be right up."

Amazed, I ask him to repeat himself: "*Zarb e-Momin*, really? the jihadist paper?"—and, as he confirms, I prefer to go down, quickly, the hotel is so small, two stories only, and I don't want to give him the time to come up.

The man is weird, with a shifty stare, a sugary voice, and a recently clean-shaven chin covered with nicks and razor burns.

His newspaper, English version, spread open on the table, is itself a revelation: on the left, the photo of a fallen "martyr" in Kashmir, with a letter from his mother saying how proud and happy her son's gesture has made her; on the right, a photo supposedly illustrating the "bloodbath" in Palestine, the "genocide" perpetrated by Israel—along with an editorial declaring the murder of Jews, all Jews, throughout the world, a "sacred duty" that "pleases Allah."

An old tape recorder is already running.

Several cassettes, all different kinds, normal and micro, which is absurd.

A leather bag slung over his shoulder bandolier-style, with a strap he hugs tightly.

Who are you? I ask. How did you know I was here? An interview? You really want an interview for the cultural section of *Zarb e-Momin*? Is this a joke? An error? What can the "cultural section" of a newspaper devoted to spreading the jihadist vision of the world be like?

Yes, he replies. He knows who I am. Pakistanis aren't idiots, you know. They read the international press. Why are you surprised? This paper is not what you think! Could you by chance be confusing it with *Voice of Islam*, which is the Lashkar monthly? Don't you know that the *Zarb* has a wide public, and that this public is interested in French thought?

He explains all this and adds, with a look of complicity: "The only thing is, not here, we can't do the interview here, because the police are prowling around, and unfortunately, they make no distinction between the *Voice of Islam* and the *Zarb*. Oh! What ever happened to the good old days of the 'Military-Mulla-Market Alliance'? I came, in fact, to take you to a safe house where we won't be bothered and where, given what you're looking for, you will learn a number of fascinating things."

"No thanks," I reply. "It's here or not at all—and if that's the case, why is this tape recorder on for no reason? That's stupid."

And he, then: "Well then, it's not at all, which is too bad, because I'm not allowed here. I really was told to bring you back."

And he packs up his tape recorder and his newspaper (in a plastic sack, not in the leather bag he doesn't open and holds so closely) and gets up with a knowing smile which expresses either sincere disappointment, or provocation that fell flat, or something else—but what?

I've been spotted again, there's no doubt about it.

The day before that, in Lahore, a strange conversation, to say the least, with Irfam Ali, the "Additional Home Secretary" of the State of Punjab....

Knowing I've been found out and, this time, having only innocent projects in mind (like going to Dokha Mandi, where Omar's family is from; going to see his house in the old city; and perhaps to see the grand mosque he used to attend), I prefer to be frank. As soon as I arrive I introduce myself officially to the man who is the boss of the police in the region, in his modest, slightly dirty office with metal shelves full of dusty files. All the sensitive files end up here.

I give him my usual speech.

I tell him, as I have the others: a novel, Pearl and Omar, the two characters who complement each other, day and night....

I add, especially for him: I am here to breathe in the atmosphere of Omar's father's birthplace.... It's so interesting, isn't it, the story of this captivating and diabolical individual, endearing and criminal, who passed the most significant years of his adolescence in this city that, personally, I like so well, with its flowers and greenery, its colonial houses, so full of charm....

And he, with his beady eyes in a square face, his enormous, plump hands incessantly clenching—as though crushing a nut—while I'm talking to him, and, now and then, when his irritation is more than he can stand, he rakes a long lock of hair back over his bald crown: It's practically a braid, reaching the nape of his neck and then falling back down almost as soon as he's arranged it. Then he interrupts me and starts a long, defensive speech along the lines of "I don't see how you can say that—Omar is still charming, Omar is always charming... people don't change just like that, Mr. Lévy. Here is a man who does what he says and says what he does, who fights for his principles and remains faithful to his ideas, have you no respect for that? Is that criminal?" All of this is accompanied by an incredible, almost grotesque, and extremely insistent anti-Semitic diatribe I just can't believe is spontaneous and unrelated to who I am and how I might react (unless that homonym that helped me that very first day—the famous and providential "Levy Malakind"—works again....)

"Listen," he fumes, with a lisp, furiously refusing to allow me a word in edgewise now, "don't interrupt, listen to me. Omar was convicted, and I'm not going to comment on the verdict much less criticize it. But who, in this affair, is more guilty, the one who did it or the one who, by his attitude, did everything to put himself in harm's way? Can't you see how Mr. Pearl provoked Omar, how he goaded him, how he deserved what happened to him? That's a really Jewish thing. A form of Jewish masochism. No, don't say no. There are Jewish characteristics, everybody knows it. I know that in Europe it's polite to question that. But there's no point in denying it when the charges are overwhelming. Look around you. Listen. Let's say we forget the physical traits, all right? But the moral characteristics? These traits History has given all peoples of the world, and the Jews in particular? You're going to tell me that some of these traits are common to a number of peoples. I'll grant you that as well. A business sense, for example, usury, the Jews and the Hindus undoubtedly have that in common. But duplicity.... The aptitude to lie.... The way they invented the genocide of Hitler, to better hide their own depravity. Who would benefit from the crime? In my profession, that's the question we always ask: Someone will benefit from this crime, now who is it? This particular crime, everyone knows it did Hitler no good. And everyone knows it's of extreme benefit to Mr. Sharon. Well, I'm not saying that Mr. Sharon made up the Holocaust. There are people who think America is in the hands of the Jews and the Jews are in the hands of Satan—thank God, I'm not one of those people! I'm not anti-Semitic! But think about how convenient it is. Follow my reasoning: The more we talk about the Holocaust, the less we talk about the bloodbath in Palestine. The more they show you these faked photos of Jewish children in tears, the less you worry about the carnage in Iraq and in all the Muslim countries of the world."

The police chief seems satisfied with his reasoning. More and more incessantly, as if he were keeping a beat, he makes this idiotic gesture that is starting to get on my nerves, of pulling his lone lock of hair back over the top of his head, where it never stays more than a second—but that's all right, he goes back to get it and starts all over again, and it slips back again, and he puts it back again. I'm burning to tell him, "Are you done with your hair, now? After all this time you don't get it? It'll never stay!" But no. He looks so content. And excited. Barely glancing at the note someone brings him. Not listening to the officer who just told him of a vicious crime that's just been committed in the suburbs of Lahore. Guffawing, slapping his thigh when he mentions the "faked photos" of Jewish children.

"Just a minute!" he starts up again, his face turning crimson, clutching his desk as though he were afraid of keeling over. "Now, I'm not saying the Jews haven't suffered, too. The Pakistanis are good people, they don't deny this sort of thing, they sympathize. But, it's just a question: these people who have learned suffering, why can't they learn to love? They had the entire world at their bedside, and now at their feet, why can't they pity others, the persecuted Muslims of Palestine, Iraq, and Jammu Kashmir? In short, all this, to tell you it is the key to the Pearl affair. Put yourself in Sheikh's place. He sees these images of massacred Palestinians. He knows Israel is a splinter in Muslim land. And he sees an Israeli—What do you mean, 'not an Israeli'? Ah! But yes, I beg your pardon—Pearl's father was Israeli, and his grandfather.... For me, it all adds up. Someone who has an Israeli father and grandfather is objectively Israeli and is therefore responsible for the crimes of Israel. It's logical. So, put yourself in the place of Sheikh. He sees an Israeli who comes to provoke the Pakistanis by intervening in their affairs. We don't concern ourselves with the Israelis' affairs. It wouldn't

occur to us and besides, we don't get mixed up in anyone's
affairs. But he, Pearl, does. Then, this annoys the Sheikh. He
can't stand seeing this fellow who goes rummaging around everywhere, asking sneaky questions. Because that's also a Jewish trait,
sneakiness—What? But of course. You only have to look at history. There was a Jewish English minister, Balfour, who decided,
in 1918, to install a Jewish state in Palestine. Well, right from
that moment, do you hear me, right from 1918, he had secretly
planned that the final date would be thirty years later, day for
day, to 1948, it's proven. Isn't that sneaky? Isn't that proof of
what I'm telling you? All right. The Sheikh has had enough. He's
like all of us who see the parade of snoopy Jews who come to
stick their big noses in our Pakistani affairs all the time and, now,
in the Pearl affair. But Omar is more courageous than the others.
He has principles. He sees his principles through. And so he kidnaps the Jew. But, once again: Who is responsible, huh? The one
who kidnaps or the one who is kidnapped?"

He stares at me. The expression in his eyes is suddenly nasty,
his smile venomous. Something at once brutal and weak in the
way he opens his mouth slightly. The gesture, one last time, of
pulling his solitary lock of hair back up to the top of his head.
A hiss in his breathing.

"But, really, Mr. Lévy, I hope I'm not upsetting you. I hope,
at least, that you're not a Jew. It's been amusing talking philosophy with you."

And me, dumbfounded, not believing my ears, caught
between hatred, pity, the impulse to burst out laughing, and the
desire to tell him who I am:

"And I hope you are not Muslim, for Islam is a great religion
that respects the peoples of the Book."

Still another day, in Islamabad, I have a strange meeting with Asif Farooqi, Daniel Pearl's fixer.

I've wanted to see him for several months.

Right from the beginning of my investigation, he's the first person I tried to contact.

He had always said no, up until now. He invariably told every intermediary who approached him on my behalf, "It's too hard, too painful. I feel so responsible, you understand? After all, I'm the one who made the connection between Danny and the Sheikh, aren't I?"

Once I even talked to him on the phone. I had gotten hold of his mobile phone number. I had arranged it myself, without going through Abdul. And the man who answered was polite, but strangely ill-at-ease, almost frightened.

"You have to understand, I am not alone, I have a wife and children. After Omar's trial, they told me, 'That's enough, never talk about any of this again.' And so, no, thank you, I can't see you, please leave me alone, I beg you...."

I had sent him a long e-mail, detailing the kind of questions I wanted to ask: what Danny was like, how he behaved when he was working on a story, if he was imprudent, irresponsible, courageous; the last weeks; the last day; if he was different, the last day; you always feel it, you always know when you're getting into a dangerous area, right? Did Danny feel it too? Did he know it? But Farooqi had replied with two curt lines to repeat that he had promised not to speak again and that he would keep his promise.

And then, that day, my Pakistani cell phone rings and it's the same Asif Farooqi. "In fact, I've been thinking.... We can meet, if you like."

To my great surprise, the man who had made it a point never to speak of Danny suggests we see each other that very night, in the residential area of Islamabad. "No, it's not my place, it's my office, the Japanese news agency, Jiji. That's where Danny and I used to meet, I thought that would please you."

And here he is in front of me, alone, the Japanese employee having left when I arrived. (When I got there, it seemed to me I saw a parked car across the street, with the lights out, with people inside, but I wouldn't swear to it.) And here he is, the appearance of a well-mannered young man, round glasses, twenty-five, maybe thirty, slim, with a little baby fat around the jowl, a weak chin, and a real sadness when he speaks of the good times he had with Danny and Mariane.

He has all the time in the world now.

Yes, yes, he's thought about it, he's glad to render me this service and he has plenty of time.

It's not every day you can contribute to the book of a writer, right? Ask me the questions that interest you, I'll do my best to answer.

Except that, after half an hour of conversation, an unpleasant impression crosses my mind.

His way of being constantly mistaken about all the details....

The dates that are off (the meeting at the Akbar the 13th instead of the 11th), the mistaken names (Bukhari instead of Fazal Karim), the wrong places (locating Danny's prison in Sorhab Goth, when I know very well that it's farther down the Super Highway, at Gulzar e-Hijri)....

His way, time and again, of citing one group instead of another, of attributing what belongs to Harkat ul-Jihad al-

Islami to Lashkar, or what is Sipah-e-Sahaba's to Harkat ul-Jihad al-Islami....

Or on the contrary, to mention a precise piece of information—Brigadier Ijaz; Omar's surrender eight days before his arrest—and then to glance at me out of the corner of his eye to see if I'm moved, if I express surprise, or if I let it pass without reacting.

At first, I react. I say, "Hang on, Lahori is the head of the Lashkar, not the Jaish!" or "Of course I know who Brigadier Ijaz is, I think I ran into him in Lahore...."

And then, after a while, I stop myself. I wonder if these aren't all traps or snares that I'm falling into and if, instead, I should try not to react. So I let it go, I let him talk, I see him coming with his deceptively innocent manner of talking about the "three letters," or of mentioning the names of Memon or Khalid Sheikh Mohammed to see if I'm surprised, or if I pick up on it, or if I take notes, or if I act like someone who is already aware of all this. So, I see him coming. And, smarter by half, I get up at the most opportune moment, pretending to have to make a phone call, or take a leak, or go in the next office to look at the news dispatches on the screen.

The idea occurs to me that, perhaps, Asif is there less to talk than to make me talk.

The idea occurs to me, and rapidly takes root in my mind, that he only agreed to see me to know where I am in all this, what I know, and what areas I'm looking into.

Is Farooqi working for someone? Sent to me? On a mission? Once again, it is a bad sign. Once again, it proves that no one is falling for my story that I'm a novelist fictionalizing the encounter between Pearl and Omar any more.

And then, the bizarre incident whose significance, at the time, I didn't really understand but that, in retrospect, seems to confirm these scattered impressions.

The French embassy for once arranged an appointment for me, with Hamid Mir, the former director of the Islamabad Urdu newspaper *Ausaf*, who is currently launching a private TV station.

Hamid Mir is an important man. He is a biographer of bin Laden. He's one of the few journalists who's been able to interview him in years. He did so in 1997. Then in May 1998. And while, regarding his last interview, in November 2001, some in Pakistan question the absolute authenticity of his version of the circumstances—blindfolded, shut in the trunk of a car, a scenario from an espionage novel—no one questions that the interview took place, nor the fact remains that he is one of the privileged spokesmen of the master of al-Qaida.

So I go to see Mr. Mir. I must, because I want to talk to him about all this. I must, because I want to question him about Omar who, I read somewhere, he had known and found unstable, intellectually disturbed, dangerous. And I must, because I want to ask him at last about his appointment with Danny the day of the kidnapping, or the eve of it, or even before—I have to verify it, but no matter, that's a detail: What's essential is that he is the only public person to have seen the two of them, the victim and the executioner, at such a brief interval, and for me, this is priceless.

So here I am, a few minutes before noon, in the restricted parking area in front of the offices of Geo TV, the new Urdu satellite television station Mir is starting with a few others.

A group of five men, some in *shalwar kameez*, another in a *djellaba*, are standing there in front of the building, watching me approach.

A little farther away are three other men, clean shaven, apparently cops or bodyguards, all carrying arms, keeping the immediate area clear.

Obviously, they're all there for me, because, as soon as I get to the stairs leading up to the entry of the building, the man in the *djellaba* strides up and takes me wordlessly by the arm, scarcely giving me time to protest, and forces me down to the cellar as the others, the bearded men and the security men together, rush down behind us.

Once downstairs, a stern-faced orderly frisks me, takes the card I show him, disappears into an office at the end of the hall and returns a few seconds later.

"Mr. Mir is not here. Mr. Mir does not have time to see you. Mr. Mir says he knows nothing of this appointment with you. Mr. Mir demands that you leave immediately."

And with that the bearded men and the body guards take me by the arm again, in unison, without listening to my protests, ignoring the typed memo confirming my appointment with Mr. Mir that I've taken from my pocket, and push me towards the stairs, manhandling me out to the sidewalk, to my car.

It all happens very quickly.

Very quickly as well, I call Mir whose mobile phone number I had taken the precaution to note and who answers on the first ring.

"Mr. Mir?

"It's me."

"I'm ...."

"I know...."

"I'm here, right in front of the building, there must be some misunderstanding."

"There's no misunderstanding."

"Yes there is. We had an appointment at twelve sharp and—"

"Your embassy tells me you want me to set up a meeting with Gilani. Well, in that case, the appointment is off, I refuse categorically to see you. I have nothing to say to you."

"I'm flabbergasted, the embassy couldn't have told you that—there was never any question of asking you for the least contact with Gilani!"

"Yes there was. That's exactly what your embassy said. I have nothing to say to you, don't try to contact me, that's it!"

The embassy—I immediately made sure—had obviously never spoken of a contact with Gilani.

Hamid Mir—I'm convinced, thinking it over now—spoke very loudly, to an audience, and with a brutality that can only be explained by the fact that he was not alone and wanted to convince the people around him of his determination.

Who? It doesn't matter. The fact, once again, is there. I prefer not to insist.

It's raining in Karachi. Under my window, I can hear the call of the ragman mixed with the *muezzin*'s. Tomorrow is Christmas. I think of Pearl's last Christmas. I think of Mariane and this sad year's end she must be going through. Who told me she was leaving to spend the holidays in Cuba, with little Adam? It was probably her. It was her without a doubt. And me, here, following in their footsteps, at the tail end of this terrible comet, with all the bad signs accumulating.

Better, of course, not to give them more weight than they necessarily deserve.

And to avoid the trap that would consist, here as elsewhere, of giving meaning to things that have none, and to exaggerate the importance of an incident....

But at the same time, I can't help but be surprised that all this is happening this way, a spate of things, all in such a short time....

These doors that shut and then, on the contrary, open, but in a way that is even more suspect.... These small provocations.... This phony proposition for an interview.... It's hard not to think that there's a thread that runs through all that, and that this thread is a message someone is trying to send me.

What message?

Without a doubt, that they've seen right through me.

That no one here is fooled any longer as to the real nature of my investigation, that also is without a doubt.

Well. We'll see. For the time being, I'm not dissatisfied with the progress I've made in the past year, it's true.

I began on the assumption that Omar was undoubtedly guilty, guilty and convicted, but without being able to completely exclude the possibility that he is too perfect a culprit, too little for a crime too great—and that focusing on his name could have the effect of throwing back into the shadows other names, names more important than his, more embarrassing. The Oswald syndrome, in a way, after the death of Kennedy. The eternal "it can't be him... there must be forces behind him that surpass him..." described by Norman Mailer.

Today, at the end of 2002, at the point of the investigation where I find myself, I know that's not true and that Omar, far from being this small-time criminal, this figurehead, this underling, is a considerable culprit, a prince in the universe of Evil, an absolutely central character since he stands at the exact intersection of some of the darkest forces of our times. I know that this name, Omar Sheikh, far from being advanced in order to protect others from being pronounced, is an enormously important name, much more significant than I had imagined in my most audacious speculations, and whose effect is not to hide but to summon some of the most terrifying figures in the modern encyclopedia of death. I know that, with Omar, we are in the presence of an unprecedented criminal configuration, where the two mutually exclusive theories of the Oswald case are simultaneously true: it's him and not him... not him because it is him... considerable forces, indeed, but his own force at the same time, which is their condensed version. I say "Omar Sheikh," and when I utter the words, I am naming the synthesis, in him, of the ISI and al-Qaida—that is the truth.

PART FIVE
"OVER INTRUSIVE"

CHAPTER 1 A FELLOW OF NO
COLLECTIVE IMPORTANCE

So the question is, why?

Yes, why al-Qaida? Why first, the ISI and now, al-Qaida? More precisely, why the ISI inside al-Qaida, or al-Qaida inside the ISI? Why are they intertwined—why did they combine forces to set a trap for a lone man?

Not that the combination is, in itself, anything surprising.

And one theory of this book is that this union is in the nature of things, in ordinary life and politics here. The thesis of this book, if one can call it a thesis, is that there exists an axis, a bond of flesh and, alas, of blood between these two forces that dominate Pakistan, and that no one can tell any longer which is in command of the other. My thesis—but do we even need to call it a thesis, when it's a fact that's obvious with every step, at every instant!—is that there exists, in the way they exchange their crimes and their powers, a reflexive relationship that often makes them merge into one, which is an essential feature of this country and what makes it so dangerous.

But a thesis is one thing; experience another.

It is one thing to know something patently obvious; it is quite another thing to put this obvious fact to a concrete test.

It is one thing to say, as I often have during this investigation, and as others have before me, that there's been an intentional confusion of roles, an incessant passing off of responsibility from one to another: You look for the ISI, you find al-Qaida; you look for al-Qaida, you run into the ISI; the bearded men are free-floating agents, and the agents are bearded men without beards or turbans; when you think about it, was the Hotel Akbar run by one or the other? The Brigadier Ijaz, the Shah Sahab of the Indian kidnapping cell, Saud Memon, Masood Azhar—are they the service's men, or bin Laden's? And Khalid Sheikh Mohammed, who was he really working for, and who abandoned him at the last moment? It's one thing to say all this, to see all these questions cropping up—but quite another to see the grand alliance, this pincer action in the actual case of an actual man.

And most of all, we may well have a thousand examples of this consubstantiality. We may well try to remember everything of the Taliban's history and their manipulation by the intelligence services. We may well recall the case of Hamid Gul, head of the ISI at the time of the Soviet war who, no sooner fired and relieved of his duty to preserve secrecy, immediately offered his services to the jihadist cause, never missing an occasion in the past few years to proclaim his love for bin Laden, Mullah Omar, and the jihad. We may well consider the case of Mahmoud Ahmad, Director General of the ISI on September 11—did he approve the transfer of $100,000 to Mohammed Atta in the name of the ISI, of which he was still chief at the time, or in honor of the jihad, for whom he would become an official propagandist as soon as he resigns from his post? I can't say. We may well consider Ahmad again, hand in hand with the rector of Binori Town, leading the delegation of holy men on a last-chance visit to Afghanistan to tell Mullah Omar his only

remaining means of avoiding war was to hand over bin Laden—
and we may well know that, on that day, both in what he said
and in the way he said it, he was more jihadist than the
jihadists, and perhaps blew on the flames instead of putting
them out. Intelligence agencies of the West may well know, as
does Islamabad, that on 8 October 2001, the day after
Musharraf's new Chief of Staff, Mohammed Aziz, took office,
his first act was to meet with the leaders of all the jihadist
groups of the "Army of Islam," some of which, like the Jaish,
were already on the Americans' blacklist of organizations linked
to al-Qaida. We may well be aware of the personal role of
Aziz—in principle a secular, military officer—in setting up the
Harkat ul-Mujahideen in 1998. We may well have no doubt as
to how things really are. It's nonetheless the first time the two
organizations actually meet, combine their efforts, and concert-
edly mobilize all of their respective powers not in order to
destroy a country (Afghanistan), or an empire (the United
States), or even a symbol (the Assembly of Kashmir at Srinagar,
or the Parliament of New Delhi), but a man (Daniel Pearl).

Of course there have been other cases of journalists kidnapped in Pakistan by ISI agents suspected of being backed up
by al-Qaida: Husain Haqqani (of the *Indian Express*); Najam
Sethi (of *The Friday Times*); Ghulam Hasnain (*Time* magazine).
But none of them was executed.

On the eve of the American war in Afghanistan, there was
the case of another lone man, Abdul Haq, who, having been sent
to the interior of the country to negotiate the surrender of
some Pashtun tribes, fell into a trap set by either the Pakistani

intelligence services, bin Laden's foreign combatants, the Taliban, or all three—to this day, no one knows which. But it was, precisely, on the eve of a war. And there were military stakes involved in the liquidation of Haq.

There was also the example of Massoud, another man alone, abandoned by all, the elimination of whom, it is less and less in doubt, was the collective effort of the same ISI and al-Qaida. But Massoud was a military commander. He was alone, but he occupied an essential place on the board of the grand game at the time. He was weak, practically disarmed, but there was a considerable strategic interest in eliminating him and decapitating the Northern Alliance two days before September 11.

Daniel Pearl—he was nothing. To all outward appearances, he was neither what was at stake nor one of the targets. He was unarmed. Inoffensive. His vocation was neither that of martyr nor of hero. To quote the famous epigraph of Sartre's *La Nausée,* borrowed from Céline, Pearl was "a fellow of no collective importance, just an individual," who had no obvious reason to see this colossal, two-fold machinery set in motion before him. And the more I turn it over in my mind, there is something that seems enigmatic to me in this massive conspiracy against an individual of no importance, who represents only himself.

Political philosophers have contemplated the mystery of this "counter-one"—the production of a victim, a slave, or, quite simply, an "other," a mirror image of the despotic, dominating "One."

The theory of the scapegoat tells us about the mimetic urge that fixates on the blind spot embodied by the sacrificial victim:

an innocent, sometimes anybody—and, at the end of the sacrifice, the calculated miracle of the group reconciled and producing its own innocence.

My generation (that of the struggle against totalitarianism) has known in the U.S.S.R. and elsewhere the case of these other solitary men, belonging neither to a community nor a party, without a clearly articulated political agenda, forbidden to express themselves, and incapable of airing their alternative point of view regarding the subjugated and sometimes dismembered society. We knew of so many of these individuals who were chosen, so to speak, by chance, without consideration of any real danger they may have represented. We called them "dissidents," but there was something almost inappropriate about this term and the way it suggested a split, even a subversion, that actually threatened the existing powers. And there was something especially disturbing about the spectacle of these immense, all-powerful, machines expending so much energy to silence adversaries that they had begun to exhibit and almost construct.

We knew (the same years, the same combats and, basically, the same pattern) the case of Cuba and its tropical Gulag. On one side, the "one man too many" (a saying of Solzhenitsyn's that Claude Lefort used in his commentary at the time)—a man condemned, thrown into prison, executed, for futile and often perfectly mysterious reasons. On the other, a politico-legal apparatus (the "granite ideology," from Solzhenitsyn again) throwing its enormous power into motion, against all reason, despite inevitable international disapproval and the resultant discredit, despite, as well, the political uselessness, demonstrated a hundred times over, of this polarization around the case of a simple individual—in order to shore up this regime of proscription. In short, the whole of Cuba transformed into an immense inverted pyramid resting, with all its enormous weight, not on the base, but on the point: the tortured or paralyzed body, the suffocating soul, of a poet, a homosexual, a Catholic, a Cuban.

Could Daniel Pearl be the equivalent, without the literature and in the landscape of the new world, of a Solzhenitsyn, a Pliouchtch, a Valladares—these other men alone, these "beings apart" of Mallarmé, these victims at once absurd and necessary, whose cause inspired our youth and who were like the mirror image of the almighty tyrant?

Perhaps. I don't know. But we must admit, Pearl's is a decidedly strange situation.

All the more so because there's still something else.

In the course of telling this story, we have seen the protagonists emerge.

We've seen them introduced, one by one, as the investigation progressed, and then all together, in the organization chart of the crime.

Yet there is a detail I haven't discussed before, perhaps because, up until now, it wasn't entirely clear to me: It's the odd and, come to think of it, unprecedented fact that, when you consider the biographies of all of Omar's accomplices, when you go down the list of the names and the chief to whom each one, like all jihadists, has sworn allegiance, we realize that these seventeen men are not from one group, nor from two, but from all the groups, all the parties, all the factions of the Islamist movement of Pakistan.

Usually, there's one particular group behind a particular crime. For the Sheraton, it's the Lashkar.

For the grenade attacks or the bomb at the bus stop of Kupwara, or the market at Chadoura, in Cachemire, it's the Jaish.

For the suicide bombing against the American consulate of Karachi, it's the Harkat ul-Mujahideen.

The Harkat ul-Ansar, become the Harkat ul-Mujahideen, for the kidnappings of tourists in Kashmir, at the end of the '90s.

Sometimes, as in the case of the 13 December 2001 attack on the Parliament in New Dehli, two groups join forces, in this case the Jaish and the Lashkar e-Toïba. But that's rare. Very rare. These organizations despise one another. They fight among themselves as much as they fight the common enemy. Remember the conflict over the control of the goods and real estate holdings of the Harkat ul-Mujahideen when Fazlur Rehman Kahlil and Masood Azhar split up, early in 2002. Consider the way the ISI itself operates, and the energy it spends not to unite, but to divide the groups that might be tempted to gain too much importance and do without its supervision.... And there's the case of the Jamiat ul-Ulema e-Islam splitting, under the influence of the services, into three groups (the JUI-F of Fazlur Rahman, the JUI-S of Sami ul-Haq, and the JUI-Q of Ajmal Qadri) which, though ideological triplets, are engaged in a struggle that is all the more bitter. In short, it's every man for himself. The logic of a sect with schisms, crimes among friends, rivalries of proximity, mutual denunciations—to such a degree that the absolute rule is that of permanent and ferocious competition between organizations pursing the same goals *but* fighting over the same territory and the same sources of funding. The rule, with very few exceptions dictated by circumstance, is "one crime, one group"—one beautiful jihadist crime, like a rare resource not to be shared, at any price, with the brother enemy.

But here....

The strange thing about this particular crime is that it is impossible to attribute to this group or that; its distinctive characteristic in the history of Pakistani or bin Laden-style terrorism is that it has given rise to a concerted effort on the part of groups that are otherwise divided in every way.

Hyder, alias Imtiaz Siddiqui alias Amjad Hussain Farooqi alias Mansur Hasnain, is a member of the Harkat Jihad e-Islami.

Arif, alias Mohammed Hashim Qadeer, comes from the Harkat ul-Mujahideen.

Adil Mohammen Sheikh, the policeman, Suleman Saquib and Fahad Nasim, his cousins, from the cell in charge of scanning the photos and sending them by e-mail to the *Wall Street Journal* and to the news agencies, all belong to the Jaish.

Akram Lahori is the emir of Lashkar, which is also the group Fazal Karim and Bukhari belong to.

Asif Ramzi, Lahori's lieutenant for the Pearl operation, is the boss of the Qari Hye which is a sort of subsidiary of the Lashkar.

Abdul Samat, as far as we know, is a member of the Tehriq e-Jihad, a small group founded in 1997 by dissident elements of the Harkat.

Memon is from the Al-Rashid Trust.

And as for Omar, he has his own personal group: the Movement for the Restoration of Pakistani Sovereignty.

In short, every group, it seems, is there.

It's like a parliament of Pakistani Islamism.

It's a crime syndicate united around Pearl's body in life, and then his cadaver in death, as it has never gathered for any other.

On one side a lone man, fragile, representing only himself.

And on the other, the ISI, and al-Qaida—and now, the jihadist syndicate in full force.

Never seen before.

A matchless alignment for a murder that is decidedly one of a kind.

CHAPTER 2 THE MAN WHO KNEW TOO MUCH

One initial explanation is obvious. Pearl was a journalist. Just a journalist, working in one of the countries of the world where it is least propitious to be a journalist, where all journalists are, as such, in permanent mortal danger. Because they are insubordinate? Free agents? Because of their annoying tendency to disobey, to refuse to toe the line? No. The real reason is that they are perceived, on the contrary, as not being free, not in the least independent—the real problem is that, in the imagination of the Pakistani military man with the low forehead, or the Islamist militant on fire with his saintly hatred, they are, by definition, spies, and nothing distinguishes a *Wall Street Journal* reporter from a CIA agent. A free journalist? Contradiction in terms. A journalist who is not linked to the intelligence agencies, the "three letters," of his country? An oxymoron, unthinkable. I've seen what I'm talking about. I've felt it myself—the extraordinary difficulty of gathering information in Pakistan without giving the impression that you are an informer. I've observed it every time, these last few trips, when I tried to explain that, all right, perhaps this wasn't a novel in the classic sense, but at least I was independent, investigating on my own and researching only the facts. Every time I met the officials, the chiefs, and deputy chiefs of this insane police force, I observed the eyelids heavy with suspicion, the tarantula-like stare, the ill-humored air of mistrust dripping with sly innuendos, that seemed to say: "Cut the crap, we know very well that an independent writer is a term that makes no sense...." No one doubts that this is why Danny died. No one doubts that the bloodthirsty cretins who made him say he was a Jew actually believed he was also an agent of the Mossad or the CIA. From this standpoint, his death makes him a martyr for that grand cause which is freedom of the press. We have to add his name to the long list of journalists, Pakistani and non-Pakistani, imprisoned or dead so that the press, and its freedom, might live. To salute Daniel Pearl, to honor his memory and his courage, is to pay tribute to all those living who, after him, accepted the same risk as he had in going, whatever the cost, to do their jobs in Karachi: Elizabeth Rubin, Dexter Filkins, Michel Peyrard, Steve LeVine, Kathy Gannon, Didier François, David Rohde, Daniel Raunet, Françoise Chipaux, Rory McCarthy, and others whose names I am forgetting—the hot iron in the wound of Pakistan, the honor of this profession.

A second good explanation is that this entire event happened in a country—a region? a world?—where, since the Afghanistan war and in anticipation of the war in Iraq soon to come, Washington was generally looked upon as the capital of the Empire of Evil, the home of the Antichrist and Satan: Daniel Pearl was American. A good American? There are no good Americans, the sects of the assassins think and say. Opponent of Bush? Democrat? Appalled at the blunders of Dostom and of the American Special Forces at Mazar-e-Sharif? An American who, according to Danny Gill, his friend from Los Angeles, probably would have joined the clan of liberal minds who would have thought twice before supporting George Bush's absurd war? "Exactly," they insist. "That's almost worse. It's the Devil's greatest ruse, the trick of the Demon. It's the ploy they've found to disarm the Arab nation...." Wasn't he sympathetic to you? A friend of the dispossessed? Wasn't Daniel Pearl one of those Americans who object to hateful stereotypes, reject chauvinism, and take the defense of the downtrodden? "Right, thanks, we know. During those eight days, we had plenty of time to see that this sap wasn't even hostile towards us. But that's not the question. We don't care what an American does or doesn't think, because the crime isn't thought, the crime is America. We don't give a damn about what your Danny did or didn't do, because America isn't a country but an idea, and it's not even an idea but the very countenance of hell." Pearl was killed less for what he thought or did than for what he was. If he was found guilty of anything at Gulzar e-Hijri, it was the singular, unique, ontological crime of simply having been born. Guilty of being, and of being born.... Guilt without a crime, essential, metaphysical.... Doesn't that remind us of something? Can't we hear, behind this kind of trial, the voice of another infamy? Pearl is dead because he was an American in a country where being American is a sin, stigmatized with a rhetoric that echoes the sin of being a Jew. Pearl was the victim of this other crap called anti-Americanism and which also makes you, in the neo-fascist eyes of the fundamentalists, the dregs, the scum, a subhuman to be eliminated. American, hence a son of a bitch. America, or Evil. The old, European anti-Americanism blended with that of the religious fanatics. The rancid hatred of our French *Pétainists* given a third-world damned-of-the-earth makeover. I finished this book at precisely this moment. In my ears, the planetary clamor, that made of America a region, not of the world, but of the spirit—and the blackest spirit, at that. Better to live as a serf under Saddam than free thanks to Bush, the global crowd proclaimed. One could, like me, refuse Bush's war but, nonetheless, find this clamor despicable. Daniel Pearl died of this.

And then, finally, there's a third reason. Pearl was a Jew. He was a Jew in a country where Judaism is not a religion, and even less an identity, but another crime, another sin. He was a positive Jew. He was a Jew in the way Philip Roth or Albert Cohen are Jews. He was proud of it. Affirmative. Didn't one of his colleagues tell me the story of this scene in Peshawar, an Islamist fiefdom, where, in a group of journalists asked about their religion, he placidly replied "Jewish," which turned the atmosphere glacial. He was a Jew like his father, like his mother. He was a Jew like one of his grandfathers, Chaïm Pearl, who gave his name to a street in B'nei Brak, Israel. He was this sort of Jew able, at the moment of supreme martyrdom, to proceed in the sanctification of the name of Jew. And he is most surely a victim of modern anti-Semitism, the anti-Semitism that starts, in fact, with B'nei Brak, ties the name of Jew to the name of Israel and, without renouncing any of its timeworn clichés, readapts them to a new set of charges, reintegrates the whole thing into a system where even the name of Israel has become a synonym for the worst of this world—making the figure of the actual Jew the very face of crime (Tsahal), of genocide (the theme, trotted out ever since Durban, and even before then, of the massacre of the Palestinians), of the desire to falsify history (the Shoah as a lie designed to conceal the reality of Jewish power). From Durban to B'nei Brak, the new clothing of hatred. From "one Jew, one bullet," chanted by some NGO members in Durban, to the Yemeni knife that actually murdered Daniel Pearl, a sort of a sequence. Daniel Pearl is dead because he was a Jew. Daniel Pearl is dead, victim of neo–anti–Judaism that is blossoming before our eyes. I've been talking about this neo–anti–Judaism for the past twenty-five years. There are a few of us who have sensed that the processes of legitimization of this ancient hatred are being profoundly reworked, and who have written about this fact for the past quarter century. For a long time, the rabble said the Jews are hateful because they killed Christ (Christian anti-Semitism). For a long time because, on the contrary, they invented him (modern, anticlerical, pagan anti-Semitism). For a long time it was because they are supposed to be a race who will always be foreigners in any land and this race must be erased from the face of the earth (birth of modern biology, racism, Hitlerism). Well, my sense is that that's all over. I have a feeling we will hear less and less that the Jews are hateful in the name of Christ, the anti-Christ, or racial purity. And what we see is a reformulation, a new means of justification for the worst which, as in France during the Dreyfus Affair, but on a more global scale this time, will associate hatred of Jews with the defense of the oppressed—a terrifying stratagem. That, against the backdrop of the religion of victimization, using this transformation of the Jew into executioner and the Jew-hater into the *new* Jew (that's right, the rabble is intimidated by nothing, slander is nothing new to them, they can very well lift towards real Jews the pure image of a victimized "Jew" now embodied by others) will legitimize the murder of a Jew as the henchman of Bush and Sharon: "Busharon" as they would say. Again, Daniel Pearl died, of this.

So there are three explanations that might satisfy me.

Three reasons to kill Daniel Pearl, each one separately and all the more so together, are adequate to explain the outcome of this drama.

Except that it doesn't work.

No, none of these reasons, however strong and solid they may be in and of themselves, manages to convince me.

None of them explains why it is this particular Jew, this journalist, this American, and not some other, whom al-Qaida, the secret services, and the entire syndicate decided to eliminate on the morning of 31 January 2002.

And that, because of a detail which, for the past year, has unceasingly intrigued me: Daniel Pearl was kidnapped on the 23rd; on the 23rd, the kidnappers know that he is a Jew, a journalist, an American; on that day, they are perfectly conscious of this hyperbolic triple guilt; and yet, they wait until the 31st, eight days after the kidnapping, to decide to punish him for being this triple culprit, which is bound to mean that something happened during those eight days—an element appeared that was not there on the 23rd but that would be there on the 31st and would make the ultimate decision to kill him inevitable.

I know what they say: The assassins didn't discover that Danny was Jewish until the 30th, from an article by Kamran Khan in the *News*—that's the new element, then, his Jewishness, that they weren't aware of before. But it doesn't jibe. Knowing

Danny, knowing, through all those who knew him, especially in Pakistan, that he made a point of honor of never dissimulating his Judaism, I cannot for an instant imagine that he didn't inform Omar of this during their initial meeting, at the Hotel Akbar. And isn't that what Omar himself declared to the police? Isn't it what Fazal and Bukhari also said, during their respective interrogations: "Omar called to tell us, there's a man here who's an American and a Jew... come quickly, we're going to kidnap him"?

I know what they say: It's the escape attempt that set everything off; when he tried, for the second time, to escape, his jailers lost patience and decided to put an end to this—that's the new element, that's where everything went haywire, right? Isn't it, according to the FBI people, the absolute rule in these cases: "never try to escape! Never, never ever!" I don't believe that either. First of all—as I said—these escape attempts are not confirmed, especially since the bullet in the knee hasn't been found by any of the coroners' teams that have examined the dismembered body. And, beyond that, because I can't imagine Bukhari, Lahori, Farooqi and the others reasoning like this. We are talking about, I repeat, the Karachi chiefs of important groups, the best of jihadism, serious people, militants, the Pakistani representatives of al-Qaida—who could imagine they would follow such a puerile line of reasoning? Who could convince us that they said to themselves, "as punishment, we'll kill him"? How could anyone suppose a murder of such importance, decided and committed by men of this caliber, could be decided on the reaction of an annoyed jailer?

It's also been attributed, I've heard it said myself, to the passing of time: it's just the time that elapsed... the lassitude... the impasse... here we have this guy on our hands, we don't know what to do with him any more, so let's kill him and cut him up into ten pieces and then put them all back together again, that will be the simplest thing to do.... Right. Once again, anything is possible. Except that this scenario isn't plausible either. Don't forget, until otherwise informed, we have to assume these were Yemenis who killed him. But someone had to make the decision to send for them, these Yemenis. They had to be located, contacted, brought to Gulzar e-Hijri and, finally, ex-filtrated again. How could this have been done lightly? How could this succession of tasks have been the result of a fit of anger and impatience? Does one actually set in motion such forces and events, expend the necessary amount of energy, just like that, on a whim, by default, or out of sheer irritation?

No.

Anyway you look at it, you cannot avoid thinking that something else happened during those seven days of detention other than a wave of weariness, an aborted escape, or an article by so widely respected a journalist as Kamran Khan.

Better still: Since all of this is happening in seclusion, since they are all, captors and captive, living in total confinement, cut off from the world, since all they have to do for seven days is to talk and talk and talk, one can't help but wonder if this other thing was something that was said rather than something that happened, and that it's something Danny said that led his jailers to conclude that he could not walk out of Gulzar e-Hijri free.

Then what is it that was said? What could Pearl have said that would have prompted his captors to call for three professional murderers to come execute him? Since I can't imagine it had anything to do with small talk, life in Los Angeles, his profession, or even his general perception of Pakistan, the United States, or the world, and since I think as well that Pearl took advantage of that time to continue his work, and advance his research into the Islamist milieu—in short, to pump these political and human specimens, which bad fortune had put in his way, once more, I can think of only one solution.

At the same time that he got them to talk, they, in turn, made him talk.

When he asked them questions, he revealed himself, through his way of questioning.

He thought he would get the truth from them, but they, in a sense, and without his necessarily being aware of it, verified what he knew and thus debriefed him.

Or else, another aspect of the hypothesis, slightly different but equally credible: given his extraordinary professionalism, he attracted confidences, confessions, details—it's entirely possible that he succeeded beyond his expectations, and that his captors, without realizing it or at least without really wanting to, gave him sensitive information that, afterwards, they regretted having so blithely offered.

My feeling is that, during their conversations, during the long nights of collective solitude, in the heat of his exchanges, for example, with Fazal Karim, his guard, it became evident either that the prisoner of Gulzar e-Hijri already knew far too much, or else that he had succeeded in gleaning still more from his jailers—and that, in either case, there was no longer any question of letting him walk out of there, carrying his secrets.

Danny died of what he knew.

Danny, the man who knew too much.

I am convinced that his was a journalist's death—dead not only because of what he was, but because of what he was looking for, and perhaps finding, and planning to write about.

Isn't that, incidentally, what President Pervez Musharraf himself said when, the day after the murder, in an astounding, angry outburst, he exclaimed that Daniel Pearl had been "over intrusive"—too curious, sticking his nose in places he shouldn't have?

Didn't Musharraf give it away when, in a comment cited in the *Washington Post* (among others) on 23 February 2002, he dared to declare, "Perhaps Daniel Pearl was over inquisitive; a mediaperson should be aware of the dangers of getting into dangerous areas; unfortunately, he got over-involved in intelligence games."

That's my hypothesis.

That's the conclusion I have come to.

So the question then becomes: Why? What had Pearl discovered, or what was he in the process of discovering, that condemned him to death? What is the stolen secret that, for his captors, was out of the question for him to walk away with?

The relationship between al-Qaida and the ISI, of course.

The tight web of relations between the two organizations, the two worlds.

This holy alliance that condemns and executes him—we can presume that, yes, he was on their trail, and that, precisely, was his fatal error.

But all of that is not saying much.

You don't execute a man because he evokes in a general way the ties between an intelligence agency and a terrorist organization.

You don't expend so much effort to kill him, you don't send an entire syndicate into action because he might develop some thesis about the underbelly of an important country.

The real question, obviously, is what, precisely, had he discovered in all this that was new and that would have caused difficulties for all of them?

This is where the reign of the uncertain begins.

This is where witnesses are rare and, if they exist, they are silent, or out to disinform.

So, like a detective following his hunches, I move forward now, sifting through clues and speculations, for the over-riding truth.

I have two hypotheses, in fact.

Two distinct hypotheses, in no way contradictory.

But first of all—a question of method—one last detour. Daniel Pearl's schedule in the weeks, the days, the hours preceding his kidnapping. Who he saw. What he read. The articles he wrote and those he was working on. This intrigue, in a word, woven with the threads of a life, where (as in a tapestry, is hidden the motive that secretly inspires it) lies, quite probably, the explanation for his death.

CHAPTER 3 IN THE FOOTSTEPS
OF DANIEL PEARL

First, my sources:

The account of Pearl's fixer in Islamabad, Asif Farooqi, given during our meeting in his office at the Japanese press agency.

A conversation with Jamil Yusuf, former businessman now heading Karachi's Citizen-Police Liaison Committee.

That of another Pakistani, from Peshawar, who asked not to be identified but whose information I have good reason to believe is credible. Let's call him Abdullah, and let's say also that he's the kind of journalist who works under his own name for the Pakistani press and, anonymously, for visiting journalists—both bold things to do in Pakistan.

And the memorandum written 27 January, four days after the kidnapping, by Mariane Pearl and Asra Nomani, Danny's colleague and tenant of the house where the couple stayed in Karachi: This twenty-page memorandum, written in great urgency, before anyone knew the tragic outcome of the kidnapping, sheds the most light on Danny's movements and is obviously the most precise, the most precious source.

Daniel Pearl, I repeat, arrived in Pakistan for the first time in October, just before the beginning of the American air strikes in Afghanistan. He stayed there for two months. He wrote three or four major articles. He returned at the end of November to Bombay, which was his actual base. On 15 December he returned to Islamabad for what would be the final time.

He is alone this time.

Mariane, pregnant, stays in India for a few more days.

"It's sad," says a Pakistani *Dawn* journalist Danny and Asif run into in the bar of a grand hotel in the embassy quarter. "It's almost Christmas and you'll be alone." Danny smiles, ever faithful to his penchant for openness on the question. "Oh, Christmas—you know I'm not Christian, I'm Jewish. The Jews aren't that big on Christmas."

With Steve LeVine, the *Journal's* central Asia correspondent visiting Pakistan, he starts an investigation on the risks of the transfer of nuclear know-how from Pakistan to Afghanistan and the Taliban. In particular, the two journalists are tracking an NGO supposedly engaged in humanitarian programs but which, in reality, serves as a cover for this kind of trafficking: the Ummah Tameer e-Nau, whose honorary president happens to be General Hamid Gul, a former head of the ISI. I've come across his name often over the past year. Pearl is also looking into a certain Dr. Bashiruddin Mahmood, a Pakistani scientist won over to the Islamist cause who, in August, had visited Osama bin Laden.

On the 23rd or the 24th, he starts a second investigation, without LeVine, into the illegal trafficking of electronic equipment between Afghanistan and Pakistan. He goes to Peshawar. He hangs around the vast Karkhano Market, where he finds imports from Afghanistan of almost everything the Taliban prohibits, but which he discovers, to his surprise, they now make a fat profit on by exporting: from a country of bearded men, Gillette razors; from the country where smoking is prohibited, Marlboro cigarettes; from the radically iconoclastic country where images are forbidden, all sorts of video cassettes, and the latest model Sony televisions. What hypocrisy! For the sarcastic journalist he knows how to be when the subject lends itself, a godsend.

The next day he starts a third investigation into the fundamentalist groups Musharraf has just outlawed, but which continue to operate in Kashmir, and, he thinks, also in Lahore and Karachi. For that investigation he goes to Bawahalpur where he plans to interview Masood Azhar, the head of Jaish and, I recall one final time, the friend, master, and tutor of Omar Sheikh. But Masood has been arrested again, along with other militants whose calls for the anti-American jihad have begun to clash with the image of Musharraf's grand antiterrorist alliance. So he has to settle for Masood's brother whom, incidentally, he suspects of involvement with the Air India hijackers of Kandahar. He also visits the Jaish offices which are supposed to have been shut down but which he notes continue to function rather openly, recruiting and organizing meetings. The visit is short and somewhat tense. He stays only thirty-six hours in Bawahalpur.

On the 27th, his article co-written with LeVine on nuclear secrets having appeared three days earlier, Danny is contacted by a shady individual who pretends to have read the piece and to have in his possession a case of fissionable material from a Ukrainian nuclear power plant, which he is ready to sell for $100,000. Danny smells a scam. In Karachi he contacts a staff member of a large Western embassy who is familiar with these things, who tells him not to follow up. But Danny is sufficiently intrigued to check his notes on the subject. It's strange, he tells Asif, how little impact our article has had. Maybe the timing, just before Christmas. Or the tone. Or maybe, let's be honest, we've got less than Seymour Hersh had in his 29 October *New Yorker* article, "The Risks to Pakistan's Nuclear Arsenal," or than Douglas Frantz and David Rhode had in the 28 November *New York Times* article "Two Pakistanis Linked to Papers on Anthrax Weapons," or than Molly Moore and Kamran Kahn in their 12 December *Washington Post* article, "Two Nuclear Experts Briefed Bin Laden, Pakistanis Say." It bothers him not to have the goods, or to have less than *The Washington Post, The New York Times,* or *The New Yorker.* It was even more annoying because for the final few days, Farooqi remembers, he was getting e-mails from his paper urging him to move, to get some information, to be more exclusive. The spirit of competition. The pressure of the information-market. He decides, without LeVine, to return to investigation number one.

On the 31st of December, Mariane arrives.

He's there at the Karachi airport to meet her, happy as a kid.

The next day, New Year's, they fly to Islamabad, meet up with Asif, and settle into their usual guest house, Chez Soi, at the top of Murree Road.

In Islamabad with Asif, he starts a fourth investigation, this time on something very different—a comparison of television programs in India and Pakistan, and how they inflame the passions of both countries and affect the culture of war. What is the war's lexicon? What kind of images, and what kind of commentary? Is there a journalistic responsibility for the military escalation between the two nuclear powers?

On the 6th, an article in the *Boston Globe* reports on a little-known figure of Islamist radicalism, Sheikh Mubarak Ali Shah Gilani, leader of the sect al-Fuqrah, and the guru of "shoe bomber" Richard Colvin Reid. It's the kind of story Pearl loves. Gilani is exactly the type of character he is looking for in his investigation covering the outlawed Islamist groups. Find me someone, he tells Asif, who can contact this Gilani! Find me someone who can take us to him!

On the 7th, Asif calls one of his colleagues whose name—bizarrely—never appears in the official accounts of the investigation or even in the press. He is Zafar Malik, of the Urdu newspaper *Jang*, a journalist who is very close to the jihadist groups engaged in the armed struggle in Afghanistan and Kashmir. "Maybe," he tells Asif, "maybe I have what you're looking for. His name is Arif, I've met him four or five times. The first time was a year ago in the offices of Harkat ul-Mujahideen in Rawalpindi... I don't know him well but I'll see if contact is possible...."

Two days later, the 9th, Zafar Malik succeeds in making contact. Danny hires a taxi that picks him up in front of Chez Soi. Accompanied by Asif, they take Pindhora Road to the midpoint between Islamabad and Rawalpindi. There, he finds a man of about twenty, bearded, wearing the traditional *shalwar kameez*, who introduces himself as the boss of a clothing manufacturer in Rawalpindi. This is the Arif that Malik spoke of. He gets into the taxi with Danny and Asif. Of course, he says, Gilani.... Nothing easier than to go see Gilani. I'll take you there right now, to his house in Chaklala, in the suburbs, right near the Islamabad military air base. (Always this proximity, both symbolic and physical, of the two worlds: that of Islamism and jihad on one side, and the army and the ISI on the other.)

Except, when they arrive, the house is empty and, according to the neighbors, its owner has just left for Chak Shazad, a quarter on the opposite side of the city. They don't know the exact address. Was Gilani getting nervous? Had he heard about the article in the *Boston Globe* and started to worry? Or is this the trap they have begun to lay for Danny?

Still, on the 9th, first at 13:58, then again at 15:34, Danny calls former Afghanistan mujahid, ISI agent, and bin Laden pilot, Khalid Khawaja, the confirmed Islamist, whom he visited in his office upon first arriving in Islamabad. He had been given Khawaja's name and address in Washington. "The man is complicated," they said. "He's the one who practically announced the attack on the World Trade Center in a declaration on CBS, in July 2001. But he's paradoxical, provocative, he has interesting contacts, he might be able to help you." So, Danny went to see him. Khawaja is even one of the first people he contacted when he arrived in Pakistan. And to his surprise they got along well. Danny didn't dislike him—this secular Islamist, this beardless fundamentalist, this anti-American steeped in American culture and even molded by it, who embodied all the ambivalence, all the hardened hatred of the most radical part of the Muslim world toward the West. So, now, Danny calls him again. And as he has just read in the *Globe* that Khawaja is a friend not only of bin Laden, but also of the famous Gilani, he asks him, "Do you have any way to help me meet Gilani?"

The 10th, at 12:21, he calls Khawaja again. The conversation is short, 37 seconds. Two hypotheses. The first: Gilani again, still Gilani—he learned the night before through one of Asif's sources that Gilani had married a cousin of Khawaja's wife, and even if he has since married a few other women, he has never divorced her—Danny learned, in other words, that the two men have closer ties than indicated by the *Boston Globe*. So he calls the former pilot to ask again, insistently: "Gilani, this is very important to me—I have to leave in a few days and I want this meeting with Gilani before I leave." The second hypothesis: Danny's investigation of the transfer of nuclear expertise, something I myself wonder if Khawaja isn't well informed about; and if I ask myself this question, I imagine that a journalist of Danny's caliber asked the question before me. Following this hypothesis, he calls Khawaja to ask him not just about Gilani, but about Sultan Bashiruddin Mahmoud and Abdul Majid, the two nuclear scientists most up-to-date on the techniques of uranium and plutonium enrichment and whom the CIA knows had contacts in August with bin Laden and his lieutenant, the Egyptian Ayman Zawahiri.

Pearl doesn't lose sight, in the meantime, of investigation number 2, into the culture of war and propaganda. So, still on the 10th, he meets Naeem Bukhari, a courageous and independent television producer, who tells him, "You should follow this Pakistani television crew—they are shooting right now, some man-in-the-street interviews on the theme, 'What do you think of the situation? How do you see your Indian neighbors? Do you think Pakistan should do more, speak and act more strongly?' You should follow them and see how they work." Which Danny does. He spends the better part of the day, pencil in hand, with the crew. He is horrified by the way the journalist asks his questions—appalled at how the tone of the questions themselves orient the answers. Shameful! he says. What kind of television station tells people: "It's difficult to love your country without hating your neighbors"? That "A good Pakistani must scorn Indians and Jews"? Isn't it just a disguised way of inflaming passions, of calling for murder? Why not just say up front "produced and directed by the army"?

Still on the 10th, in the afternoon, while Danny and Asif are in a bazaar in Rawalpindi, Asif gets a call from Arif, the man who took them the day before to Gilani's empty house. Essentially, Arif says: "Tell your boss not to worry, he's got a raincheck. I know someone close to Gilani who will set up the meeting you're looking for." This someone, supposedly called Bashir, is in reality, Omar Sheikh.

On the 11th, the big meeting with Bashir, alias Omar, takes place. A taxi, like two days before. Another meeting on Pindhora Road. Arif meets them at the same intersection, but this time he is accompanied by a bearded friend, who remains silent as Arif takes them to the Hotel Akbar, room 411, where Omar is waiting. The long conversation to gain his confidence. The club sandwiches. The iced coffee brought up by the little man in the *djellaba*. The atmosphere so dreary that Danny oddly doesn't notice the ominous aspect, or if he has, it hasn't discouraged him from his quest for Gilani.

"Bizarre, this Shabir," he says to his fixer as they leave. "Why do you say 'Shabir'?" asks Asif. "He said his name was Bashir." "No, I distinctly heard him say 'Shabir,'" says Pearl. In fact they are both right. Because Omar got tripped up in his own lie. One time he said Shabir and another, Bashir. So that the next day, trying to cover the slip, he signs his first e-mail with the odd, rather un-Pakistani name, "Bashir Ahmed Shabir Chowdry." It should have raised suspicions, if not for Pearl, at least for Asif. Was this Asif's real mistake?

On the 12th, Danny is still in Rawalpindi, in the smugglers market. Mariane wants a CD player. So he asks for a CD player. But when he is ready to pay, he asks for a receipt. What are you talking about? asks the merchant. How can you expect a receipt when you're in the smugglers' market and you're buying stolen goods? The scene will be repeated throughout the day, all over Rawalpindi. Danny, a man of principle, demanding the receipt, and the merchants, incapable of giving him one, persistently refusing. Mariane, in the end, is deprived of her CD player. And his ongoing investigation of the contraband trade between Afghanistan and Pakistan (an excellent first article in the series has already appeared on the 9th, three days earlier) continues steadily to enrich itself with experience.

From the night of the 12th to the 16th, he's in Peshawar. Does he want to go into Afghanistan, like fellow journalist Michel Peyrard? Is he looking for traces of al-Qaida and its ties with Pashtun gangs in the tribal zones? I don't think so. Let's not forget, Daniel Pearl was not a war correspondent. Proposed an assignment in Afghanistan in November, he answered, "No, that's not my field. You need special training to be a war reporter. I don't have that training." Why would he have changed his mind? Why would he do now, what he didn't want to do yesterday? He's smart enough to know he's ill-trained for the job—why would he want to play the hero now? No, I think there are two reasons he's here. His ongoing investigation into the smuggling networks between Afghanistan and Pakistan. And the other is for the story we know he was conscious of having missed in part, the one that would inevitably take on full dimension in Peshawar, the strategic center of Afghanistan-Pakistan relations: the investigation of the possible transference of nuclear technologies organized by elements of the ISI for al-Qaida.

On the 18th he is back in Islamabad, where he will stay till the 22nd. These are the days, we recall, he receives a series of e-mails from "Bashir," alias Omar. These are the days, in other words, when the Gilani trap begins to close around him. Asif finds him suddenly strange. At once feverish and evasive. Enthusiastic yet absent. He's hiding something. Asif can't get anything out of him, but he can see that something has happened and Danny's hiding it.

"I'm going to Karachi," the reporter finally admits when cornered. "Why Karachi? Whatever for?" "Because from there I'll take a plane to Dubai and then the United States." "But there are flights from Islamabad! Why go by Karachi?" "All right," Danny says, giving up, "Let's say I've got something else to do in Karachi. I have to meet Gilani there, OK? But it's a secret."

Asif is suddenly very ill at ease. Almost angry. First of all, why the secrecy? Why go to Karachi without him? Why split up now, only a few days before his departure? He has become attached to this enthusiastic, principled American, so different from the Americans he's known. And there's another thing: he is the one who introduced Danny to Arif, who brought him to Bashir. When he thinks about it, it's the first time in his life that he's introduced one of his sources to a client. And that makes him feel, without knowing how to explain it, vaguely uneasy, almost afraid.

On the 22nd, Pearl is in Karachi.

On the 23rd, at 11:30, he sees Syed Zulfikar Shah, head of immigration at the city's airport. Then, between noon and 13:15, brigadier Tariq Mahmoud, director of civil aviation. Mariane, from her memorandum, speaks of two interviews on the issue of cyber-crime. I myself saw the subject of the second. He was cautioùs, of course, embarrassed, when he understood why I was knocking on his door. But we did speak. I asked him what he had discussed that day with the murdered American journalist. And my feeling is that here again Danny was interested in the movements of Richard Colvin Reid, thus still and always, although indirectly, Gilani.

We know the rest.

We know the schedule, hour by hour, from the end of the day of the 23rd. Between 14:30 and 15:30, Randall Bennett, head of security at the American embassy, now posted in Madrid, told him: "Don't go to this meeting... we don't like the way it looks." To the Marriott on foot. A phone call at 15:30 to Steph Laraich, chief of police at the French Consulate, who never found out how Danny got his number and still, to this day, regrets not having been there to take the call himself and say: "Watch out! Don't do it! Or at least, arrange a cover, a car to follow you, something." Danny makes another call at 16:00, to Asif, in Islamabad, who remembers an uncharacteristic anxiety in his voice. "I'm suddenly asking myself, is it safe to see this Gilani?" And Asif, not wanting to seem jealous or vexed: "He's a public person, not well known, but public; if you meet him in a public place, I guess it's OK; one thing though, Mariane; don't take Mariane; the public place might be a mosque or a *madrasa*, and it wouldn't be a good idea if Mariane were with you, dressed European and pregnant."

Mariane and Asra Nomani from 16:00 to 17:00. The cybercafé in Lakson Square Building, because he's still on the Reid affair. A telephone call to Jamil Yusuf at 17:10. The rendezvous a few minutes later at his office in Governor's House, where Yusuf will also tell Danny he doesn't feel right about the 19:00 rendezvous at the Village Garden. A call to Asra, who is hosting the Pearl's farewell dinner. "Start without me, I have one more appointment. I'll be there soon...." And then the Village Garden, finally, where he leaves Nasir Abbas's taxi, and where, at exactly 19:00, a car, maybe followed by another, and preceded by a motorcycle, stops for him.

If we add it all up, Daniel Pearl was obsessed by two great questions during his last four or five weeks, and I think we must look where he was looking, to uncover the reasons he was put to death—to understand, we have to follow him and try to resume those two, final investigations.

The elusive Gilani.

And the nuclear question.

CHAPTER 4 THE ASSASSINS ARE AMONG US

Gilani.

Why this fixation on Pir Mubarak Shah Gilani?

Why him, Pir Mubarak Shah Gilani, rather than, say, Masood Azhar, or Ramzi bin al-Shibh, or even bin Laden who, during those weeks, was roaming between western Afghanistan, the tribal zones of Pakistan, and, perhaps, Karachi?

It's been said: Richard Reid.

It's been said—Pearl himself thought—that the "shoe bomber" on the Air France Paris to Miami flight was a disciple of Gilani; that it is he, Gilani, who may have given him the go-ahead for action; and that Pearl was interested in Gilani because he was investigating the case of Richard Reid.

Fine.

But was Richard Reid really worthy of so much attention? Would Pearl have searched so thoroughly, mobilized so many contacts and so much energy, taken such risks, if it was just a question of reconstructing the itinerary of a London car thief, even one who has gone through a conversion to terrorism?

Who is this man, who is this mysterious character that Pearl, on the last day of his stay in Pakistan, ignoring all the rules of security he knew better than anyone, wanted so much to interview, even if for just a few minutes?

Moinuddin Haider, Minister of the Interior, at the time of my November trip, pretended he had never heard of Gilani, nor his movement, the al-Fuqrah, literally, "The Poor," or, better still, "The Impoverished."

The Brigadier Javed Iqbal Cheema, his assistant, had developed a slightly different line, but one that didn't get me any further: "What is this business about going through fifteen intermediaries to get to Gilani? When we arrested Gilani, he told us, 'OK, gentlemen, I am available, I am not underground; if there's a journalist who wants to see me, I'd be thrilled; but this Mr. Pearl never called me, he never telephoned.' Now I, Brigadier Javed Cheema, put the question to you: Why did Mr. Pearl never call Gilani?" And when I immediately said: "If it's that easy to interview Gilani, you're on! If Daniel Pearl's sole fault was that he didn't ask politely, I'm asking you now: could you set this up for me? with your help, could I meet Mr. Gilani?" Cheema became rather flustered and suddenly found all kinds of reasons to carefully sidestep the question.

We recall as well the episode of Hamid Mir, the official biographer and interviewer of bin Laden, and of his odd way of ignoring all polite conventions, especially by referring to a request I had never made as a pretext for canceling an appointment that he had actually confirmed.

I took up the investigation from there.

I began again, at the point where Pearl had left off.

Like him, I went to Chakala, near the Islamabad air base where the mysterious Gilani was supposed to have resided but where I found a house that was not only empty and closed but, according to the neighbors, had been sold to "a Kuwaiti" who planned on "doing some remodeling."

I went to Chak Shazad where I saw his other house; the one Asif, Arif, and Danny had searched for in vain during their outing on the 9th—not as nice as the first one, a one-storey dwelling with walls of exposed bricks, windows protected by painted wood shutters, abandoned as well.

I also went to Lahore, to the old city, where Gilani's real, much nicer home, is located, surrounded by high walls and guarded like a fortress—as is the grand and prestigious *madrassa* of Jamia e-Namia, which has a dome engraved with the names of Gilani's first American disciples, converted in the early '80s, as described in Farah Stockman's article in the *Boston Globe* which had made such an impression on Pearl.

I met one of the disciples of the master, Wasim Yousouf, son of a Rawalpindi merchant, for whom belonging to al-Fuqrah is an honor, and who talked to me about it willingly.

And then, finally, I went to the United States, the source, as we shall see, of some of the trails that lead to Gilani and to his organization.

1. The first thing I realized is that Gilani is the head of a small group. A very small group, one that is little known. Nothing like the great jihadist organizations I've encountered, or that Pearl was investigating during the few days he spent in Peshawar. Nothing comparable to the Lashkar, Jaish e-Mohammed and other Harkat ul-Mujahideen that were, or at least aspired to be, mass organizations. In terms of goals or recruiting, nothing like these vast structures, these armies fighting for control of the people of the martyrs of Allah. A few hundred members. Maybe two hundred, with the core fol-lowing concentrated solely in the city of Lahore where Gilani

has his principle mission, his four wives, and the places where he teaches.

Outside this small following, the man expresses himself very little. He's a secretive person who claims to be a direct descendant of the Prophet and whose last interview, prior to Pearl's interest in him, dated from the early '90s. In short, this native of Kashmir, this forceful Islamist, who, in the rare photos of him that I've been able to find, appears to be a sort of giant, imposing, with a reddish beard, and a look of unbearable intensity, is the leader of a sect, with followers who change their names when they are admitted, as in all sects and in the training camps as well. (Richard Reid, for example, became Abdul Rauf—"Brother Abdul.") And, as the head of the sect, he is a sort of guru whose functions bear little in common with others such as Nizamuddin Shamzai and Masood Azhar, the mass orators who preach the jihad in full view of the press, in popular assemblies that are often gigantic.

It's not surprising that the Pakistani newspapers, so prolix when it comes to other groups, seemed caught off guard the day after the kidnapping, when this group suddenly appeared. Not surprising either that Moinuddin Haider, Minister of the Interior, told me that before the Pearl affair, he had actually never heard of al-Fuqrah.

2. This small, obscure, and mysterious sect nonetheless has ties, as they all do, with the intelligence services. Perhaps not with Haider, but with the services most certainly. They may be unknown in the police files, that's possible—but ties to the country's "invisible power" is without a doubt.

Omar admitted as much when, after the Rangers came to arrest Gilani at his home in Rawalpindi, he said that the sect's chief—to whom he had a brief introduction when he took his first guerilla training—had rendered "unexplained services to Islam and to Pakistan" (*The News,* 15 February 2002).

Khalid Khawaja, the former pilot for Bin Laden and ex-ISI officer who did not wish to see me, but told my fixer over the phone that we should "watch out for Gilani," because the guru was sick of being "mixed up in this unfortunate Pearl affair all the time"—Khawaja, in declarations made right after the kidnapping, when he and Gilani happened to be under scrutiny of the FBI, confirmed Gilani's ties to the services, probably to protect himself and to protect his friend (*Dawn,* 23 February 2002).

Same message from Vince Cannistraro, former counter-terrorism chief of the CIA now working in television, who immediately said, in the first feverish days of the search for Pearl, and, for once, without the usual cant: Gilani is "untouchable" because he counts "on the board of his organization" several "senior ISI officials" (NewsMax.com wires, 31 January 2002).

And as for Gilani himself, when the Rawalpindi police came looking for him, he did exactly what "Tariq" told me all the jihadists do when they are arrested: He immediately changed from his venerable master persona to that of the Mafioso who's been nabbed and he gave up the names of his contacts as well as a house secret or two, and declared that, during the '80s, he had informed the services of what he saw and heard during his then-frequent stays in the United States—in exchange for which, Pir Mubarak Shah Gilani, Daniel Pearl's last known contact, his last appointment before the kidnapping, the man he wanted to see and thought he would see when he arrived at the Village Garden, was out on the street after a few days, and would never to be bothered again (*The News*, 31 January 2002).

3. Gilani's al-Fuqrah is also linked to Osama bin Laden, like most of these groups, though probably in a more intimate and organic way.

Gilani, of course, denies it. He denies it today, now that he is in the limelight. But Khawaja told CBS News reporter George Crile, whom he led to Gilani a few days after Pearl's death: "I am telling you, I am sure of one thing, Osama does not have even one of his followers as committed as Sheikh Mubarak Gilani" (CBSNews.com, 13 March 2002). And, in a Canadian TV film shot in Khartoum in 1993, we see (Mira L. Boland, "Sheikh Gilani's American disciples," *The Weekly Standard*, 18 March 2002) the boss of al-Fuqrah at the "grand summit of terrorism," sponsored by the Sudanese strongman of the time, Hassan el-Turabi.

There are Afghan and Iranian mullahs. Delegates from George Habache's movement and Nayef Hawatmeh's. People from Hamas and Islamic Jihad, from the Lebanese Hezbollah. The aristocracy of world terrorism. And also, hand in hand with Gilani, a Saudi entrepreneur, little known at the time, veteran of the anti-Soviet jihad, Osama bin Laden.

Is it true, the journalist asks the Pakistani, that the two men recently arrested in relation to an investigation of plans to attack Indian targets in Toronto are your followers? And he responds, with an unbearable mixture of guile and insolence: one or two of them, yes.... I admit that one or two of them studied at our school in Lahore, but they're the exception... because, "once people join our university, they become real good citizens; they stop smoking, they stop stealing, they stop living on welfare, that is what I teach them."

Bin Laden, at the time, is beginning to weave his network. In Gilani, he has an ally, an antenna in New York, and perhaps more.

4. Why more? Are there different kinds of links to bin Laden? Of course. There is a major distinction to which very few European commentators pay enough attention. And that is the distinction between al-Qaida itself, which is a purely Arab, even Saudi organization, with several hundred members directly linked to bin Laden, responsible for his personal protection and constituting, in Afghanistan, with the backup of some Algerians, Moroccans, Palestinians, Egyptians and, especially, Yemenis, the famous "055 Brigade," which was "lent" to the Taliban in 1997 for the capture of Mazar e-Sharif; and there is the International Islamic Front for the Jihad Against the United States and Israel, which is, as the name indicates, an international organization, a federation of related groups, tied, of course, to the emir, but kept at a distance from the hard core—a sort of a Comintern of jihadism with several tens of thousands of combatants gravitating around a Center that, modernity dictates, no longer has a territory.

Well, Gilani is not a member of the International Front. Nor is he, of course, a "direct adherent" of al-Qaida; but he has a distinct status in comparison with the heads of the other groups which means that he is not, like them, a member of the terrorist Comintern either. "Pir Mubarak Shah Gilani is a master," al-Fuqrah member Wasim Yousouf told me. "Even Osama bows before Pir Mubarak Shah Gilani. Do you know that *Pir*, in

Urdu, means 'venerated master'?" A way of suggesting a tie of a different nature. A way of saying that Gilani enjoys a sort of an ideological, even political influence upon Osama.

The master of al-Qaida is a war lord. He is undoubtedly a good financier. But is he, by the same token, an ideologue? A spiritual master? Is he even a particularly enlightened reader of the Koran? Those who know him doubt it. All of those who worked on the founder of al-Qaida's discourse and on the evolution of his style over the years strongly sense that this master has had masters, some high-flying prompters, some ideological and political tutors, some more or less secret sources of inspiration that have helped him to become what he is.

We remember, for instance, this near-comic dialogue with his official interviewer, Hamid Mir, in November 2001: Mir, in reference to the Twin Towers attacks, asks him about the basis for a *fatwah* against American civilians and, in the heat of the discussion, asks him how, theologically, he resolves the thorny question of Americans who are Muslims but who nonetheless died in the attack; "I see you're trying to set a trap for me," says a suddenly disconcerted Osama, who seems to be caught off-guard, "I shall consult my friends and give you my response tomorrow morning."

We know that the Mufti Nizamuddin Shamzai, rector of the Binori Town mosque, is one of these "friends."

We know that Sheikh Abdullah Azzam, the Palestinian fundamentalist who created the al-Kifah Center in Peshawar in the early '80s and who was considered, until his death in 1989, one of the re-inventors of an authentic, transnational jihad, was another of these secret mentors.

Well, perhaps Gilani is still another. Perhaps that's what the Canadian tape of the Sudanese summit says when it shows the chief of al-Qaida, so good, so modest, next to the master from Lahore. And perhaps that was one of Daniel Pearl's hypotheses as well.

5. What is al-Fuqrah's ideology? And what distinguishes it from the ideology that motivates other jihadist organizations?

I have had access to two documents: a little propaganda pamphlet, in Arabic, that gives the Gilanian vision of the holy war; and then a map of the world, distributed to the faithful, entitled "The United States of Islam," outlining, colored in green, with a green flag planted squarely in the middle, the Muslim universe, from the Philippines to Xinjiang, from West Africa to Turkey and the Middle East.

This map is interesting, of course. And, even more interesting is another, smaller map, an insert at the lower right, displaying the same "United States of Islam" in twenty years: the entire planet is colored green—the last infidel has fallen! The global *Oummah* has come to pass! But the important thing is the propaganda book itself, full of "poems" by the master, in the purest sectarian style, whose major motifs are trifold.

First, the jihad; the hymn to the "sub-machine gun," the "true believer's" strength; and the exhortation of "our Sheikh Gilani" to "prepare one's head for sacrifice"; nostalgia for the days when the "warriors of Allah" brought Europe to its knees; and the idea that, with the fall of the Soviet Union, a third world war had begun, from which Islam would emerge victorious.

Next, the theme of purity; the idea that Islam has been "corrupted" by too long a contact with the West and with Westerners; the obsession with a return to the sources of the true Faith, in spite of all these heretics who have sold their souls to the Zionists and the Crusaders; the idea that this return can only be effected through violence.

And then another theme that seems less usual in Islam, dealing with the presence of the "forces of evil" or "forces from below," that constitute the invisible underside to the visible world; magic Islam, esoteric and black, an almost Satanic Islam that warned the Americans in the early '90s that occult forces lay in wait for them, that innumerable tornadoes, terrifying earthquakes would be unleashed against the signs of their power and their pride.

Let us add (from the Anti-Defamation League report, "Muslims of America: In Their Own Words"), the strange vision the sect has of Christians: "By having put their God on the crucifix, as opposed to executing Satan, they not only have blasphemed against the Wisdom and Judgment of God Almighty, but reduced Him to a role of subservience to Satan." Attacks against homosexuals: "A perfect example, of unspeakable crimes against humanity." This declaration expressing an unbridled anti-Semitism: "As we all know, the Jews are master conspirators; they plot and plan for a century ahead." This other: "Every God-fearing individual, whether in America or abroad, must become informed of the heinous, barbaric, and purely subhuman nature of Zionism and all of its offshoots." This one again: "Jews are an example of human Satans; this is why Jews are the founders of Satan worship and are now trying to take over the entire globe in which the global religion is to be Satanism...."

I don't dare speculate any further, of course, concerning Daniel Pearl's hypotheses. But my own is that there is a tone, a morbid power, in these strange writings that Osama bin Laden can only have found compelling.

6. But that isn't all. And here is the essential point, the one I cannot imagine having escaped Daniel Pearl's notice, the one that must have intensified his interest in meeting with Gilani.

This little group, the al-Fuqrah, this sect of hand-picked fanatics, may number only two or three hundred in Lahore. But there is a country in the world where they are more numerous and more powerful, where they recruit on a vast scale and enjoy a popularity never achieved in Pakistan. This country is not Yemen, nor Indonesia, not Iraq or any of the other countries constituting Mr. Bush's "axis of evil." It is the United States of America itself.

The story begins early in the '80s in a Brooklyn mosque where a young imam named Gilani is taking his first steps as "venerated master." The war in Afghanistan has just begun. American public opinion is solidly behind the freedom fighters who, from Kandahar to the Panshir, resist the Soviet army. And here is Gilani, more loquacious than he is today, noisier, generally dressed in fatigues and wearing ammunition bandoliers, who, from his mosque in the heart of New York, founds al-Fuqrah, whose purpose is to recruit volunteers for the jihad amongst black Americans, often the poorest, sometimes ex-convicts, preferably "converts," who seem to be his specialty, his breeding ground, during these years.

Twenty years later, the Afghanistan war is a thing of the past. The al-Fuqrah sect has finally been outlawed in the United States. And Gilani himself, after the first World Trade Center attack in 1993, after at least one of his faithful, Clement Rodney Hampton-el, alias "Abd al-Rashid Abdallah," has been alleged to have been part of the attack, preferred to leave the United States and continue to direct his network from Lahore.

But the fact remains. Al-Fuqrah was born in New York. Al-Fuqrah is originally an American organization. Its first acts of violence, its first murders, its bombs in hotels, stores, cinemas managed by Indians, its intercommunity settlings of scores that led to the execution of, among others, an imam in Brooklyn and another in Tucson—all took place in the United States. It still has today between two and three thousand followers in the United States.

7. Gilani, probably realizing that one day al-Fuqrah's violence would attract, if not America's federal antiterrorist authorities, then at least those in charge of combating organized crime—such as the FBI and the local New York City Police—took precautions as early as the beginning of the '90s by establishing another organization, then another, the sect's democratic fronts. Both were still going strong when Pearl wanted to see Gilani and both are still flourishing today, as I resume Pearl's investigation. One is called Muslims of America, the other the International Quranic Open University.

Their main purpose is to pursue, among all the activities of al-Fuqrah, those that will never be considered unlawful and could, consequently, possibly serve as a cover for other activities. Teaching, of course. Consciousness-raising campaigns centered upon the "martyred Muslim peoples." Bosnia. Chechnya. Intellectual resistance to the "Zionist lobby." And, finally, one of al-Fuqrah's long-standing goals, perhaps its "holiest" mission and, in any case, the one Gilani seems proudest of, the establishment of small *"jamaats"* or "communities" of the faithful who have in common the teachings of the master and constitute a religious commune in the countryside, far from the urban gangrene of moral pollution and a climate of decadence, whose members live according to the precepts of Islam.

Phalansteries of this type already exist, in Virginia, Colorado, California, Pennsylvania, South Carolina, in Canada and in the Caribbean.

There are dozens, perhaps thirty, of these strange "green bases" whose existence supposedly follows Koranic precepts which, in fact, have been largely reinterpreted and revised by Gilani-think—several thousand "brothers" dispersed from one end of the North American continent to the other.

They are model villages, Islamic *kolkhozes* in the middle of enemy territory, hundreds of acres often in deserted regions, purchased and offered to the faithful who have heard the call to leave the cities of the Demon and return, if not to the desert, at least to the earth and its truth, to create, in the sight of Allah, these counter-societies protected from the corruption of this materialistic, Godless world—these are the Islamist enclaves in the heart of George W. Bush's America that allow us to say that the organization Pearl was investigating is still, more than ever, an American organization.

8. I visited one of these enclaves. I went, in the Town of Tompkins, Delaware County, New York, to the place where a handful of faithful, twenty years ago, established one of these model villages, since expanded to a population of around 30 families and two hundred people.

A countryside of hills and forests. A two-lane road, Roods Creek, not a soul on it, which leads to a simple gate. Before the gate, a small wooden sign indicating, on one side, "Muslims of America," and, on the other, "International Quranic Open University." A little sentry shack, with a cheerful old man who serves as guardian. Trailer homes planted in a circle like Conestoga wagons in a western. Others scattered up the hill. We're in the heart of what other people in neighboring Deposit, or in the little hamlet of Trout Creek, call, with a trace of fear or suspicion, "Islamberg."

The circled trailers are the school, and the women's quarters. Beyond them is the former mosque. Farther off, in an old quarry carved out of a hillside, will be the new mosque, larger, built on a foundation and still under construction, the ground floor in concrete block with a wooden second story. A similar building nearby is a general store that provides basic necessities and allows the "Brothers" to avoid going outside the compound and to live, if they choose, in quasi-autonomy. Higher up the hillside is the school for older children, and nearby, on another hill, a workshop for repairs or recycling or both. A small pond serving as a fish farm, on the edge of which is kept like a relic the trailer of the founder—he is still here, and still running his security guard company in New York. And, back down the hill, on the right, a ramshackle building whose walls are covered with silvered insulation panels, and which serves as both a dining hall and a library.

"We have nothing to do with al-Fuqrah," insists a big, friendly, athletic, black man who has lived here with his family for the past eight years. "We're related to Muslims of America, which is quite another organization, and advocates study and prayer."

Another man, a lawyer who commutes every day to New York City, and adopts the same look of a cool, ecologist pioneer, adds: "We aren't involved in terrorism; none of our members has ever been implicated in any act of the kind; did you know the kids from our community school went to New York as early as 12 September to help the firemen clear up Ground Zero? You won't find anyone more patriotic than we are."

Right. No doubt that's all true. And it's a sure thing that in the bucolic world of Islamberg, with its back-to-the-earth-and-the-great-outdoors utopian feel, in this isolated community that seems miles from the world of crooks and losers that was al-Fuqrah's lot in the beginning and of which Richard Reid is nonetheless still representative, things fit more easily into the pattern of a nineteenth-century utopian society than they do into that of an Islamist training camp. Except that....

9. Except that the sect has another face. I won't enter into the details of the criminal past of al-Fuqrah in and of itself, of no concern to the people of Islamberg, as they would insist that they belong not to al-Fuqrah but to the Muslims of American and the International Quranic Open University. I'll skip over all we know today about the thirteen assassinations and the seventeen bomb attacks committed by Gilani's men in the '80s on United States territory. I won't emphasize the 1989 police raid on one of his hideouts in Colorado that turned up an arsenal of semiautomatic weapons, fifteen kilos of explosives, blank social security cards and birth certificates, fake drivers' licenses, blueprints of New York bridges, photos of power stations and oil installations, guerrilla manuals, and notes indicating assassination plans targeting Rashid Khalifa, the imam of Tucson, Arizona, which, incidentally, were effectively carried out. I'll pass over (although we're not talking about al-Fuqrah here but Muslims of America) the NGO system implanted in the '90s

that functions today as a series of bogus associations that have managed to embezzle $1.3 million in the state of California alone—all of it sent directly to the home office in Lahore. The important thing is that the friendly rural communities of Muslims of America and of the International Quranic Open University continue to adhere to the teachings of the master of al-Fuqrah, as though nothing has happened.

The important thing is that the acronym of the sect still appears on the gates of some of the villages, including Islamberg.

The important thing is the video, presented during one of the innumerable court actions brought against the organization in the past few years in North America, in this case in Canada. Here we see Gilani, battle dress over his *shalwar kameez*, presiding over a military training session in a green-hilled setting that could very well be Islamberg, and declaring to the camera: "We give recruits highly specialized training in guerilla warfare; we are at present establishing training camps; you can easily reach us at the Quranic Open University offices in upstate New York, or in Canada, or Michigan, or South Carolina, or Pakistan; wherever we are, you can reach us" (Mira L. Boland, "Sheikh Gilani's American disciple," *Weekly Standard,* 18 March 2002).

Still more recent is the 2001 FBI investigation of the murder of a deputy sheriff in the county of Fresno, near the community of "Baladullah" (in Arabic "City of God") in the Sierra Nevada foothills, that concludes (Knight-Ridder Newspapers, 25 December 2001) that the alleged murderer is a member of both organizations, Moslems of America and al-Fuqrah.

And then, finally, the sniper that terrorized the Washington, D.C. area, John Muhammad, a convert who left the Nation of Islam and whom the FBI suspects had joined not only al-Fuqrah, but also Muslims of America (which, thus, would appear to be an organization linked to assassins; is not Wadih El Hage, the African embassy bomber, and former personal secretary to bin Laden, also suspected to be linked to al-Fuqrah, the parent organization of Muslims of America? And similarly, as we saw, is not Rodney Hampton-el, convicted along with Sheik Rahman, not only in connection with the first World Trade Center attack, but in a plot to bomb New York City's bridges and tunnels, a known member of al-Fuqrah?)

I know the conclusions of Douglas Wamsley, a prosecutor of the case the Attorney General of Colorado, concerning the murder of Rhasid Khalifa, in Arizona in 1990. I also know the reports of Thomas Gallagher, special agent with the U.S. Bureau Alcohol, Tobacco and Firearms about another Muslims of America compound in Virginia. I know the conclusion of the 2002 investigation of Jonathan Bernstein, executive director of the Anti-Defamation League's Central Pacific region, about the links between Muslims of America and al-Fuqrah in the area of Fresno, especially in the education field. And finally, there is the note of the Department of Law regarding Colorado's prosecution of James D. Williams, condemned to sixty-nine years of prison for attempted murder and extortion.

No one believes in the actual autonomy of al-Fuqrah and its front organizations. No one doubts that Gilani is the inspiration behind the American utopian communities of Islam as well as the assassins' sect. And no one doubts that the division of roles between them is in large part fictitious.

10. Which leads one to the simplest and also the most troubling question: Why doesn't the United States do anything? Why

do the authorities tolerate the Muslims of America? And as for al-Fuqrah itself, the parent institution, of whom the State Department annual report, *Patterns of Global Terrorism,* said, "Its members have attacked several targets considered to be enemies of Islam, among them Muslims known as heretics, and Hindus," why did it take the United States so long to outlaw the organization?

Perhaps because, the targets were "only" Muslims or Hindus....

Respect for the law and due process was also probably a reason, as well as the fact that in many cases, at Islamberg, for example, it was impossible to prove the least connection with any concrete terrorist plot or activity whatsoever....

But I wonder if there is not another, still deeper reason, one that would take us back to those times long ago and almost forgotten when the American government supported all the forces that, one way or another, opposed the enemy in its global struggle against world Communism—beginning, we recall, with the fundamentalist Muslim movements of Uzbekistan, Tajikistan, Turkmenistan, Afghanistan and, of course, Pakistan.

The era of Zbigniew Brezinski. The period of William Casey, CIA Director from 1981 to 1987 and responsible for the green light given the ISI to recruit, arm, and train tens of thousands of Arab fighters who would struggle to break up the "Empire of Evil" while simultaneously fighting for their faith.... Following that, the era where America supported the FIS in Algeria, the Taliban in Kandahar and Kabul, the Muslim Brotherhood and the Wahabite tendencies in Arab countries, as well as the most hard-line Chechen groups.... The time when, in Afghanistan, long before the Taliban, they played Gulbuddin Heykmatiar against Massoud, the religious fanatics against the democrats.... The era when it seemed like a good idea to push the most radical Sunni groups throughout the world, to counter the Shiite revolution in Iran.... And the era when, as a result, insane things happened within the United States, things that, retrospectively, make the head spin: Ramzi Yousef, the future mastermind of the attack against the World Trade Center, recruited by the CIA... the U.S. embassy at Khartoum issuing a visa to blind sheikh Omar Abdel Raman, already implicated in the assassination of Sadat... two international conferences at Oklahoma City (better than the "terrorist summit" of Khartoum), in 1988 and 1992, summits of radical Islam, where some of the architects of both Trade Tower attacks attended and were speakers.... Azzam, the Palestinian *eminence grise* of bin Laden, authorized to open a recruiting office for his al-Kifah Center in the middle of New York.... And Pir Mubarak Shah Gilani, linked to the Pakistani secret services and—who knows—perhaps to the American intelligence agencies as well.

Was Daniel Pearl investigating the American branches of al-Qaida? Is the key to the mystery of his death also in the closets or on the hard disks of the intelligence agencies of Washington? We're still waiting for a clear and public admission, by those responsible, of this extraordinary historical error in which the leaders of the free world welcomed to their breast and sometimes generated the Golem that we must now drive out from one end of the planet to the other. Perhaps that is what Daniel Pearl was waiting for—perhaps that's what he wanted to provoke.

CHAPTER 5 THE BOMB FOR BIN LADEN?

"There are newspapers in the West that say that you're in the process of acquiring chemical and nuclear weapons. Is there any truth to these reports?"

"Yes, I heard the speech by the American President Bush yesterday. He's trying to alarm the Europeans by telling them that I'm going to attack them with weapons of mass destruction. Well, I would like to state that yes, if America started using chemical or nuclear weapons against us, we would retaliate with chemical or nuclear weapons. We have the weapons for that. We have the means to be dissuasive."

"And where did you get these weapons?"

"Let's go on to the next question . . . ."

The person speaking is Osama bin Laden.

It's his first interview after September 11 and the attack against the World Trade Center and the Pentagon.

The man he's speaking to is Hamid Mir, the former managing editor of the Urdu newspaper in Islamabad, the man who so strangely canceled our meeting, claiming that I was trying to get to Gilani through him—and also the man who with Khawaja was one of Daniel Pearl's very first contacts in Islamabad.

So, is that the other key to the mystery?

The question that bin Laden evades in his interview with Mir—is that the very subject that Pearl was working on?

Did Pearl have part of the answer to the terrifying question of whether the emir of al-Qaida is bluffing, or whether he really does possess (and if so, how? where? thanks to whom?) weapons of mass destruction, able to topple, in his favor, the balance of power with the civilized world?

My hypothesis is yes.

I think, or rather I suppose, that Pearl was also on this track.

And that, if true, would be another possible explanation for his death.

The point of departure, the most solid clue I have, is, of course, the 24 December article he wrote with Steve LeVine and which he regretted had not had more impact.

What does this article say, exactly?

It reports how, I repeat, the authors came across one of those Pakistani NGOs that was supposedly developing aid projects in Afghanistan under the Taliban, called UTN, Ummah Tameer e-Nau, the "Reconstruction of Muslm Ummah."

It recounts how the "honorary" president of UTN, responsible mainly for attracting Pakistani and Arab investors to the big agricultural development projects supposedly being launched in the Kandahar region, is none other than Hamid Gul—the former boss of the ISI, who has been retired for twelve years but has maintained, as one does, connections to his former profession.

It reveals furthermore that the operational boss of the organization is a certain Bashiruddin Mahmoud, 61, Islamist, disciple of Israr Ahmed, that other *uléma* from Lahore who is said to be, like Gilani, one of the more or less secret gurus of

Pakistani fundamentalism and of bin Laden in particular. Mahmoud is, in addition, and this is an important point, a very famous scientist—in charge of the plutonium factory built, with the help of the Chinese, in Khusab, and head of the Pakistani Atomic Energy Commission until 1999 (at which time his political leanings, his vehement and public protests against his country's ratification of the nonproliferation treaty, started to worry American intelligence and caused him to be sent into retirement).

And finally the article reveals that the two men, Gul and Mahmoud, the General and the Scientist, got together in Kaboul in very strange circumstances at the end of August 2001—after Mahmoud had already, at the beginning of the month in Kandahar, met not only the Taliban leaders but also bin Laden in person....

So it is useless for Gul to deny—and Pearl and LeVine's article says as much—that he was ever informed of a meeting between Mahmoud and bin Laden.

It is useless for Mahmoud to claim: "No! My trips to Afghanistan, my meetings with this man or that man, have nothing to do with my old job and therefore nothing to do with Pakistan's nuclear secrets; I wanted to participate in the development of this poor country; finance windmills; think about the exploitation of the oil and gas reserves, its iron and coal mines; accompany my son who had a bank project in Kabul."

It is useless for him to say to those who criticize him for meeting with the Emir of al-Qaida: "We are not talking about the same man; the man I met is a friend of humankind, good, generous, spending without limit to renovate schools, open orphanages, set up funds to help war widows—God save Osama."

And, most of all, it is useless for the Pakistani government, under pressure from the "friendly" intelligence services and notably that of the Americans (who, incidentally, a few days before the article was published, seem to have managed to get the UTN's accounts blocked), to have arrested Mahmoud, interrogate him, keep him a few weeks in prison, then under house arrest—and, finally, liberate him.

The reality is there.

Bin Laden had contact with one of the fathers of the Pakistani bomb.

There had probably been—another item from the Pearl-LeVine article, contributed by an unnamed "former ISI colonel"—a first meeting the previous year.

And Afghanistan being what it is, and given the secret services' vigilant watch over the comings and goings of scientists involved in the nuclear network—and Mahmoud is not just any scientist! Pearl and LeVine insist—it is unthinkable that these trips to Afghanistan, these meetings with bin Laden, these conversations, would take place without the knowledge of Islamabad.

Pearl is right to regret that his article did not make more of a splash, because he and LeVine had a double scoop: The interaction between an atomic scientist and al-Qaida; and that such interaction had the blessing of the Pakistani state, which the West believes has put its most sensitive weapons under lock and key.

From this point I tried to find out a little more—as with the Gilani dossier, I tried, with my own means, to go a little further....

Mahmoud, for instance—the character of Mahmoud, concerning whom I quickly make two further discoveries. The first:

Far from being an Islamist like any other lost in the swamp of the movement's innumerable sympathizers, he is an active militant in one of the most radical and, as we now know, most bloodthirsty groups of all those which populate the country—he is an activist in the Harkat ul-Mujahideen, which we understand had a central role in the abduction and execution of Pearl himself. The second: Far from being a matter of conscience with no effect on his scientific activity, Mahmoud's Islamism contaminates everything, infects even his scientific work and inspires him to hold a terrifying theory—of which those in the West who live in the cozy certainty that Pakistani may have flaws, but it has its arsenals locked up, should be aware—it inspires him to think that the Pakistani bomb is not Pakistani but Islamist and, therefore, belongs by right to the entire community of believers, to the *Oummah*.

Next, Abdul Qadir Kahn, Mahmoud's boss, and thus the genuine father of the bomb tested for the first time on 28 May 1998. Pearl and LeVine don't talk about him, but. . . . He's a popular national celebrity. A new Jinnah. A star. He's the man credited with having restored the country's honor and pride by giving it the bomb. Songs have been composed about him. He is cheered on the streets of Karachi. His birth is sanctified in the mosques of Pakistan. And I've never been able to mention his name without seeing the face of the person I'm addressing, no matter of what background, origin or sensibility, light up as if I were talking about a saint or a hero. Well, the man is a member of the Lashkar e-Toiba. This scientific expert, this Pakistani Oppenheimer, this genius who in his lifetime has had the country's biggest nuclear laboratory named after him, is officially a member of a terrorist organization which constitutes, as does the

Harkat, the innermost circle of al-Qaida. A believer in nuclear weapons and a fanatic. Holder of the true secrets of the bomb, and clearly linked to bin Laden. We don't have to scare ourselves thinking what would happen if, by chance, Musharraf were overthrown and replaced by a clique of religious fanatics. The clique is already there. The religious fanatics are in the arena. They have, because they invented them, the key, the access codes for the Pakistani silos, transmission systems and warheads.

Public opinion. More precisely, the opinion of the jihadist groups in the company of which I have been living, closely or at a distance, for nearly a year, and which I suddenly discover have not only an opinion on the jihad, a position on social questions, on the status of women, on the great debates around the interpretation of the Prophet's words—they also have, with equal certainty, a line, an orthodoxy, a conviction about nuclear issues. For example, at the Peshawar mosque, when I was there in November, a Lashkar e-Toiba preacher cautioned Musharraf against the crime of "selling off the country's nuclear heritage." Another example: in the issue of *Zarb e-Momin* which my strange visitor in December had finally left on the table: an "editorial" where the emir of Jamaat e-Islami warns that "the whole nation" will rise up if they give in to the "American Zionists" and renounce the "Islamic bomb." What a pretty sight, he thunders, to see the Muslims being treated like dogs, yet again! The Jews have the bomb; the Americans have the bomb; even the French have it; why should we be the only ones forbidden to have the bomb! And finally, two years ago in another newspaper of the movement, a declaration by the Mufti Mizamuddin Shamzai, rector of Binori Town whose "elevated spirituality" I no longer much believe in, but whose statements still come as a shock: the Koran orders

Muslims to give themselves "a strong capacity for defense"; should our leaders be renouncing this, signing treacherous non-proliferation treaties that the Zionist enemy is imposing on them—it would be an act of "high treason," a "non-Islamic" action, "a rebellion against the commandments of almighty Allah." Is there another country in the world where the question of the bomb has the status of a great national cause? Another country where the day of the first nuclear test—28 May—has the unofficial status of a religious holiday and where people parade under banners adorned with the "Hatif," the Pakistani nuclear missile? Is there a more nightmarish situation than when an atomic arsenal becomes an article of faith, in the heads of religious zealots? And yet that is Pakistan.

And on the al-Qaida problem, finally, specifically on the question of where bin Laden is, exactly, in his quest to acquire weapons of mass destruction, three pieces of information that I imagine Daniel Pearl had, plus two personal recollections. . .

The case of Mamdouh Mahmoud Salim, the bin Laden lieutenant, co-founder of al-Qaida and involved as such in the bombing attacks on the American embassies in Kenya and Tanzania: arrested in Munich on 25 September 1998 as he was trying to make a deal with Ukrainian intermediaries for nuclear material and enriched uranium.

The 1998 book by Yossef Bodansky, director of the Congressional Task Force on Terrorism and Unconventional Warfare of the U.S. House of Representatives, which recounts how bin Laden paid $30 million cash plus the value of two tons of heroin to a group of Chechens who were supposed to provide him with the makings of one or more "dirty" bombs.

The statements from General Lebed revealing to American authorities, not long before his death, that the government of the Russian Federation had lost track of about a hundred nuclear explosive devices among the seven hundred that had been miniaturized by the Soviets in the 1970s: these bombs, he said, fit in a suitcase; they can be smuggled into any enemy territory, and therefore into the United States, through the exact same channels as any contraband goods; some have a shelf-life sufficiently long that they could be there already, sleeping, since the last years of the Soviet era, waiting to be reactivated; these micro-bombs, said Lebed, these atomic suitcases capable when they explode of killing several tens of thousands of people, maybe a hundred thousand, are the ideal weapon for a terrorist group.

And accordingly two personal recollections, which bring me back from the ex-Soviet republics of Central Asia to Pakistan, and from Pakistan to bin Laden, corroborating the intuitions of Daniel Pearl....

A conversation in the spring of 2002 with Moshe Yaalon, nicknamed "Bogey," who has just been appointed chief of staff of the Israeli army. I had met with Ariel Sharon the day before. I see Yaalon that morning at the Ministry of Defense—an enormous fortified complex, cheerful atmosphere, a very civilian aspect to the offices, few military emblems and female soldiers at reception. We talk about Arafat. I tell him about my indestructible commitment to the Israeli cause, and about the strong reservations I nonetheless have about the kind of response chosen to deal with the second Intifada. We also talk about Iraq, which seems to me, compared to the real threats that weigh upon our world, to have all the characteristics of a false target, a red herring. I put in a few words about Pakistan, naturally. I evoke, referring to the book that is taking shape, that nest of vipers, that powder-keg, about which I imagine Israel has an opinion: "The missile sites, for instance, the places where fissile materials are stored—are they not far more dangerous than Saddam Hussein's? As a result, hasn't the international intelligence community lost control of the situation?" And he, surprised, and then vaguely mocking, with a gleam in his eye that makes him look like the young Rabin: "So, you are interested in Pakistan? How about that, so are we... but don't get it wrong—the international community knows, down to the single unit, where the warheads are in that country... if one budges, if it moves a single millimeter"—he holds his thumb and index finger apart to indicate a millimeter—"we'll know how to operate." And now me: "Does that mean there could be a Pakistani Osirak? Would that kind of operation—the destruction of a nuclear installation while under construction—be conceivable in the world of bin Laden and post–September 11?" He laughs: "That's a good question; but I don't have the answer." An Osirak in Kahuta, Chagai, Khushab? An Israeli commando unit capable of parachuting onto a nuclear site if a hijacking were imminent? The thought is both reassuring and terrible. Because just the fact of contemplating it means that the problem could arise.

And furthermore, a few years earlier, when I visited the Panshir, that other even more explicit conversation with Mohammed Fahim, who was then the head of Massoud's secret service. We are in the Northern Alliance's guest house, at the entrance to the valley. We're waiting for Massoud. Fahim is thinner than he is today, less formal, outspoken in a way that is lost to the marshal-minister he has become.

"The West," he tells me, "is once again underestimating the enormous danger that the Pakistanis represent. They created the Taliban. They're now creating bin Laden. Did you know that bin Laden has a laboratory near Kandahar where he's trying to make weapons of mass destruction, and that he's doing it with the full knowledge of the services, who are providing him with everything he wants—first-hand information, visits from scientists, samples of fissile materials, help with smuggling?" I don't pay very much attention to this information at the time. As with the revelation of bin Laden's Kandahar address, which I cite, but offhandedly, in my travel chronicle for the newspaper Le Monde—part of me attributes these disclosures to the Alliance's anti-Pakistani para-noia, and even more so their secret services. But I go back to my notes from that time. I read them again in the light of both Pearl's investigation, and of my investigation of his investigation. Fahim, that day, gave me the location of the laboratory: forty kilometers from the airport, west of Kandahar. The salary of the Russian or Turkmen engineers hired by bin Laden: $2,000 a month, double what the Russian Federation would pay them at the time. He also told me that one of those Turkmen scientists had worked in Baghdad in the '80s, on that same Osirak reactor; how strange.... But most significantly he explained to me that all these weapons are too heavy, too hard to transport and then to maintain, that their locking mechanisms are too complex, for al-Qaida to get very far with the Ukrainian or Chechen networks.

"Maybe a dirty bomb," Fahim told me. "Maybe from those countries they can make nuclear devices without launchers that they'll set off in Kabul the day we go in. And obviously we are taking that possibility very seriously. Except that for the serious business, they'll do it with them...."

He points with his chin in the direction of Pakistan.

"It's only them, the ISI people, who can give them the know-how, and the maintenance, and the hardware necessary to put together an arsenal of weapons of mass destruction."

And he adds, "We have all the data on that; we know the process is ongoing...."

Several hypotheses, from that point.

One can suppose that Danny found out more about this "ongoing process."

One can suppose that he extended his investigation to Hamid Gul and his possible ties to the supposedly secular and Kamelist branch of the services.

One can imagine that he was establishing the list of ISI superior officers who, faithful to the Gul line, that is to say to the doctrine of the Islamist bomb, were busy proving Mohammed Fahim's analysis and were willing to close their eyes to a technology transfer to terrorist groups.

Was Pearl getting ready to give exact locations for the war-heads and launchers of the Islamabad arsenal—and thus to provide the proof that the information was within the reach of the first terrorist to come along?

Did he have information that disproved the reassuring declarations that Musharraf kept making at that time, about his complete control over the nuclear chain of command and the deactivation of storage and launching facilities?

Had he seen in Peshawar one of those MK 47 nuclear suitcases marked "made in U.S.A." or "in U.S.S.R." that representatives of several Western special services had talked to me about—big-bellied gray or black canteens, padded like military canteens, double metal handle on the sides, a cap like the cap on a gas tank, and inside, a twentieth or a thirtieth of the Hiroshima bomb?

One can imagine, too, that after the Gul and Mahmoud trails he opened the Khan trail—after Abdul Qader Khan, the real father and boss of the Islamist bomb—and one can imagine that he scratched below the surface of the hero's official biography to find other feats of arms, carefully hidden from the outside world and particularly from the Americans. The cooperation programs, for instance, from 1986 to 1994, with the Iran of the Ayatollahs. The memo from the Iraqi secret service, dated 6 October 1990, a copy of which was shown to me in New Delhi, in which is described the Pakistani proposition to help Saddam Hussein, through Kahn, build a factory to enrich uranium. One can also imagine that he came across the dossier on Khan's contacts with the North Korean nuclear industry. I stumbled across this open secret in India, concerning the exchange of courtesies, through Khan, between Pakistan and North Korea, one side offering their know-how, the other delivering their missiles—why wouldn't Danny have been on that also? Why wouldn't he have been on the verge of presenting, in line with his 24 December article, but this time on the front page of the *Wall Street Journal,* an account of the secret agreements on this issue signed between Pyongyang and Islamabad?

If he studied the biography of Abdul Qader Khan, if he ended up, as I think he did, realizing that Khan's role was much more crucial than Mahmoud's or Gul's, I can't see him not getting interested in the scientist's peculiar status after his forced retirement in 2001: out of the loop, really? Taken off sensitive dossiers? A citizen like any other, just a little more acclaimed than most—the kind whose restaurant check is picked up for him when he's recognized, or his taxi ride offered for free? Or else, as I believe, and as I think Danny must have if he had the time to push the investigation that far: an emissary, unofficial but busier than ever, for the Pakistani nuclear lobby? I cannot help but conclude that the logical outcome of Pearl's investigation was leading him in the direction of the scientist's last trip to North Korea, which was recent, after his retirement and unnoticed: an Abdul Qader Khan, a minister told me, who no longer represented anyone but himself, going on a nice tourist visit to Pyongyang; an Abdul Qader Khan who, a friend insisted, had been on an official mission there previously, and it so happened that he liked it, he kept friends there and went back for purely personal reasons—would you hold it against a scientist who has given his life to his country if he goes to have a good time with his friends in Pyongyang? Yes, I think that's exactly the kind of, not reproach, but at least question, that Daniel Pearl would have been formulating on the eve of his abduction; I would bet that Pearl was asking himself, a I do now, what kind of tourism one indulges in these days in Pyongyang, what kind of friends you keep there when you're the world champion in making plutonium out of uranium—I would bet on an investigator attempting to find out what North Koreans would have to say at this time to a man who, for years, taught the scientists of a country barred from nuclear research the art and craft of circumventing embargoes....

In other words, I bet on a Daniel Pearl busy gathering proof of Pakistan's collusion between the leading rogue states and terrorist networks of the world.

My hypothesis is that he was writing an article on Pakistan's duplicitous game, whereby it posed on one hand as a good ally of the United States, and on the other lending itself, through its most prestigious scientists, to the most fearsome operations of nuclear proliferation.

To put it simply, was Pearl breaking the taboo?

Entering this sinister world of mad scientists and Islamist fanatics, taking steps into this dark night where secret services and nuclear secrets exchange and share their shadowy realms, working on this highly sensitive and explosive material—was Pearl violating the other major prohibition that weighs upon this part of the world?

I'm doing it, anyway.

Following Danny, in his wake and, in a way, in homage, I bring this modest contribution to the cause of truth that he loved more than anything else.

I assert that Pakistan is the biggest rogue of all the rogue states of today.

I assert that what is taking form there, between Islamabad and Karachi, is a black hole compared to which Saddam Hussein's Baghdad was an obsolete weapons dump.

The stench of apocalypse hangs over those cities; I am convinced that Danny smelled that stench.

CHAPTER 6   GENTLE ISLAM

One year already.

One year since—sitting in President Ahmid Karzai's office in Kabul with Karzai and his ministers, Fahim and Qanouni, remembering Commander Massoud—I learned of Daniel Pearl's death.

A word to Mariane whose pain and sorrow, on this anniversary day, I can only imagine.

Trying, with friends, to relay to synagogues in France word of the day of prayer and remembrance Ruth and Judea, Danny's courageous parents, have organized in Los Angeles.

A book that comes to an end with its blanks, its hypotheses, its zones that remain obscure.

And then, this last trip to Karachi. I had promised myself never to return. At least for the duration of this regime. But it was a message from Abdul that decided me: "Memon... the owner of the property at Gulzar e-Hijiri... the missing piece of your puzzle.... I think I've found Saud Memon, come...."

Go to the Islamic bookstore in Rawalpini, to the first floor of a building on Murree Road, which serves as an office for al-Rashid Trust and where I can meet the man who knows the man that knows the man who will lead me to Saud Memon. The same dance of the bearded ones hesitating as usual between the amiable and the veiled threat. The same courteous but cold looks, as if to signify how far is too far. The same smugness about being right, to the point of daring to say that, "The journalist's killer, whoever he is, will go to paradise." And, again, the same promises as always, the same way of opening the door a crack, knowing they'll slam it shut just as quickly: "Yes, of course... nothing simpler... our friend Memon isn't hiding, he's in Karachi... there's no place on earth he'd be safer than in Karachi, especially not in the Arab countries collaborating with the Americans, the dogs!"

Go to Karachi then. Try this last trail, Sorhab Road, on the way to Gulzar e-Hijri, but deep into the neighboring slums, a maze of alleys and dirt paths in the heart of the metropolis, landscape of empty farms, ruins, shanties of corrugated iron and cardboard, bursting open-air sewers, makeshift bridges over pools of mud. "Who is he?" a skeletal Afghan refugee looming up from behind a crumbling wall, asks Abdul. "No one; a European; a Muslim from Bosnia; he's one of us." And there, in these end-of-the-world surroundings, a house, not unlike the one where Pearl was held and where I see a man lying on a rope bed, wearing a jacket with ragged cuffs over his bare skin, a chamber pot at the foot of the bed, his eyes feverish, and a voice not long for this world. "I'm not Saud Memon. I'm his uncle. Saud was here. He'll come back. But the American police just arrested Khalid Sheikh Mohammed. They're everywhere. He had to escape. Leave me alone. Can't you see I'm sick."

Call Rawalpindi then, try to find out more about the story of Mohammed's arrest. According to the latest news, he's Pearl's assassin. Him, the "Yemeni" who held the knife. There's even an ex-CIA agent, Robert Baer, now a writer, who says: "That's what

Pearl was doing... looking for Mohammed... he was on
Mohammed's trail... well, Mohammed didn't like it...
Mohammed got revenge.... Mohammed, with Omar, planned
the kidnapping and killed him with his own hands...." To me
the idea is less than plausible. I can't believe that bin Laden's
number-three man, chief of al-Qaida operations, this rather distinguished Kuwaiti intellectual, could have done the job himself.
I look at his official photograph, the one the CIA has circulated
for the last two years and that everyone knows, neatly trimmed
beard, pitiless but intelligent eyes, impeccable turban, and I say
to myself: "No, not possible, I can't see this particular man carrying out the sentence." But I turn to the other picture, the new
one, published in this morning's papers, where we see him just
out of bed, in the instant, I imagine, the Rangers burst in, his
hair a mess, his eyes swollen and haggard, black body hair showing through a dubious undershirt, the grim mouth; this is not
the same old Mohammed... for a moment I even think we
might be in the midst of an umpteenth manipulation, another
identity switch... but if it's really him then, yes, why not... *this*
Mohammed could have killed Daniel Pearl... wasn't it said of
Saddam Hussein that he reserved the privilege of killing with his
own hands those opponents who personally offended him?

Besides, the whole Mohammed affair is bizarre. The officials
in Islamabad crow. More than ever, the Pakistanis play the good
allies, America's pals, antiterrorist, virtuous. Except that no one
is able to say where he was arrested. Or how. Or even when. That
is what is most extraordinary. Nobody seems to know if it
happened today or eight days ago, or fifteen, or six months ago
The number-three man of al-Qaida is arrested on the sly, secretly
detained, "held but not charged" in the manner of most of the

suspects in the Pearl case: and the authorities pull him out now, this devil, like a rabbit out of a hat, or an opportune gift to their great friend, America. When is the Security Counsel session on the war in Iraq? And how exactly will Pakistan vote? Once again, the impression of a wily power, expert at the double and triple game, having its secret stock of terrorists ready to trot out according to the needs and circumstances, the well-understood interests of the "three letters," the political market....

Three photos of Hadi, Omar's baby, this morning, in my e-mail. He has a nice, round face. Big eyes. A white T-shirt, with "Hello Kiki" in green letters across the front, shows his plump arms. In one of the pictures he is strapped in his baby chair. In another, he cries, his little fist wiping a tear. In the third he chortles happily—but behind him, on the wall, is a large dark shadow. Who sent me these? How strange.

News of Omar himself. Also in my e-mail: the same sender, a London address that I try to reach, but no answer—a fictitious site that quickly disappears. It's a long interview given from his cell to an Urdu newspaper. The prisoner of Hyderabad recalls the death of Pearl. He talks about what he was doing in Kandahar, in "the house of friends," on the eve of September 11. He talks about his experience in Bosnia, and India. He speaks as well of the war in Iraq, which clearly infuriates him. And what does he propose to stop this war? What is the ultimate weapon of the "favored son" of bin Laden to prevent this forthcoming "massacre"? His *idée fixe*. Always the same. This man is decidedly a maniac. I'd laugh if it weren't tragic—he suggests kidnapping the sons of Bush and Cheney.

Another man, one of my informants from last year, from whom I learn the existence of a new suspect, the eighteenth, a certain Qari Asad, emir of Lashkar i-Janghvi for the eastern part of Karachi, secretly arrested on 18 February, who gave the police a different version of Daniel Pearl's kidnapping. One car, not two. No Bukhari on his motorcycle. A second meeting, halfway, at the "Snoopy Ice Cream Parlor," near the Sohrab Goth mosque, where Pearl has some ice cream before getting back in the car and leaving for Gulzar e-Hijri. I look for the "Snoopy Ice Cream Parlor" and can't find it.

If I add it all up, have I made much progress in a year?

Do I see things more clearly than at the very beginning of my investigation, when things seemed simpler—an American Jew, Muslim extremists, a video playing in a loop in the militant shock mosques?

Sometimes I think yes. I hang on to my conclusions. I remind myself it's not every day you find a killer who is both in the upper ranks of al-Qaida and agent of the ISI. And I think that the Pearl affair is much more than The Pearl Affair and that we're here, between Washington and Islamabad, against a backdrop of weapons of mass destruction gone mad, in the very eye of the hurricane.

Sometimes, on the contrary, I wonder if I didn't go too far in this investigation; if I haven't been sucked into a whirlpool; if I shouldn't have left Omar to his banality and his oblivion; if, by wanting too much to untangle the web, peel away too much, I didn't lose myself in a dust storm of facts; I wonder if I wasn't a victim of my own fascination for crime writers, piling up notes, poring over reports, obsessional clerks, rummagers of overlapping clues that contradict each other, eternal seekers of inconsequential witnesses, people mad for the reverse side of things and the depth of souls, these dreamers who incessantly rerun the film searching for the ignored detail, the unseen connection, the perspective that could pry open the truth, the fortuitous corroboration, the forgotten thread—but who, in the end, see the mystery unravel only to resurface further on, from another angle, misleading in a new way.

For the last time I'm in front of the Marriott.

For the last time, in front of the Village Garden, the first station of Daniel Pearl's cross, with its sign in red letters that, from a distance, resemble Chinese characters.

I know now that I'll never return to Karachi, or not for a very long time—I know there's little chance, after this book, that I'd still be welcome. So I fill my eyes and ears with the life of this city that I detested, where I was afraid, where it was often gray and dreary, where I met so few friendly faces but where I also have a few good memories and that I sometimes liked very much.

The face of Jamil Yusuf, head of Karachi's Citizen-Police Liaison Committee, relentless in his high-risk quest for Danny's killers and those of others.

The journalist and the embassy employee whose names I can't cite but who helped me so much and who I know are among the last of the just in this modern Nineveh.

The airport road where this time I find the guest house I had looked for in vain the first day, when the cop with the kohl-lined eyes stopped my taxi before letting the representative of the Levy Malakand go his way.

My chauffeur today, with his forthright look, his jovial smile, the first in a year not to ask the eternal questions: "Where are you from? What is your religion?"

And the mosque where he asks permission to stop: "It's the hour of the fourth prayer, do you mind if we stop? You can come along, by the way... two minutes... you are most welcome, anyway you're ahead of schedule...."

It's a small prayer room. A humble neighborhood mosque. But the men aren't aggressive. After the first moment of surprise, they offer me a cushion and make a motion for me to sit against the wall while they pray. And it's the first time that I enter a religious space in Karachi without feeling the wind of imprecation, of hatred.

I think, as I'm on my way again, of this other face of Islam, made of tolerance and moderation, disfigured by the fanatics of God, or rather the Devil.

I think of this familiar Islam, steeped in life and piety, friendly toward others, consoling to the humble, tolerant of man's weakness, but sullied by the gang of "combatants of the true faith."

I remember my friends in Bosnia and Panshir: Izetbegovic and his citizen Islam; Massoud on a mountain over the plain of Chamali praying to his God, facing the most beautiful view in the world.

I remember my Bengali friends who, already thirty years ago, warned against the Torquemada they saw rising in their ranks. They are an insult, they said, to the God of knowledge, of wisdom and of mercy who is the God of Muslims.

I remember the blue domes of the mosque in Mazar e-Sharif, the arabesque arches of Boukhara and their columbine sweetness, the marble lacework of the Saadian tombs that Michaelangelo would have admired—I hear the murmur of water from a rivulet in the Ghardaia oasis and the sage ecstasies of Sohravardi whose beauty cedes nothing to the greatest passages of Isaac Luria or of Pascal.

There is this other face of Islam.

There is this gentle Islam towards which, in spite of everything, until the last minute, Daniel Pearl wanted to believe, as I want to believe.

Who will prevail, the sons of Massoud or Pearl's killers?

Who will prevail: the heirs of this ancient commerce of men and cultures that stretches from Avicenne to Mahfouz by way of the sages of Cordoba—or the madmen of the Peshawar camps who call for jihad and, belly strapped with explosives, aspire to die as martyrs?

It's the beginning of the grand struggle of the century.

I think it was, in fact, that grand struggle for Pearl when he inveighed against the ideologues of a war of civilizations that promises the worst.

It was the true subject of this book—homage to my posthumous friend and a call for the sharing of light.

Bernard-Henri Lévy is France's leading philosopher and one of the most esteemed and bestselling writers in Europe. He has also served on diplomatic missions for the French government—most recently, to Afghanistan after the fall of the Taliban. He first wrote about the region in 1971, as a war correspondent covering the conflict between India and Pakistan over Bangladesh. The first of his 30 books, *Red India*, was also about that conflict.

James X. Mitchell is a screenwriter and translator living in Paris.